Under
the
Bombs

Under the Bombs

The German Home Front 1942-1945

Earl R. Beck

THE UNIVERSITY PRESS OF KENTUCKY

627012

Copyright © 1986 by The University Press of Kentucky

Scholarly publisher for the Commonwealth,
serving Bellarmine College, Berea College, Centre
College of Kentucky, Eastern Kentucky University,
The Filson Club, Georgetown College, Kentucky
Historical Society, Kentucky State University,
Morehead State University, Murray State University,
Northern Kentucky University, Transylvania University,
University of Kentucky, University of Louisville,
and Western Kentucky University.

Editorial and Sales Offices: Lexington, Kentucky 40506-0024

Library of Congress Cataloging-in-Publication Data
Beck, Earl R. (Earl Ray), 1916-
    Under the bombs.

    Bibliography: p.
    Includes index.
    1. World War, 1939–1945—Germany.   2. World War,
1939-1945—Aerial operations.   3. Bombardment—Germany.
4. World, War, 1939-1945—Destruction and pillage—
Germany.   I. Title.
D757.B42   1986   940.54′4943   85-24681
ISBN 0-8131-1567-1

**To Marjorie, for forty-one years
my partner in everything**

Contents

Illustrations follow page 148

Preface

Early in 1946, I traveled by train from Bavaria to Bremerhaven to return home to the United States. As the train passed by the great cities along the Rhine and through northern Germany, I saw for the first time the full extent of the bombing war against Germany—the endless line of skeletonized buildings rising grimly across the skyline of an entire city. The questions that arose in my mind were haunting ones: "How did the Germans survive this kind of devastation, live amid these endless blocks of shattered homes, and emerge themselves unshattered by the terror and dread which this kind of war must have occasioned?" And accompanying this question, a more unpleasant one: "Could Americans survive this kind of challenge, this kind of devastation of our cities?" This book, completed forty years later, seeks to answer the first question. The second one will, I hope, continue to remain only a subject for speculation.

The search for materials upon which this book could be based was a frustrating one. The number of wartime diaries detailing the personal experiences and thoughts of those who lived under the bombs was relatively small. This was not surprising. Keeping diaries in the Nazi period was dangerous. One could neither write nor speak one's intimate feelings without danger of persecution and punishment. Postwar accountings of wartime experiences by Germans have also remained relatively scarce. Recent efforts to add to these through personal interviews had only modest beginnings. And recollections set forth forty years later are likely to be distorted by the postwar experiences.

But the Nazi regime itself kept myriads of reports on the feelings and thoughts of the people. The *Sicherheitsdienst*, the security service of the dreaded SS, had agents all over Germany. They were responsible for providing detailed reports of the passing comments of the inhabitants of the cities and towns where they were stationed—comments not only about the regime itself, but about food supplies, work problems, entertainment, propaganda success or failure, and so on. Strangely enough, some of these agents seem to have found some pleasure in retelling the critical comments they heard.

Other government agents, local and regional officials, school officials, agents of the regular police, labor leaders, and court officials were responsible for providing similar reports. Some of these found their way into the party archives or the ministries in Berlin. Others remained in local or regional archives. Those in the central archives of the party and in the Berlin Document Center are available in the rich microfilmed records in our National Archives. I am grateful to the Strozier Library for having purchased through the years an extensive section of these materials.

I was able to supplement these through the reports of the regional court presidents available in the federal archives of the Federal Republic of Germany in Koblenz. Some records of the party not available to me at home I found in the collections of the Institute for Contemporary History in Munich. Also helpful there was a large collection of books that are no longer widely available. The publication of the local and regional records of Bavaria by the institute provides a rich storehouse of primary materials available to scholars. Recent publications dealing with Württemberg, Munich, Augsburg, Essen, and Duisburg have also been helpful.

I am grateful to the history department at Florida State University for granting me the necessary time for research. I am also grateful to the Federal Republic of Germany, which provided the rich opportunity of a "study trip" in 1981, which I extended for research purposes. The officials at the Bundesarchiv in Koblenz and the Institute for Contemporary History in Munich were capable and helpful in every way. I also met with a friendly reception and excellent working conditions at the Institute for Newspaper Research in Dortmund. I recommend its resources to students examining the Weimar or Nazi periods.

What I have written remains an impressionistic view of the

course of events during the years concerned. I have sought to tell a story, not to provide an analysis of those events. In a book dealing with such complex and varied matters, definitive conclusions are not possible. I have sought to provide for Americans who have never really experienced a war in their own homeland some feeling for what it was really like to be "under the bombs."

1. The End
of Optimism

It was a warm Saturday evening in May in the great industrial city of Cologne. The people, as they strolled home, looked forward to a pleasant Sunday outside. The year was 1942. Germany was now well into its third year of war. There had been air raids before. Cologne itself had suffered a mild attack in February and a more severe one in April. But the midnight sirens on this late spring night called the city's inhabitants to something new and more dreadful. The thoughts of a pleasant Sunday in the green environs of the city were to be bitterly obliterated.[1]

The great searchlights blinked on. The heavy antiaircraft batteries opened fire, followed later by the light ones. The fire was continuous, but so was the creeping wall of flame from the line of dropping bombs. A thousand silver shapes high above unloaded a thousand loads of bombs. They dropped on homes and churches. They dropped on the very old and the very young, on women as well as men. The British Royal Air Force had launched its first successful thousand-bomber raid on Germany. Its purpose was the destruction of the homes—and the lives—of those who worked in munitions factories and the creation of an aura of fear and disillusionment that would cripple the German war effort.

In the ninety minutes shortly after midnight on this night of May 30/31, 1942, 1,500 tons of bombs fell on the city below—8,300 small (stick) incendiary bombs, 90 explosive bombs, 116 phosphorus bombs, 81 fire bomb canisters, 4 liquid bombs, each with 125 kg of incendiary fluid, and 3 heavy mines were counted by those below, a small beginning to the totals of those dropped later on other German cities. But 100,000 inhabitants of the city lost their homes temporarily; 227 businesses were damaged, but only 16 were destroyed and 55 severely damaged. The face of the city had been totally altered, however. Whole streets had disappeared. Old monuments, museums, and churches lay in ruins. The fate of Cologne was a harbinger of worse things to come.[2]

The British bombs were not aimed at the harbor installations or the bridges on the Rhine. Nor were they directed at the armament factories or military installations in the area. Their target was the center of the city. For by this time the British military planners had come to the conclusion that the only effective usage of their bombers over Germany was in direct night attacks on the urban population centers. Before the war, Prime Minister Neville Chamberlain had told the House of Commons that in the event of a war, Britain would bomb only purely military objectives and even in this endeavor would take due care to avoid civilian casualties. But the exigencies of war forced the British to reconsider such prewar promises. Daylight bombings over Germany in 1940 and 1941 proved extremely costly. German flak and German fighter planes took an excessive toll of British raiders on their relatively lengthy pathway to targets within the Reich. By 1942, the British had turned to the much criticized decision that the bombers had to go at night and had to attack the only objectives suitable for nighttime bombing—the centers of the cities.[3]

The pertinent directive, developed by Secretary of State for Air Sir Archibald Sinclair and the British Defense Committee, was issued on February 14, 1942, eight days before Air Marshal Sir Arthur Harris became commander-in-chief of the bomber command. The key words of the directive indicated that the "primary objective" of British bombing in Germany "should now be focussed on the morale of the enemy civil population and, in particular, of the industrial workers." A list of important industries in the roll of targeted cities was drawn up, but Sir Charles Portal in a memorandum to Harris's predecessor on February 4, 1942, wrote: "Ref the new bombing directive: I suppose it is clear that the aiming points are to be the built-up areas, not, for instance, the dockyards or aircraft factories where these are mentioned in Appendix A. This must be made quite clear if it is not already understood." And even at the outset, the city of Lübeck was included in the list of cities to be bombed, not because it was important industrially but because it was especially flammable.[4]

To his full acceptance of the above directive, Sir Arthur Harris added a propagandist advocacy of the independent employment of bombing forces with the assurance that they could win victory on their own. There was also in his use of these forces a kind of joy in his work that gave him the nickname "Bomber Harris" and turned an operation that could not avoid connotations of barbarism into one of routine. The number of planes to be used was constantly increased. The size of the biggest bombs dropped rose from 900 kg in the spring of 1942 to 1,800 kg in the summer of that year, to 3,600 in the fall, and eventually to 10,000 kg by the end of the war.[5] The number of small stick incendiary bombs dropped rose so high that in the last part of the war, Berlin and Munich were each the target of over two million of them, Frankfurt and Nuremberg of well over a million each.[6] The use of incendiaries became more sophisticated, with rubber and liquid asphalt being added to make them cling to their objectives and to add to the difficulty of extinguishing them.[7]

From the beginning, this policy was criticized in England itself and later on by some Americans. But with the continent shut off from attack in Hitler's vaunted Fortress Europe, the United States only beginning to enter the fray, the British land forces confronting formidable opposition in North Africa, and Britain's ally, the Soviet Union, struggling to maintain itself against the powerful attack of massive German armies, Great Britain desperately needed a means of convincing its allies and its own people that it could punish its enemy. Air photos of burning German cities horrified few British citizens, who had experienced the bombs and fires of London and Coventry, seen the early war photographs of a Warsaw wrapped in billowing clouds of black smoke, and read of the ravaging of the Russian countryside by the advancing German armies. For that matter, few Americans were shocked by those aerial photos. They, too, had seen the burning areas around Pearl Harbor ravaged by Germany's ally, Japan. Warfare, especially a war against an enemy genuinely conceived to be evil and monstrous, hardens those who are involved. Against an evil enemy even evil means can be justified.

Lübeck and Rostock had been targets of what Goebbels was to label British "terror bombing" before Cologne.[8] During the remainder of 1942, only Bremen became the target of another thousand-bomber raid, and even there the number of planes actually reaching the target fell three hundred below that mark. But attacks by smaller bands of planes showered bombs on Essen, Emden, Hamburg,

Duisburg, Düsseldorf, and other cities.[9] The full effects of this mode of bombing were not, however, to be realized until a year later when Hamburg underwent the "July catastrophe" of a devastating firestorm. In any war, there is always a "home front" responsible for the direction of the war effort and its supply and provisionment. But from this time on there was a "homeland war" for Germany in addition to the wars it was waging in Russia, on the Atlantic, and in Africa.

World War II initiated the concept of "total war"—a war that involved all, civilians and military alike, in the war effort. This was not really new. Lazare Carnot had anticipated it during the French Revolution with his call for "a nation in arms." But never before World War II had nations been required to draw so heavily upon the total human resources available to them. In each country, there was a propaganda effort to portray every person in the state as personally involved in the struggle being waged. In the United States, "Rosie the Riveter" was as much a part of the picture as "G.I. Joe." The German "Rosies" were not so likely as their American counterparts to be working as riveters, but from 1942 on, they and their children were to face terrors of war as severe as those experienced by their front-line soldiers. Shivering from fear of being buried alive in the cellars that served as air-raid shelters, they had to emerge from those areas of modest security to extinguish the fire bombs that sizzled in the attics above before entire houses were incinerated. Each explosive bomb that fell could mean life or death for each person who heard it coming, depending on where it fell and how big it was.

There is no rational way of rendering judgment on the moral aspects of the Allied bombing. It did, of course, kill Nazis and anti-Nazis alike; women and children as well as men; prisoners of war and foreign workers as well as Germans; professors, artists, musicians, and farmers, as well as workers in munitions factories. And the mode of death, as will be seen, was often shocking and gruesome. But it is faulty to assume that without the bombing all those who perished would have survived and would have met death more peacefully. Land invasion would have meant the ravaging of cities by heavy artillery, tanks, and flame throwers, the desperate flight of thousands of civilians (which indeed occurred on Germany's eastern front), and the ultimate collapse of all forces of order, with internecine fighting, famine, and disease as likely accompaniments. Neither can one assume that more churches, famous monuments, paintings, library books, and so forth would have survived. That those who dropped the bombs had pangs of guilt in respect to the suffering they caused and the cultural wealth they destroyed is a credit to their humanitarian sensitivities. But sentiments of revulsion are more appropriately directed at war itself, which inevitably brutalizes those involved, destroys normal sensitivities, and opens the way to rape, pillage, and wanton destruction. A "clean," "humane" war is an impossibility.

But if this seems to apologize for the bombings, there is also ground for admiration for those who were under the bombs, who kept working in the factories even though their homes were in rubble, who kept working in the fields although every kind of labor help shrank away, who kept government offices running although they had to deal with increasingly angry and desperate people. The story told in this book is not meant to condemn the bombers or to defend the Nazi officials who dealt with the damage the bombers wrought. Rather it seeks to portray the last stage of the death struggle of a nation that had been misled, had sowed the dragon seeds of destruction, and now confronted the monsters that had sprung from them. And there is a clear portrait of heroism attached to the German people, a heroism not ideological in either its origin or its persistence, a heroism that personifies the basic strength of the human personality under the severest form of stress.

Those who were under the bombs were not living in a free society. They lived, worked, and played under a regime that sought to direct every aspect of their existence. The essence of that regime was a complex amalgam of ideology and bureaucracy. The ideology had brought the regime to power. Its adherents claimed their right to posts in the bureaucracy. Bureaus and bureaucrats justified their existence on an ideological basis. But bureaucracy always creates for itself a place separate from ideology or political affiliation. It is a kind of separate world of memos, correspondence, directives, and orders. In this nether world there is conflict and rivalry—the search for more power, more things to do, more personnel, more visible significance. The Nazi bureaucracy was incredibly complex, with many areas of conflicting jurisdiction, a great deal of personal rivalry, and a leadership that fostered internal rivalries and conflicts. Nazi bureaucrats, like most bureaucrats, followed orders from above, sought to meet goals and set standards, and enjoyed the paper work that was the sign of their profession and the innumerable titles attached to their functions.

A description of this bureaucracy and an analysis of the varying importance of particular bureaus and bureaucrats would require a separate book. It would also divert attention from the people themselves, who are the centerpiece of this study. But a few brief notes are unavoidable. Hitler was the Führer, leader of the Nazi party and also head of the German state. He was the source of all authority, the determiner of both military and political policy, the spiritual guide of his people. Even as late as this time of crisis, he combined elements of the human and the divine. "The Führer is always right" was more than a political chant—it still had broad popular acceptance. But the Führer became increasingly wrapped up in military strategy and decisions. The god spoke less frequently to his troubled followers.

By this time, party and state were to all intents and purposes one, although some state titles remained alongside the party titles. The party leaders of the central government, the Reichsleiters, were also ministers of the Reich. Beneath each Reichsminister was a complex bureaucracy headquartered in Berlin. The old states had virtually disappeared; they had been replaced by the Gaus, which had once been the regional divisions of the party. The Gauleiters exercised the administrative powers of the state within each Gau and were also designated, in most cases, as the coordinators of the defense of the Reich within their Gaus if military danger required this. Beneath the Gauleiters were county leaders (Kreisleiters), city or town leaders (Ortsgruppenleiters), and in the larger cities block and cell leaders. But within each of these divisions, there were also leaders charged specifically with the affairs of labor, of farming, of propaganda and cultural affairs, of welfare work, and so forth. The lines of authority between these officials and the respective offices in Berlin as over and against the respective Gauleiters, Kreisleiters, and so on could never be clearly and formally defined. And there was a very large police organization inextricably interwoven with the dreaded SS organization of Heinrich Himmler.[10]

The major figures at the center of the bureaucracy were Himmler, now heading all of the police forces of Germany; Joseph Goebbels, with an extremely extensive and active bureaucratic organization for propaganda; and Martin Bormann, who had greatly increased his influence after the flight to England in 1941 of Rudolf Hess, who had been designated as Hitler's deputy. From 1942 on to the end of the war, Bormann exercised ever greater influence on Hitler, controlling access to him and issuing decrees under his signature, some of which the failing dictator had probably never seen. Bormann was the consummate bureaucrat—in the shadows, loving paper work and the flow of reports to him. From his desk poured out a flood of materials directed to the Gauleiters, Kreisleiters, and Ortsgruppenleiters, those who were designated the Hoheitsträger, the bearers of authority—the "golden pheasants" as these functionaries were called by the people. Bormann's writings comprised a number of series: "confidential information" reports (*Vertrauliche Informationen*); "circulars" (*Rundschreiben*); "directives" (*Anordnungen*); and "publicity releases" (*Bekanntgaben*). The first three of these, in themselves confidential, also had a "secret" file for the sole information of the Hoheitsträger. Some of the Gauleiters ignored or disobeyed Bormann's directives, but by their nature, Bormann's reports provide a detailed key to the concerns and actions of the government.[11]

Other government documents reflect more clearly the concerns and attitudes of the people themselves. The party and the state exercised power through fear—the threat of extreme punishment for disobedience. But the party also lived in fear—fear that the power gained after such a long struggle would disintegrate; fear that opposition groups would undercut their popularity; and a basic, unwritten, and unadmitted but very real fear that ideology would lose its power. This fear is witnessed in the great variety of reports on the popular mood required by the regime. The best known of these "mood" or morale reports are those of the Sicherheitsdienst, the intelligence service of the SS.[12] Throughout Germany, agents of the SD reported on rumors circulated, critical comments made, reactions to new government directives, the reception of speeches of the party leaders and of new movies, and so forth. Similar reports were made by various government leaders, school administrators, labor leaders, and court officials. In a society in which diaries could seldom be kept for fear of their being used as evidence of antistate feelings, these mood reports give insight into the thoughts of the people. It was a sign of the vigilance of the observer to report evidence of discontent. Although these reports seldom make clear the extent of such discontent, they allow us as in a mirror darkly to see some of the reality lying beneath the humdrum of orders and regulations.

It might be added that the newspapers of the period were a part of the bureaucratic apparatus. Their editors were, to all intents and purposes, government agents, accepting both the news itself and directions for its presentation from propaganda ministry handouts. As a consequence, the only nonofficial reflection of the life of the people in the newspapers of the day is to be found in the advertisements for the exchange of goods and in some details of local news. After all, the details of bombing damage could be hidden in national press releases but not from the inhabitants of the cities themselves, and dispositions in respect to transportation and other local matters had to be made known to them.[13]

In one of his fairly frequent gaffes Hermann Göring, the Reich air minister, had, in 1939, assured the inhabitants of Germany's cities along the Rhine that they would never have to fear British air attacks.[14] The air defenses, he thought, were so strong that if British planes penetrated them, the German people could call him "Meier." This was, of course, an invitation that got much use during the war, but there was some justification for Göring's confidence. A million men were deployed in antiaircraft defenses. The German apparatus for tracking and countering invading planes was relatively sophisticated. But Göring had not anticipated night attacks, and the German air force was very heavily committed in the campaign in the east, so much so that, by 1942, the defense of Germany in the west was entrusted to just twenty-five squadrons of fighter planes (250).[15] Field Marshal Erhard Milch gave increasing attention to the production of fighter planes after November 1941, but the effort came too late, was constantly hampered by changing battle strategy and Hitler's personal interference, and in the long run proved futile, since lack of fuel for pilot training prevented many of the new fighter planes from being used in combat.[16]

Bureaucratic arrangements for civilian defense against air attack had begun in 1935, and much had been accomplished before the beginning of the war. Plans for alarms, shelters, first-aid services, degasification groups, and so forth had been made. A considerable effort in respect to air-raid shelters, including experimentation with various types of above-ground tower shelters, had been carried out. But in September 1940, the work of civilian defense was greatly expanded by an emergency decree of Hitler's designating eighty-two cities in which air-raid shelters and other emergency installations were to be built.[17]

The results of these measures can be seen in the example of Cologne. Prior to the thousand-bomber raid, five hundred air raid shelters, secure against bomb fragments, provided places for 75,000 people. Fourteen auxiliary hospitals with 1,760 beds had been built. Twenty-seven emergency first-aid stations and fourteen stations for secondary medical assistance were in place. Twenty-five bunkers secure against direct hits provided shelter for 7,250 people. Twenty-nine more were under construction. These projects and auxiliary provisions had cost twenty-four million marks and involved the movement of 200,000 cubic meters of earth and the use of 100,000 cubic meters of iron and 35,000 tons of cement. Emergency water supplies had been provided. Forty-two thousand private air-raid shelters were being built in private homes. In all, thirty-nine million marks had gone for air-raid protection. And the bombs fell, buildings were destroyed, and there were 460 dead—not a heavy toll; more a victory for the defenders than for the attackers.[18]

Within a few hours after the May 30/31 attack, the roads to Cologne were filled with trucks bringing 61,000 sheets, 100,000 meters of curtain material, 34,000 pieces of clothing for men and women, 50,000 pieces of clothing for boys and girls, 90,000 boxes of soap powder, 700,000 cakes of soap, and ten million cigarettes. Three hundred seventy-four workers dealing with claims for war damage were aided by 43 from Bonn and Düsseldorf, 160 more from the Interior Ministry, and 150 court agents, and before a month had passed, 140,000 claims had been handled. The final total of claims presented mounted to 370,000 and 126 million marks were paid as damages. Five thousand two hundred workmen from Cologne itself were backed up in the repair work by 3,400 glaziers brought in from outside, 10,000 building advisers, 25,000 soldiers—in all 16,500 auxiliary aid.[19]

These figures present in brief summary a part of the story to follow. The bombings were to prove damaging to the houses and buildings of the cities but took a relatively minimal toll of people and had a relatively insignificant effect upon war production. The bureaucracy made heroic efforts to deal with the bombing damages as they occurred. But behind the figures lies the story of lost homes, of constant fear and uncertainty, of the movement of thousands of people to unfamiliar places and often ungracious hosts. Each bomb that fell shrieked the word "defeat," although those beneath the bombs scarcely dared whisper it.

During the remainder of 1942, there were thirty-two more attacks on German cities. Approximately 12,600 tons of bombs fell on nineteen different targets, with Bremen being attacked five times, Duisburg four times, and Essen, Hamburg, and Emden twice each. But this was only a modest beginning to the hail of bombs released in 1943.[20]

These attacks contributed to a decline of morale that had many other sources as well. As early as Rudolf Hess's precipitate flight to England on May 10, 1941, and the rumors of increasing difficulties with the Soviet Union, party officials had noted "a not insignificant decline" of popular optimism.[21] The early shock of a two-front war had been increased by news of the hardships of the Russian winter and the shortage of winter clothing for the German troops.[22] By 1942, the homeland skies no longer reflected the earlier rosy glow of optimism. Shortages of food, clothing, and household utensils became ever more apparent. The party began a new and darker drive against the Jews and the established churches. The conduct of justice became still more severe and arbitrary. The countryside and the cities filled with prisoners of war from the east as well as the west and with foreign laborers in the millions, some recruited on contract but most engaged in forced labor, unwilling guests in a hated land. And Germany confronted a new foe in the United States and began to doubt the value of its Italian allies. The gnawing doubt of ultimate victory began to spread rapidly, a doubt that could not be expressed without danger but still came increasingly into the reports on the popular mood made by the police and government agents watching over their assigned areas of surveillance.

Potential food shortages were the most serious concern both of the people and of the government bureaucracy. By this time, of course, Germany was well into its third year at war. Germany's home production was supplemented by considerable imports from the occupied portions of the Soviet Union and from other parts of eastern Europe. Wheat, butter, and considerable quantities of sunflower seeds, which helped to supplement food oil supplies, were imported. But the needs of an army deep in foreign territory and the problem of feeding constantly increasing numbers of foreign workers for the armament factories placed an ever heavier strain upon Germany's food producers. The regime was haunted by the specter of the turnip winter of World War I, when Germany hovered on the verge of starvation, and it was determined that the population, which still remembered those bitter days, should not confront a similar challenge.

As early as the middle of 1941, there were serious shortages of beer, wine, and tobacco in Germany. A secret situation report from the Sicherheitsdienst depicted the supply situation in the great cities as catastrophic, with long lines waiting for hours to obtain fruit, vegetables, and, above all, potatoes. And, noted the writer, even without Jewish influence the Germans were becoming a nation of black marketeers and influence peddlers.[23] The black market was due partly to the effects of price controls, which kept food prices at prewar levels while the cost of shoes and other needs of the farmers doubled or tripled.[24] As a consequence, many farmers felt badly treated by the system and justified in bettering their income illegally. By early January 1942, Bormann was seriously concerned about the availability of vegetables during the coming year. The meat ration had already been reduced, and the harsh weather was threatening the potato crop so that other vegetables would become an even more vital part of the diet during the coming year. The party sought to make sure that available vegetables got into the rationing system and also took steps to facilitate the use of "wild foods." For two days in April, the women teachers from the party's division concerned with household welfare collected the vegetable products available in Germany's forest areas. These included figworts, yarrow, goat's-rue, stinging nettle, dandelions, sorrel, broad and pointed-leaf plantain, carnation roots, parsnip, parsley, and chives. A bread spread, they demonstrated, could be made from sorrel, yarrow, parsley, and chives with vinegar and salt, or a spinach substitute from stinging nettle, goat's-rue and plantain, or soups from combinations of these "natural foods." There were no reports on the tastiness of these concoctions, but the party never aroused much public enthusiasm for the suggested grazing of human cattle. But in times of need, the availability of these "wild foods" was again suggested. Meanwhile, Bormann sought to prohibit party members from taking advantage of their positions to obtain meals without ration cards.[25]

The shortages of alcoholic beverages had also increased. Brandy was now to be distributed only by the glass, some to workers in the munitions factories but most of it to mine workers. Beer production was to be reduced from fifty million hectoliters to forty-four million. Moreover, the greater part of this would be at the 3.5 percent alcoholic level.[26] At the same time, cuts in the level of fat in milk and an increase in the water content of butter and margarine were ordered, but absolute secrecy was enjoined in respect to fat shortages.[27] In a desperate effort to increase the production of potatoes, the price was raised by .75 marks per *Zentner* (110 lbs.). This was one of the few increases in the cost of food allowed during the war, and it was adopted only after considerable debate and justified by its importance for the raising of swine both for meat and for fat products.[28]

Bormann also emphasized the need to limit the use of tractors on farms to those converted to methane gas. At this time, in March 1942, he noted, only engines using this form of fuel were being produced. A company, Generatorkraft AG, was preparing the wood to be used for these engines.[29] Shortages of wood could be avoided, he suggested, by using the stalks of potatoes for the production of cellulose for paper. The major unions of potato producers were to arrange for the collection of these in the fields, where they were to be dried before being shipped to a cellulose factory in Weimar. Two marks per one hundred kilograms were to be paid to the farmers.[30]

That these signs of food shortage should engender beefing was unavoidable. The weak beer was received with derision, especially in southern Germany, where beer was regarded as part of the diet.[31] Observers reported that heavy penalties reduced the prevalence of black-market slaughtering but also crowded jail facilities for long-term imprisonment. Perhaps, suggested one judge, those guilty could be castrated near sausage factories to add to meat supplies.[32]

In February, Goebbels declared that German civilians had no reason to gripe about food, since those at home had borne few sacrifices.[33] But by the time of the thousand-bomber attack on Cologne in May, bad weather raised urgent fears of a complete crop loss. Goebbels worried that the bread ration would have to be reduced and barley mixed into its production. And potato raising would require the use of reserves as seed potatoes. If the English, as some reports were indicating, dropped the American potato beetle and the Texas farm pox on German fields, there would really be a critical shortage.[34]

At this point, in May 1942, the official monthly rations for the "normal user" (there were higher rations for those engaged in "heavy" work in the munitions factories and mines), which had early in the war been 10,600 grams of bread, 2,000 grams of general foodstuffs, and 130 grams of sugar, were reduced to 8,000 grams of bread (a little better than half a loaf per day), 1,200 grams of meat (less than a tenth of a pound per day), 600 grams of general foodstuffs, and 900 grams of sugar (about two pounds) for the entire month.[35]

The summer of 1942 found Nazi officials sharing the concerns of ordinary citizens about the food supply for the coming year.[36] There was an effort to tighten the regulations in respect to the slaughtering of swine, since these were a major source of fat supplies. Extra care was to be exercised to be sure that the weights of those slaughtered were properly recorded and the meat ration of farm workers was to be raised to 750 g per week (equivalent to the category of a heavy worker in industry) in an effort to reduce cheating.[37] Party members or leaders also became subject to expulsion from the party "in serious cases" for breaches of war regulations.[38] The distribution of food cards was now assigned to the party officials (Hoheitsträger) along with instructions that no cards were to be issued to full Jews or first-class Mischlinge (half Jews) or to households in which there were full Jews or first-class *Mischlinge*, or to Aryan husbands or wives who had not divorced their Jewish spouses.[39]

Jews were to receive special ration cards from a Jewish agency. These were to be stamped *"Jude"* in a color standing out from the background, and from October 19, 1942, on were not to be valid for meat, wheat products (cookies, white bread, and so on), full milk, skimmed milk, or eggs. Jewish children over ten were to receive the full bread ration of the Reich but only in rye bread. Jewish children over six would receive the normal fat ration of the Reich but no artificial honey, cocoa, or marmalade. Packages for Jews were to be opened prior to delivery, and if they contained coffee, cocoa, tea, or other products not allowed Jews, the whole package was to be confiscated. If no prohibited products were in the package, it could be delivered, but the contents were to be deducted from the ration allowances even if they had spoiled on the way. The only exception to these severe regulations applied to Jews who had been wounded in military service in World War I and their families.[40]

At the same time, many other shortages plagued the people at home. Clothing shortages had begun, although they were to be much more severe during the following year. When rumors arose that the soldiers on the eastern front still needed woolen clothing and that a new collection would be started, Bormann denied that this was necessary, since new uniforms designed to meet the Russian winter were being distributed.[41] But the processing—fumigation and repair—of the woolen clothing already collected was still underway and there were, indeed, notes of continued shortages at the front.[42] The need for iron led the government to confiscate a large portion of the church bells in Germany—whether this need was genuine or simply an excuse to take action against the churches, as noted below, is somewhat uncertain.[43] Other metals were also collected by the state.[44] Tobacco and paper shortages became severe. The size of newspapers was drastically reduced.[45] There were rumors of shortages of rubber nipples for use on nursing bottles, but the government denied that this vital item was in short supply.[46]

Efforts were beginning to close manufacturing plants not directly serving the war effort and to establish more efficient control of munitions production through the appointment, on February 8, 1942, of Albert Speer as minister of armaments and munitions.[47] Germany began to face, but was never to solve fully, the serious problem of eliminating normal consumer-oriented production, with the consequence of depriving many parts of the Reich of old, well-established firms, a situation which the Gauleiters resisted ferociously.[48] Attending these efforts was also a concern for maintaining exports to pay for needed imports.[49]

The party executives from this point on sought to reduce the easily criticized display of breaches of wartime etiquette by their subordinates (although they were often guilty of improper actions themselves).[50] There was to be no unnecessary use of motor cars at a time when the streets were empty because of gasoline rationing. The wearing of dress uniforms or evening clothes was prohibited. Party leaders were to avoid any sort of action likely to contribute to the general belief that party bosses were using their positions to evade the hardships of a wartime economy.[51]

A second vital appointment by Hitler on March 21, 1942, that of Fritz Sauckel as plenipotentiary for labor service, began to have serious consequences for the home front.[52] Sauckel, formerly the Gauleiter of Thuringia, created another one of those great bureaucratic complexes that characterized the Third Reich. Within the Reich, Sauckel had representatives working through the Gauleiters for the assignment and supervision of the labor of foreign workers. Abroad, his representatives were responsible for recruiting workers, some coming more or less voluntarily through labor contracts, others being pressed into service. Sauckel added a strong emphasis on the proper feeding, housing, and clothing of foreign laborers, motivated more by considerations of working efficiency than by humanitarian concerns. Although food rations were predominantly meager, housing crowded and often unsanitary, and clothing provisions desperately inadequate, Sauckel's efforts to deal with these matters, strongly supported by Bormann, added pressure to the existing shortages in each of these areas. Sauckel's first great drive to recruit foreign labor added over 1.6 million laborers to the German scene by the end of July 1942. An additional million were added before the end of the year. Another 1.4 million were brought in during 1943 and still another million in 1944 until at the end of that year there were over eight million "guests" in Germany with one of every five workers employed being a foreigner.[53]

Although the greatest concerns were yet to come, fears of this vast alien population began to appear in the mood reports before the fall of 1942. French and Russian prisoners of war along with that strange combination of "East workers" and contract workers from Holland, Belgium, and Denmark began to flood the Reich at a time when Germany was drained of its own male population to fight in the East and in Africa.[54] The organization of volunteer police to assist in control arrangements was designed to meet the danger of an uprising.[55] But almost as serious a concern as that of a possible revolt was the very real fact that German women, starved for male companionship, were making friends with these foreigners. The strongest temptation was attached to the French prisoners of war, and a long line of complaints about German women falling to the blandishments of these defeated neighbors began to fill the mood reports.[56]

In addition to the serious charges of sexual relationships with foreigners, there was the less serious but still troublesome problem of fraternization. Especially in the countryside, there were reports of POW's and foreign workers eating with farm families and sometimes sharing in the better rations they enjoyed. In Bavaria, because the Russian POW's were Catholics (Orthodox) and most of them wore crosses, the people could not regard them as undesirable and on some occasions let them join in church processions.[57]

To the Nazi bureaucracy, all of these things spoke of the need for sterner controls, and that need was met by Hitler's third major appointment in 1942, of Otto Thierack as minister of justice. This marked a renewed effort to streamline judicial procedure according to the Nazi model. Thierack became the author of a series of Richterbriefe, published letters in which he set forth the "proper" way of handling various kinds of legal cases. The major thrust of these "judicial letters" was toward increased severity. The reports to the minister from the various court administrators began to show new signs of caution in respect to criticism of the state and, of course, the proper tone of deference to the minister for his provision of clear "guidance."[58]

Adding to the growing darkness of this period were twin drives by the state against the Jews and the churches. The story of the Wannsee Conference in Berlin on January 20, 1942, at which plans for the "final solution" of the Jewish question were announced is now well known. Recent research has indicated that the strength of anti-Semitism in the prewar period was less than has been assumed and that there was more opposition to anti-Semitism within both the public and the party than seemed likely.[59] But the war provided the opportunity for the rabid anti-Semites to realize their most extreme objectives. The German public became aware of what was happening only gradually. But the general public *was* aware that the anti-Semitism of the party was finding new and crueler expression. No one in Germany could have failed to know the special ration arrangements detailed above. Some Germans helped their Jewish neighbors evade these regulations. But this was always dangerous and fanatical Nazis limited the effectiveness of this aid.[60] Some evacuations of Jews from the German cities and towns had already begun. But these became universal in 1942 and 1943. As will be noted below, they were delayed somewhat in the larger cities, especially Berlin. Although there were small incidents of kindness in some places,[61] little open opposition was displayed. Such opposition was, of course, dangerous and in the midst of wartime regulations could hardly have been organized effectively.

What the Germans believed was happening to these Jews who were evacuated from their homes has been much debated. The official line was that they were being taken east on the road to settlement deep in Asiatic Russia. But there were already rumors coming back home of "very sharp measures" being taken against the Jews in the East and a defense of the necessity to "solve" the Jewish problem during this generation "with ruthless severity."[62] Recent research suggests that the primary reaction to the Nazi measures was predominantly one of indifference.[63] The pressures of war and the absence of the Jews from the home scene allowed people to ignore what was occurring. But, as will be seen, there were those Germans who spoke the deep fears that God was punishing them through the bombings for the way they had treated the Jews.

At the same time a strong drive began against the Catholic church in Germany, whose priests, Goebbels suggested, were "loathsome riffraff" and might have to be dealt with more fully after the war.[64] Most church bells were confiscated (the Catholics did not want to ring them for Nazi celebrations); rules were issued forbidding the church to interfere with working hours on Sundays; orders were circulated that funerals for "heroes" were to follow the Nazi format; and efforts were initiated to curb clerical criticism.[65] Some of the anger probably derived from the church's effective opposition to the euthanasia extermination program of mental or physical misfits which Hitler had been forced to terminate in 1941.[66] There was also the fear of criticism of the regime on the part of the bishops—especially noted at the time of the conference of bishops in Fulda in August 1942.[67] From this time on, party notes were to reflect a sense of frustration that "a final solution" of the church question could not accompany that relating to the Jews.

There is also in the party files a directive stating that Negroes and mulattoes were to be excluded from taking part in any public performance.[68] This may, perhaps, have been part of the propaganda moves against the United States, Germany's newest enemy, which sought to emphasize its absolute lack of culture, its worship of film stars, and its quest for sensationalism, as shown in the appearance of women boxers and mud fights. The best roads and the fastest cars were to be found in the technically much more advanced home country, declared the Nazis, and the United States had no right to promulgate moral lessons for Germany. English words were ordered dropped from usage and American phonograph records were not to be played.[69]

But at the same time these unfavorable moral judgments were being made in respect to the United States, German mood reports were telling of girls as young as fourteen engaging in prostitution, others, twelve to thirteen years old, seeking to buy "Parisian rings" and knowing exactly what they wanted, and the beginning of a youth criminality to be discussed more fully below.[70]

The shadows at home were darkened by gloomy news from the battle fronts. The glamorous reports of submarine sinkings of allied ships began to disappear. There were no longer great victories in Africa, and even the amateur newspaper readers could see the signs of crisis on the eastern front. Nor were these things distant and remote. The agony in the East was perhaps most poignantly typified by the experience of a German wife who opened the letter from her soldier husband, who had been captured by the Russians, to read that all was well, but then, as she took off the stamp to save it, found beneath it the line, "They sawed off both my feet. I'll never come home."[71] How many more would it be who never came home?

2. The Last (Somewhat) Merry Christmas

By 1942, the words "merry Christmas" had lost much of their meaning in Germany. How could one be "merry" with the threat of bombing over one's head; with the news from the eastern front being dark and murky, portending difficulties which the army did not want to report; with increasing shortages of everyday articles and a homeland changing its appearance as thousands of people left the cities for a safer refuge in the countryside? Those at home could no longer find optimism in the forward push of their armies in Russia— it was clear that the German forces were meeting more difficulties than the bitter cold of another winter. Even the official army reports reflected concern for the German armies at Stalingrad. A massive British offensive in North Africa indicated that Field Marshal Erwin Rommel's victories had not ended British resistance there. Christmas brought thoughts of brothers, cousins, sweethearts suffering the privations of cold and heat with victory still an uncertain chimera after three and one-half years of bitter conflict.

But it was dangerous to be too gloomy. The newspapers carried news of serious penalties for "defeatists." And open opposition could lead to the death penalty—the Nazi regime had adopted the dreaded instrument of death of the French Revolution, the guillotine.[1] Probably more efficient than hanging, the guillotine still carried connotations of the Reign of Terror, in which thousands of political opponents in France had lost their heads. Even the solace of religion was denied many Germans as the government began a great drive against the established churches, which still constituted an irritant for a regime that allowed people to proclaim themselves *Gottgläubige*, believers in God, but sought to restrict formal church activities because of the chronic opposition of priests and preachers.[2] The Sicherheitsdienst reported on party leaders who attended church activities and church officials who tried to extend the role of the church outside the confines of their churches.

It was, therefore, a Christmas that carried little of the cheer that had traditionally been a part of the German celebration of the birth of Christ. Fritz Nadler reported that in the shops of Nuremberg nothing was left to buy—only the dummies once used to display clothing remained in the windows. For children, there were only the primitive toys made by the Hitler Youth and the League of German Girls.[3] For Bavarians in general, the approach of the Christmas season carried no emotional lift—weariness and a sense of crisis brought a "somewhat sentimental" mood, said a Sicherheitsdienst report.[4] Ursula von Kardorff spent Christmas eve in the Gedächtniskirche in Berlin, the great church crowded with women and many soldiers—"all the women were weeping."[5] The family of Josef Fischer in Cologne wondered whether they would ever really be able to think of Christmas as a festival of peace—but they did have a Christmas tree brought in by sled from the woods and decorated with six candles, which still delighted the children.[6]

One aspect of life was a little better. The regime sought to cushion coming bad news by improving the food provisions. Sugar shortages were avoided by the importation of 110,000 tons from Hungary, and the shortage of wheat in the old Reich, due to the severe past winter, was offset by the importation of 750,000 tons from the new Gaus of Posen and West Prussia created after the conquest of Poland. Fat shortages were reduced by importing sunflower seeds from the Ukraine and the Don and Kuban areas of Russia. And, best of all, the potato harvest was regarded as good enough to allow a ration increase from two and one-half kilograms to four and one-half kilograms per person, per week.[7]

Another source of food at home came with the provision of furlough packages of food for soldiers on leave. These so-called "Führer packages" included two and one half kilograms of wheat flour, one kilogram of sugar, one kilogram of meat, and one and one half kilograms of other food supplies.[8] Along with special Christmas rations, slight increases of bread and meat rations, and issues of wine, there was some improvement of morale—the people for the first time in a long while were able to eat their fill again.[9]

Children in Nuremberg got a pound of apples as a special ration. The Nadlers fell into luck when Fritz provided books for a neighbor from a farming family and received a five-pound duck for Christmas.[10] The Fischers might have bought a hen if they had got there in time—they came from Poland—but had to settle for a small rabbit, along with fifty grams of coffee per person, "booty from France."[11] The Messerschmitt works in Regensburg still had a Christmas festival for their employees and gave presents to the children.[12]

There were still some things to buy. Paintings were exhibited and, in the absence of more practical purchases, were a good investment. Most were landscapes—models for portraits or nudes could scarcely be obtained.[13] Used clothing was still being sold—the prices were not supposed to exceed 75 percent of the price paid for the items when new, but a pair of men's pants sold for thirty-two marks, an old coat without a lining for thirty- five marks, and three pairs of dirty, old socks for over three marks, all of these prices being much higher than the original cost.[14]

The cities had not yet lost all of their charm. Soccer was still going strong in Dortmund and a fabulous "Men and Animals Sensation" was scheduled for the Deutschlandhalle there.[15] In Munich, there was the beginning of a university week celebrating 470 years of the Ludwig-Maximilian University. The rector, an SS Oberführer, was to be joined in the ceremonies by the famous but fanatically pro-Nazi explorer Sven Hedin and Gauleiter Paul Giesler.[16] Goebbels visited Dresden a little before Christmas and found it "stately, wonderfully bright, and clean." On the way he had found the scenery "one of wonderful calm and austerity," which made him "happy as in times of peace."[17] A little later he visited Hannover, which looked "almost as it did in peace" with "almost no trace" of past air raids.[18] Ulrich von Hassell lectured at Stuttgart, "a really delightful city," and attended a meeting of the Dante Society in Weimar, "a pleasant oasis in this barren period."[19]

Bormann celebrated Christmas with the circulation of a lengthy propagandist essay on popular culture: "The true cultural strength of a people must make itself known in all expressions of life in which are portrayed the spiritual character, the inward feeling for life of a people." A new railroad building, said Bormann, could hold its own with an art museum, an earthen water jug with a marble statue, a cleverly written death notice with a lyrical poem. One should look for and prize the chest and chair of a farmer's home, the painting decorating the wall of a worker's dwelling, the form of a grave marker and its inscription, or the dedication of a book given as a gift. There was, he proclaimed, no more culture in a great opera that one attended in dress clothes than there was in the intimate family joy for the birth of a child. It was the task of youth leaders and teachers to awaken the enthusiasm of their audience, to bring them to sing with the joy of human hearts and souls, and to encourage and preserve the music of the home and village, its customs, and its domestic usages. To accomplish this, no doctor's gown was needed—only an honorable German heart and the healthy understanding of an old Nazi.[20]

But under the surface most people began to share a real dread of the future. Although the official newspapers still strove to preserve confidence of victory in the East, the people guessed that the shortness of news in respect to the Russian front indicated serious difficulties there. The first public awareness of the crisis at Stalingrad came with the news of Soviet attacks south of Stalingrad on the Kalinin front. This struck the Germans "like lightning out of a clear sky." Those with relatives feared that the men who had already spent more than twenty months on the front there would not be receiving furloughs any time soon. And rumors became stronger that some parts, perhaps the larger part, of the German forces in Stalingrad were trapped by Russian forces. These rumors were soon confirmed by soldiers on furlough, who also told of the thinning of the front lines by partisan activity in their rear.[21]

At the same time, Rommel's African forces began to reel back from severe British attacks, and the first direct intervention of the United States against German forces came as American and British forces joined in the North African landings on November 7 and 8, 1942. General Walter Warlimont was later to describe the month of November 1942 as marking "the real turn of the tide against Germany."[22]

Vaguely, the German people shared this realization, but the feeling remained that somehow the difficulties could be overcome.[23] The Nazis tolerated war weariness and doubts, but when a Catholic bishop proclaimed that 1943 would be a year of catastrophes, good Nazis were outraged that he was not severely punished.[24] Hitler's New Year's greeting spoke of English and Jewish designs to take away the German children, slaughter millions of young men, divide the Reich, and make it the object of permanent exploitation. But he continued to promise German victory.[25]

For intellectuals, this Christmas period of darkening shadows was a time for internal examination and questioning. Gottfried Benn, the poet, wrote to his friend F.W. Oelze that "the things about us will last a while yet before they come to an end and how this end will turn out no one knows, but it will undoubtedly bring a very decisive alteration of conditions for all of us. Only fools could deceive themselves in this regard."[26] Horst Lange wrote in his diary that his time spent in recovering from wounds incurred in Russia had left him with inner hells along with the outer ones he had faced on the battle front. But now with recovery the fears that had made him unhappy had departed—he was capable of facing the weight of the darkness and of measuring the light more clearly and exactly.[27] Ursula von Kardorff's brother, confronting service on the eastern front, took refuge in the words of the poet Rainer Maria Rilke: "The best way is not to try to work things out or to count things up, but just to go on growing, like a tree, which can stand up to spring storms because it knows that summer must follow, and so it will, but only for those who have patience, who go on living as though all eternity lay before them, quiet, carefree and vast." But for the writer there were to be neither spring storms nor a summer following—he died on February 2, 1943, fulfilling his own presentiment that death itself would be like waking from a nightmare.[28]

For most Germans, the solace for the malaise was not philosophy but religion. Much to the disgust of the Nazis, the Catholic clergy displayed renewed activity. The government reports seethed with anger at their work. The report of the Nazi county school head in Dinkelsbühl spoke jealously of the great Christmas tree in the village church, covered with angels' hair, silver bells, and candles in excess, of a huge garlanded wreath with electric lighting and above it the figure of the Christ child, of the decorations of the thirty-three soldiers' graves in the chapel, each having a small candle, and of the chapel itself lit by four great, thick, red candles.[29]

A Sicherheitsdienst report described the great activity of the clergy about Linz. The priests and sisters were, said the writer, in constant motion on the trains and other transport. They carried the confessional to the homes and even to the farmers in the fields and put pressure on the families to request religious instruction for their children. They were getting there before the Nazi officials to provide consolation on the death of soldiers and organizing elaborate harvest festivals. The only answer, said this Nazi official, was for the party officers to get busy and preempt these ceremonies.[30]

The party did seek to make sure that death notices were carried by party officials, not the clergy, but one official in Wallern paid the price of carrying bad news about a soldier when the grieving mother boxed his ears. Although she was arrested, the church service for the son had a very large attendance.[31] Clergy were also excluded from providing nonreligious instruction, and religious instruction was severely limited. No overtime schooling could be permitted for religious instruction, stated the directive, in view of the serious work pressures of the wartime period.[32] Court action against the clergy also continued. A Sicherheitsdienst report from Linz told of fifteen Roman Catholic priests tried in December 1942. Warnings and more serious penalties were assessed.[33] There were also the continued petty annoyances such as a party order that all ideologically inappropriate and undesirable literature, such as prejudiced confessional material, was to be removed from the hospitals.[34] Hereafter sick Catholics had to read *Mein Kampf* rather than the Bible.

The Christmas period also emphasized the shortage of all kinds of commonly used items. Cuts in the clothing ration cards—the new card provided for no suits or coats—brought a veritable "storm" of people into the clothing stores to get anything available which had been "saved" back on the previous ration cards.[35] Contradicting Bormann's public assurances that the soldiers on the eastern front were well clothed for the winter this time, a confidential report indicated serious shortages of wool for the army and directed that all domestic distribution was to be confined to those who had been bombed out of their homes. At the same time, directives were to be issued that people should always take their coats with them when they went into the air- raid shelters.[36] Rumors began to circulate that all men who had three suits would be required to give up one of them.[37] Marriages and burials presented clothing problems. There were complaints that funeral clothing was unavailable in this period when the number of funerals for soldiers was increasing.[38] Bridal couples also had problems, not just in respect to wedding clothes, but housewares as well.[39]

The shortage of shoes became critical. In Lambach near Wels the women lined up at four in the morning in hopes of making purchases, but in Wels alone there were 25,000 requests for shoes with only a tenth of that quantity being available.[40] Many other aspects of daily life were troubled by wartime deficiencies. Housewives in Hamburg complained of a lack of water kettles, pots, kitchen brooms, and belts.[41] During January 1943, household articles of iron or other metals became subject to rationing, including such items as cookpots, pans, frying pans, pails, and washtubs.[42] The farmers confronted shortages of hoses for their pumps and of spades, gardening forks, cow chains, and barbed wire.[43] One farmer who sought to get new milk strainers went through the maze of bureaucracy only to get permission from Berlin in the end to buy bed sheets to use for this purpose.[44] Other items in short supply were mattresses, bed linen, bicycle tires, toothbrushes and toothpaste, combs, baby powder, and delousing products (in heavy use with the entry of so many foreign workers). Restaurants began to find that their customers were walking off with the table glasses.[45] Toilet paper also became short. Mathilde Wolff-Mönckeberg spent Christmas 1942 straightening out the tissue paper in which the cookies sent her were wrapped so that it would serve this other vital need.[46] The "swap" advertisements in the newspapers increased in number, often suggesting the exchange of what once had been luxury items for the more vital needs of the day. In Munich, an advertiser offered to exchange a two-seater folding boat for a three-door clothing closet and a gas oven.[47] Other advertisements sought brides' dresses and baby articles.[48]

But party leaders could still manage. The Reich Press Chief Dr. Otto Dietrich had no difficulty fitting up a new office-residence in Berlin with a dozen white-wine glasses, a dozen red-wine glasses, a dozen sweet-wine glasses, a dozen liqueur glasses, a dozen flat and a dozen tall champagne glasses, as well as the linen and other bedding needs required. He did have to pay for the bedding, since it had his initials on it, but not for the glasses, which presumably were destined to serve his official duties.[49]

The year 1942 also saw the beginning of the evacuation of women and children from the cities most seriously endangered by the Allied bombings. Baldur von Schirach was initially in charge of the process, which had begun in 1940 before the heavy bombing. He had gained Hitler's approval of the term *erweiterte Kinderlandverschickung,* ("expanded sending of the children into the country,") as a means of treating this process as a sort of continuation of the rural vacations of the children rather than as an evacuation of them from the cities.[50] By November 27, 1942, Schirach was able to report that 335,409 youths from ten to fourteen years of age were in camps of the Hitler Youth and that the Nazi Welfare Agency was caring for 862,968 mothers and children, for a grand total of 1,198,377 persons evacuated from the cities. A total of 1654 special trains and 78 transports by ship on the Rhine and Weser rivers had been required for this move. One hundred twenty-seven thousand tubes of toothpaste, 7,500 first-aid kits, 9,900 musical instruments, 140,000 complete clothing outfits for boys, 130,000 for girls, and 110,000 pairs of wooden shoes had been provided for these new residents of rural Germany.[51] These staggering figures were, of course, to be enormously exceeded during the following years.

But the complaints of the rural folk about the problems occasioned by these new guests also began, and the state threatened penalties of imprisonment for those chosen as hosts who refused to accept persons who had lost their homes in the bombing.[52] Problems with respect to other groups also existed. The state had placed some thousands of Slovenes in Bavaria, and the local populace showed no evidence of accepting the party's indication that these people were worthy of German respect and good will.[53] A similar effort to place Poles of German descent in the area around Danzig gained even less acceptance. The local populace thought that the idea of making Poles into Germans was a poor one—these new immigrants were lazy, came late to work, and then did not do their jobs, and they added to the existing crowding of the area.[54]

Relations with Soviet and French prisoners of war and with the growing numbers of foreign workers also continued to pose problems. At the end of 1942, ten German women and girls in the Augsburg area were sentenced to jail for terms of four to ten months for having sexual intercourse with prisoners of war.[55] In Augsburg itself, a Polish worker killed a twenty-one-year-old German girl because he feared punishment if their love affair was discovered, and on January 20, 1943, at Ebersbach in the Württemberg area, a young Polish farm worker was hung because of improper relations with a farmer's daughter. In this latter case, foreign workers from the area five kilometers in all directions were brought in to see the penalty for getting involved in such a heinous crime.[56] The Germans continued to be shocked at the susceptibility of their women to the charms of French prisoners of war. Although there is no indication of actual sexual intercourse, a police report from Schwandorf in Bavaria reported on December 13, 1942, the case of a farm girl who committed the sacrilege of embracing one of the prisoners of war who worked on the farm and of sharing her food. When the husband returned from the service and forgave her derelictions, the police were unimpressed. It was obvious that he was just too kind and good or his wife would never have been involved in such transgressions in the first place.[57]

Women also presented another problem to the party and state. They were extremely reluctant to work in the armament factories and when they did so, made use of any kind of excuse or reason to get free of that obligation. Bureaucrats talked of *Frauenflucht*, the flight of women from this service.[58] The wives of soldiers had financial support from the state and did not need to work, and women evacuated from the bombed-out districts used their children as an excuse. In the long run, the Nazi effort to recruit women for the labor service was never fully successful. The Nazi ideology had tended to inculcate the old ideals that a woman's place was in the home—Kinder, Küche, Kirche (children, kitchen, church). And although the state favored the organization of women and their political input, it never succeeded in bringing them fully into the work force.[59]

But labor shortages contributed to the second major drive launched by Fritz Sauckel to recruit foreign labor. Party directives conveyed Sauckel's efforts to see that camps for these workers had provision for heat and food storage, arrangements to improve cleanliness, and gardens that might help supplement food rations. Party leaders were enlisted to help in checking on the effectuation of these objectives.[60] These party directives were, of course, part of the effort launched by Sauckel and partly supported by the food ministry to improve the food rations of foreign workers. Obviously, the motives related to the improvement of production, not to humanitarian concerns. But in spite of all efforts, the provisioning of foreign workers throughout the remainder of the war continued to be less than adequate, especially for those lodged in camps and working in factories.[61] The "pay" of foreign workers was negligible. There were deductions for food and lodging, and the employers helped them "save" their money by deducting a portion of their wages for that purpose. The consequence was that even those foreign workers who came in on a contract basis became virtually slave laborers.[62]

German workers in the armament factories also complained of low pay. During the remainder of the war, inflationary pressures existed because the buying power could not be satisfied with the normal process of purchasing. Efforts to link wages to production quotas were strongly opposed, especially in South Germany.[63]

By the end of 1942, there was also criticism of the regime that went far beyond simple defeatism and beefing about the war. From this point on, the number of Germans who were no longer prisoners of Nazi ideology grew rapidly. But the extent and degree of opposition to the regime cannot be assessed with any degree of validity. A large section of the population trusted and defended Hitler and those who served him to the very end of the war. A larger portion of the population lapsed into a fatalist attitude, thinking only of survival. "It's easier to believe in victory than to run around Berlin without a head," was a joke that caught the spirit of people in the capital.[64] A minority of critics now rejected the party and Hitler's leadership, but it was an even smaller minority that planned or supported plans for the overthrow of the regime.

Sometimes the opposition was quiet and revealed only in secret diary entries. Ruth Andreas-Friedrich, who became associated with underground resistance demonstrations later, wrote at this time that only with a lost war could the Nazi regime be brought to an end and that love of her country meant hatred of Hitler.[65] Friedrich Reck-Malleczewen, as he watched the bombing of Munich from a distance, wrote: "And so we continue to vegetate in our life of shame, our life of dishonor, our life of lies. And our protest, at least the protest of our cowardly bourgeoisie, is in the retelling of old jokes about the regime, while their remaining days are spent swallowing propaganda."[66] But Reck- Malleczewen's own courage was restricted to his diaries. The only public courage displayed in this period was that of a small group of students at the University of Munich. A brother and sister, Hans and Sophie Scholl, their close friend, Christoph Probst, one of their professors, and other less closely associated friends were involved in the best-known public protest of this period, that involving the circulation of the "White Rose Pamphlets."[67] Those properly bearing that title were circulated on the campus of the university before the Allied landings in North Africa on November 8, 1942. "It is certain that today every honest German is ashamed of his government," proclaimed the first of these pamphlets. And it raised the question, "Who among us has any conception of the dimensions of shame that will befall us and our children when one day the veil has fallen from our eyes and the most horrible of crimes—crimes that infinitely outdistance every human measure—reach the light of day?"[68] The third pamphlet followed up with the words, "But our present 'state' is the dictatorship of evil," and proclaimed that failure to resist involved the guilt of those who accepted the system. The authors admitted, however, that passive resistance and sabotage were the only means of opposing the Nazis.[69]

The last of the White Rose pamphlets and the two "letters of the resistance" that followed were written as the dimensions of the army difficulties in Russia began to be known. They were more vituperative in language. "Every word that comes from Hitler's mouth is a lie," shouted the last White Rose publication. "His mouth is the foul-smelling maw of Hell, and his might is at bottom accursed." Hitler was the antichrist leading Germany into ultimate tragedy in

Russia: "Neither Hitler nor Goebbels can have counted the dead. In Russia thousands are lost daily. It is the time of the harvest, and the reaper cuts into the ripe grain with wide strokes. Mourning takes up her abode in the country cottages, and there is no one to dry the tears of the mothers."[70]

The "letters of the resistance" were issued in 1943—one before the tragedy of Stalingrad was known, the second afterward. The first presaged the news of defeat and warned the German people that "a criminal regime cannot achieve a German victory— *Hitler cannot win the war; he can only prolong it.*" Calling for opposition, it asked the pregnant question, "Are we to be forever the nation which is hated and rejected by all mankind?"[71] The second pamphlet suggested less accurately that "the frightful bloodbath [of Stalingrad] has opened the eyes of even the stupidest Germans."[72]

The official reaction to the White Rose pamphlets came a month before the public was informed of the defeat at Stalingrad. The Gauleiter of Bavaria, Paul Giesler, spoke to the students of the University of Munich on January 13, 1943. By this time, he knew of the White Rose pamphlets although he was not aware that those responsible for their circulation were among his listeners. Although the occasion was a celebration of the university's 470th anniversary, Giesler's speech was simply further evidence of the strong anti-intellectual attitude of Nazi fanatics. University students, he said, were wasting their time in school when they should be serving in the armies or working in armament factories. They should be ashamed to be spending several hours a day in study and lazing around the rest of the time. He was particularly critical of the coeds. They should be in the home having children, preferably sons, for Hitler. He considered an annual contribution to the fatherland "appropriate." "Of course," he added, "a certain amount of cooperation is required in these matters. If some of you girls lack a sufficient charm to find a mate, I will be glad to assign you one of my adjutants for whose ancestry I can vouch. I can promise you a thoroughly enjoyable experience."[73]

Even before this final insult, students, especially the coeds, had begun to leave the hall. When the SS guards tried to bar the doors and began to make indiscriminate arrests, many of the wounded soldiers in the audience who were enrolled in the university protested and helped to break the restraints. Large numbers of students joined arm in arm to march through the streets of Munich. Order was restored by the use of riot police and a declaration of a state of emergency.[74] The Scholls and their friends were to pay for their protests with their lives. But under the surface, there were others who shared their hatred of the regime. Placards began to appear, hung silently during nighttime hours, labeling Hitler "a mass murderer," and party leaders began to receive anonymous letters criticizing the regime.[75] And the organization of conspiracy against the government began a slow and uncertain pathway that was not to reach fruition until the middle of 1944.

In November, the former ambassador to Italy, Ulrich von Hassell, wrote that there was a "further drop in the barometer. Stalingrad has begun to play a part like that of Verdun."[76] But von Hassell was not optimistic about moves against Hitler by either the people or the army generals. In this he was correct. Lt. Col. Claus Schenck von Stauffenberg, later to be the main figure in the assassination effort of July 20, 1944, was beginning his strong opposition efforts at this time, seeking to get Field Marshal Erich von Manstein to join opponents of the regime but finding little support.[77] The so-called "Kreisau circle" of conservative opponents led by Helmuth James Count von Moltke had begun its series of meetings and drafting of plans for a non-Hitler government.[78] Dietrich Bonhoeffer and Dr. Hans Schoenfeld, two well-known clerical opponents of the regime had met with the British Bishop of Chichester in Stockholm, seeking to obtain outside support for an opposition movement in Germany in the form of concessions to be promised if Hitler were overthrown. But the results were disappointing.[79] Joined to the Kreisau circle at least in consultation were prominent Catholic bishops, Graf Clemens von Galen, Bishop of Münster, and Cardinal Michael Faulhaber, Archbishop of Munich, both of whom had gained the reputation of being anti-Nazi, and Protestant bishops Hans Meiser of Bavaria and Theophil Wurm of Württemberg, who had moved to protests against the persecution of the Jews.[80]

The party leaders were not unaware that the dangers of opposition were increasing. As has already been noted, both Hitler and Bormann were increasingly worried by the evidence of disenchantment. On December 18, 1942, Bormann, in a circular to party leaders, spoke of the critical notes appearing in the mood reports. He attributed these to fear, cowardice, and opposition to the party's ideology. All of the difficulties of the *Kampfzeit*, the time of struggle, were reappearing, he noted, and had to be met with the spirit and methods of that period—good answers or more convincing measures.[81]

These "more convincing" measures had, of course, been much employed since the beginning of the war. At the start of the Polish campaign, there were only 25,000 prisoners in the concentration camps. Those numbers had greatly increased during the war. The war had brought the great expansion of the "special courts," which operated alongside and often in place of the regular court system. By 1940, there were fifty-five of these special courts. Presided over by younger justices, they were more willing to follow the party dictates. In April 1942, Hitler had denounced the courts for their mildness in dealing with wartime cases. He had threatened to act against the jurists who, he said, "must be defective by nature or become so with age." More and more cases were decided by the special courts—by 1943, they were dealing with 73 percent of all legal cases concerned.[82] The number of "not guilty" verdicts brought in these courts shrank until less than 8 percent escaped the condemnation of these tribunals in 1942.[83] And Thierack, as already noted, belabored the regular court judges with his juristic letters telling them how to interpret cases appearing before them.[84] Thierack was an ardent executor of Hitler's ideas of justice. "Now the situation in every people is like this," Hitler told Thierack, "the broad masses are neither good nor bad. They possess neither the courage nor the wickedness for fully good or fully bad actions. The extremes dictate the outcome. If I decimate the good [extreme] while I save the bad, then that will come which took place in 1918 when five or six hundred bums destroyed a whole nation. The war brings the severest losses exactly to the elite groups. Therefore, it is necessary that justice not conserve the negative elements but rather eradicate the rotten elements. It must in this fashion work against the negative selection [of the best] which war carries with it. The judge is the bearer of the nation's self-preservation."[85] As a result, justice was not only severe and fanatic but often petty and humorless. This is typified in the report of action against a complainer who had been required to report to the local Gauleiter every day for four weeks. The Gauleiter would then ask this troublemaker, "How are things going?" The man concerned replied, "Everything is going fine for me." At the end of the four weeks' time, the critic appeared before the Gauleiter with a rosary entwined in his fingers. When the Gauleiter asked him why, he said, "I've been lying for four weeks—now I must repent." For his "penitence" he received a jail sentence of three and one half years.[86]

In a sense, the judges were like other bureaucrats under the Nazis—the prisoners of bureaucratic procedure as well as ideology. Their actions were judged by the standards set by the regime. Those who failed to conform faced penalties of removal from office, enforced retirement, or personal punishment by the regime. One author lists 20 justices who lost their lives by opposition and 207 who lost their positions.[87] But this list includes some Jewish judges and others connected with the assassination plot of 1944. The record seems to indicate that most judges carried out their duties as directed, albeit with reservations repeatedly *hinted at* in the reports of the regional court presidents.

The war tended to intensify the bureaucratic nature of the Nazi regime. One Sicherheitsdienst report noted that workers in the construction business had to fill out six forms for sickness insurance, sixteen forms for the work offices, eleven forms for the Reich trust offices, eight forms for local government, five forms for the association of construction workers, four forms reporting themselves to the army, six quarterly forms for the federal government in Berlin, five forms for the German Labor Front, and eight forms for the economic offices—a grand total of sixty-nine forms to be completed.[88]

Early in 1943, an operation to save coal, *Aktion Kohlenklau*, was initiated with, typically, a new bureaucrat, a "town specialist for heating questions" to tell people how to set up their stoves and use them more efficiently.[89] Again more bureaucracy but with some success. Older agencies justified their work by the citation of numbers to prove efficiency and philosophic declarations to prove conformity to ideology. Thus, the National-Socialist Public Welfare Office reported that it had 80,000 paid workers helping to care for people as kindergarten teachers, youth leaders, doctors, and in similar positions, plus 1,300,000 holding honorary positions with the agency. Its "winter help work" had raised more than a billion marks and provided aid to seventeen million people, while "mother and child" work had been constantly expanded—the number of day-care centers increased from 10,829 in 1939 to 23,535 in 1943, and 1,800,000 children had been given vacations on the farms away from the cities. All of these figures demonstrated that the agency was "the symbol of a new spiritual viewpoint" that had taught Germans "an ideological lesson" and brought them to realize their "social responsibility."[90]

The Berlin bureaucracy continued to be concerned with Allied bombings. It sought to reduce the number of "study trips" being taken by local and regional officials to the bombed cities.[91] Heavy damages were reported from raids on Bremen, including severe damage to the Gestapo headquarters there. Raids there in September had left 5,300 homeless. Raids on Hamburg in July had left 11,500 homeless and 313 dead.[92] The bomb alarms were far more numerous in 1942 than the bombings. Cologne had counted 309 alarms by June, and the smaller attacks continued. But observers became aware that the Allies were using increasingly larger bombs. Fischer described the effect of a "super" 1,800 kilo mine: "Up to two kilometers doors and window frames are torn out. The roofs fly away. In a circle of fifty meters the people in the cellars suffer ripped up lungs. And it is not only the enormous pressure of the explosion which destroys and tears down. Not less strong is the suction which draws houses of many stories away with it. The pressure of the explosion goes to the sides and upwards. The hole left behind is seldom deeper than fifty centimeters."[93] And in predictive accuracy, Fischer noted that the heavy bombs, combined with a concentrated fire-bombing attack on the next night, would leave a city with the larger part of its population hopelessly lost.[94]

Before the year was out, the Germans began to realize that they would face American bombers as well as British. The propaganda office sent out instructions that the term "Flying Fortress' was not to be used for the American planes, since it was obviously a propaganda ploy and might add to popular concern.[95] But the Allied landings in Morocco and Algeria on November 7 and 8, 1942, could not be concealed from the people, and the American president, Franklin D. Roosevelt, now entered into the Nazi propaganda mills as the number one criminal and foe of humanity, the slave of world Jewry.[96] This propaganda undoubtedly gained greater credence than it might otherwise have had with the conference at Casablanca of January 14 to 25, 1943, which carried with it the adoption of the slogan that only an "unconditional surrender" by Germany was to be accepted. But with Nazi propaganda directed towards a final victory, it was somewhat difficult for them to exploit the unconditional surrender theme, except as an indication of the severity and determination of American opposition.

However, neither the United States nor England dominated German concerns in 1943. Attention was fixed on the Soviet Union, where brothers, uncles, fathers, and cousins were trapped in the "kettle" of Stalingrad. Germany was about to face its most serious loss of prestige of the entire war.

3. Stalingrad and All-Out Warfare

On February 2, 1943, the German Sixth Army at Stalingrad laid down its arms. After fighting and losing over half its personnel in the desperate effort to retain this farthest point of German advance into the seemingly endless reaches of the Soviet Union, 91,000 survivors fell into the hands of the Russians. Included in those who became prisoners were Field Marshal Friedrich Paulus, General Walter von Seydlitz-Kurzbach, who commanded the German Fifty-first Corps and might have been Paulus's successor if Paulus had gone into German headquarters, and twenty-two other generals. Only five thousand of those captured survived the war.

In many ways, the tragic fate of the German forces at Stalingrad underscored the defects and shortcomings of Hitler's Germany. The blame for the catastrophe rests clearly and squarely on the Führer himself. The outcome underscored the weakness of the dictatorial regime, dependent as it was on the unchallengeable decisions of an increasingly arbitrary, inflexible, and self-willed man. Those who died were sacrificed for the sake of a stubborn pride, not for tangible objectives. Their deaths reflected the utter inhumanity of the leader, who displayed no compassion for the sufferings and deaths of those who had carried his banners almost a thousand miles into Russia. And their deaths also underscored the weakness of those who wore the epaulets of generals but obeyed the ill-conceived orders they knew would lead to disaster. Heroism, toughness, and an amazing ability to survive hunger, cold, and suffering were displayed by the German soldiers at Stalingrad. None of these qualities were found among the Nazi leaders of the state.

It was in April 1942 that Hitler decided to initiate a great drive into the Crimean area of the Soviet Union. Stalingrad became the major goal of this thrust, although Hitler had anticipated using it as a fulcrum to occupy the entire southeastern area of European Russia. And once again, the German armies fought brilliantly but ruthlessly through the summer of 1942, reaching the outskirts of Stalingrad late in August. The French General Charles de Gaulle, when he visited Russia in December 1944, expressed his admiration for the German accomplishment of getting so deep into Soviet territory.[1]

From September into November of 1942, the fighting across the streets of Stalingrad fluctuated, with heavy losses on both sides. By November, the Soviet forces, greatly reinforced, began to hold against further German advances and gradually forged the ring of armies closing the German Sixth Army in the city into the constricted and battered trap which the Germans labeled the *Kessel*, the "kettle" or, perhaps more appropriately, "the cauldron." By this time, all common sense, all reasonable military strategy, dictated a retreat, a breakout by the trapped Sixth Army to save lives and equipment. But Hitler had dismissed as false intelligence the reports of the growing strength and danger of the Soviet forces. With German forces in the city surrounded and every general in the city and in the supreme headquarters advising a breakout, Hitler refused to allow this action. On November 24, 1942, he sealed the fate of the forces at Stalingrad by a direct order to General (later Field Marshal) Paulus to hold his ground. In spite of efforts by his own generals to get him to disobey Hitler's orders, Paulus regarded it as his duty to follow orders he knew were disastrous. A month later, on December 21, when the situation had become still more catastrophic within the city, Hitler again refused to allow a breakout.

The soldiers in the city suffered the agonies of hunger and cold through the dark winter days of December 1942 and January 1943. The warm clothes gathered at home during the previous winter had not reached them, although great piles of them lay behind the front lines before the kettle was closed. Fur coats, caps, and boots never got to the front lines.[2] And the cold was more intense than anyone had anticipated. When dysentery affected the troops, the satisfaction of bodily needs in the open threatened quick congelation of the exposed parts of the body.[3] Efforts to supply the troups from the air were hampered by freezing motors, landing paths choked with snow and ice, and the growing strength of enemy antiaircraft batteries. Planes that did land often delivered useless supplies—sweets, contraceptives, spices, propaganda pamphlets.[4] The horses that had accompanied the troops into the city were eaten. The bread ration became a slice a day. Warm meals to cushion the cold became rare. And when the final Soviet attacks began on January 10, 1943, there was nothing for the trapped German soldiers to do but to fight to the last hand grenade or rifle bullet, to await the Russian tanks as they crashed through their fox holes and crushed those who hid beneath them, and eventually, for some ninety thousand, to join their leaders in surrendering to the Russians.

In January, just before the final battle, the troops in Stalingrad had a last opportunity to write letters home. Few of them reached their destination. Instead they were taken by the army censors and analyzed for their attitude towards the military leadership. The senseless numbers game played by the censors found 2.1 percent favorable to the war leadership, 4.4 percent doubting it, 57.1 percent rejecting it, 3.4 percent in strong opposition, and 33 percent indifferent.[5] This bureaucratic game deprived those at home of the last thoughts of their loved ones. Perhaps the seizure was meant to prevent friends and relatives from reading comments stating that although death was supposed to be heroic and inspiring, the reality in Stalingrad was different: "A slaughter, a freezing, nothing more than a biological fact like eating and drinking. They fall like flies and no one cares about them and buries them. Without arms and legs and without eyes, with ripped up stomachs, they lie everywhere."[6] Or, "The Führer has promised firmly to chop us out of here, that [message] was read to us and we believed it firmly. I believe it even today, because I must believe in something. If it isn't true, what shall we believe in? . . . If what they promised us isn't true, then Germany will be lost, since in that case no promises can be trusted."[7] But the bureaucrats also deprived wives of the last words of their husbands, such as those of one who faced death without fear and admonished his wife to "educate the children to be upright men who will hold their heads high and be able to look everyone squarely in the face."[8]

The German public did not learn the true facts about Stalingrad until the end. Until early in November, the army reports still spoke of "mopping-up" operations. Hitler himself was confident of victory until November 9. The first public notice of difficulties came on November 24, with the report of a Soviet breakthrough of German positions southwest of Stalingrad.[9] Through the desperate months that followed no mention of Stalingrad appeared in the army communiqués. On January 16, 1943, the army reports for the first time admitted that the German troops in Stalingrad were engaged in a defensive battle against an enemy "attacking from all sides." Although Paulus had warned Hitler on January 22 that the situation was hopeless, he still fired hopes on January 30, the anniversary of the Nazi takeover of power, as he wired the Führer that "the Swastika still waves over Stalingrad."[10] But by January 25, 1943, an observer in Berlin noted that the radio and the newspapers were "keeping up a kind of barrage of mourning" for the events at Stalingrad and that all bars and nonessential shops had been closed.[11] In Nuremberg, however, the radio continued to play hit music while the people were waiting to hear the news from Stalingrad. Fritz Nadler's neighbor, a blind veteran of the First World War, had to be restrained from chopping up the loudspeakers with an ax.[12] On January 27, the radio reports pictured the Sixth Army as "clinging to the ruins of Stalingrad."[13] On January 30, the party celebrations for the acquisition of power, more modest than usual, found Göring speaking of the heroism of the Spartans at Thermopylae and pronouncing the sentence—not to be reported in the newspapers—"The soldier who goes to the front must know that he must die there. If he comes back to the homeland, then he has, indeed, had a piece of good luck."[14] Goebbels more gracefully spoke of the growing faith of the people in their leaders the longer the war lasted and promised that a new life would blossom after victory "on the sacrifices of the dead and the ruins of our cities."[15]

Not until February 3 did the army reports carry the news of the surrender of Stalingrad, picturing a heroic end of the Sixth Army's resistance—"generals, officers, noncommissioned officers, and soldiers fought shoulder to shoulder until the last bullet."[16] In Nuremberg, in spite of the radio report, crowds waited outside the newspaper offices to see the story in print.[17] Everywhere, stores, bars, and businesses were closed for three days of mourning.[18] Göring proclaimed that victory would come in spite of Stalingrad and said that a thousand years later Germans would still speak of the battle with reverence and awe.[19] But Hitler drew a veil of silence over the details of the battle and its outcome.[20] If he hoped thereby to conceal news of the capture of Paulus (who had been made a field marshal just before the surrender) and the other generals, he did not succeed. Nor did he succeed in stilling the muted criticism of the army leadership for allowing the destruction of a whole army when some part of it might have been saved.[21] He could not keep down the questioning of mothers and fathers in respect to the fate of their sons either killed or in the hands of the Russians.

One outcome of the events was an increased fear of the Russians—the anti-Bolshevik propaganda, which had pictured them as cruel and sadistic monsters, now added to the concern for German prisoners of war in their hands and for the potential revenge that might be wreaked against Germany.[22] As early as the week following Stalingrad one of Ursula von Kardorff's associates told her that he had hoarded two hundred liters of gasoline for his car and twenty hand grenades so that he could escape to Switzerland if the Russians came.[23] And from all sections of Germany came personal notes in respect to those captured by the Russians—from Linz, that those captured were mostly Austrians; in Nuremberg, people believed that 19,000 of their relatives and neighbors had been trapped in Stalingrad; in Augsburg, they were convinced that many Swabians were involved.[24]

And Stalingrad was followed by other German withdrawals from less well known places—Kursk, Krasnodar, Rostov, Voroshilov, Kharkov. The rapid advance of the Soviet armies added to the sense of concern occasioned by Stalingrad.[25] From this point on, the number of Germans who no longer believed in victory rose rapidly. Even good Nazis began to lose faith in the future. Milita Maschmann, a devoted worker for the League of German Girls, reported that the press office of the Reich Youth Movement in Berlin, where she worked, "was like a termites' nest, gradually pervaded by a sense of the coming collapse without a single person daring to breathe a syllable about it."[26] The average person had to be even more careful, but the mood reports indicated a growing weariness with the war and reported unguarded critical comments, some even directly against Hitler.[27] Even before the final news of the surrender, the poet Gottfried Benn said guardedly what many Germans believed: "As for what concerns the situation, that is crystal clear. There will scarcely be more surprises. The form which the course of events will assume cannot be specified, but the outcome is unavoidably revealed."[28]

The impact of Stalingrad on the home front was profound. The whole temper of the remaining war years was set by this event. No longer were the Nazis confident in the power of Nazism. Although bulwarked against popular distrust, they adopted ever sterner measures to enforce at least outward conformity with the system. From this point on, Sicherheitsdienst reports told of increased listening to foreign radio broadcasts. The public had not been taken into the regime's confidence with respect to the affairs at Stalingrad and no longer trusted its newscasts.[29] Although the propaganda-inspired fear of Bolshevism, or better of the Russians themselves, continued to grow, the party was increasingly aware that the youth of the country had not been sold and did not wish to be sold on the Nazi *Weltanschauung*.[30] And the party symbol and the "Heil, Hitler!" greeting were no longer as respected as they had once been. A soldier on furlough in Munich boxed the ears of a man who met him with the Hitler greeting.[31]

The response of the party leaders to this decline of morale was twofold: an intensification of propaganda and of court action against defeatists and critics. Two weeks and two days after the final surrender of the German forces at Stalingrad, Joseph Goebbels made a speech often labeled the greatest triumph of his career.[32] The scene was the Sportpalast, the great sports arena in Berlin. Thousands attended but they came by invitation and by ticket. Party members in the audience wore civilian clothes rather than uniforms—the newsreel pictures would, as a consequence, give the impression of a more general audience. To all intents and purposes, Goebbels was Hitler's stand-in. The excuse, of course, was that the Führer was too busy running the war to make propaganda speeches. But already Goebbels occupied the role of the only party leader willing to deal with unpleasant subjects—the effects of the air raids, the tragically lost battle of Stalingrad. The arena had none of the gay decorations that were formerly an accompaniment of major party meetings. A grim banner blazoned the motif of this assembly: *Totaler Krieg—Kürzester Krieg* (total war—the shortest war). Goebbels admitted in his opening statement that the audience was a selected one—but one selected, he proclaimed, to reflect every class, every echelon of German society. Just before him sat the wounded war veterans, those who had lost legs or arms or sight in battle, many flanked by Red Cross sisters who had aided in their attendance. Behind them sat the armament workers, men and women from the Berlin tank factories. Further to the rear, along with party leaders, were the soldiers in active service, lesser party officials, doctors, scientists, artists, engineers, architects, and teachers. Women in large numbers were represented as well as the youth and the aged. Thus, Goebbels asserted, this was an audience which could speak for Germany as a whole. And to this group, he propounded ten questions designed to give them the opportunity to reject the "lies" and "deceits" of English propaganda.[33]

The first five questions mingled the concept of trust in the

Führer and the willingness to assume the obligations of "total war": (1) "Do you believe in the Führer and with us in the final total victory of the German people?" (2) "Are you ready to stand with the Führer as a phalanx of the homeland behind the fighting armies . . . ?" (3) "Are you and is the German people determined, if the Führer orders it, to work ten, twelve, and even fourteen and sixteen hours daily . . . for victory?" (4) "Do you want total war . . . even, if necessary, more total and more radical than we can even imagine it today?" (5) "Is your trust in the Führer greater today . . . than ever? Is your willingness to follow him and to do everything to bring the war to a victorious end an absolute and limitless one?"

The second five questions asked for more specific promises of support: (6) to provide the men and weapons to defeat Bolshevism on the eastern front; (7) to provide the morale at home to support the battle front; (8) on the part of the women, to find services they could perform so as to release men for front-line service; (9) to "sanction when necessary the most radical measures against a small circle of shirkers and black marketeers, who . . . seek to exploit the needs of the people for selfish purposes" (at this point, Goebbels made very clear what he meant as he added, "Are you in agreement that he who places himself before the [prosecution of the] war shall lose his head?"; and (10) to "accept government measures which seek to apportion equal rights and obligations to all."

Each of the ten questions received thunderous sounds of support. Some of the old magic of mass hysteria was still there. A skeptical and anti-Nazi reporter who attended found himself jumping to his feet almost ready to shout his support. If Goebbels had asked the audience, "Do you all want to die?" the reporter said, they would still have shouted, "Yes!"[34] Goebbels's speech at the Sportpalast did not mark the beginning of the drive for total war. He had already employed the term in an earlier speech at Düsseldorf, where he had joined the danger of a Bolshevik victory with the machinations of international Jewry.[35] This joining of a renewed will for victory with "the extermination and elimination of Jewry" was to characterize his propaganda drive throughout the remainder of the war.

Actual legislation implementing total war policies had begun before the fall of Stalingrad. On January 25, 1943, Hitler singled out tank production for special concern, and the party was ordered to give all possible support to increased production.[36] On January 13, he had proclaimed the total mobilization of all men and women for the defense of the Reich. This decree gained its initial order of execution on January 27 when Fritz Sauckel as plenipotentiary for the Labor Service ordered the registration of all available men from sixteen to sixty-five and women from seventeen to forty-five for potential war-related work.[37] From the beginning, there were, of course, exemptions within these groups of those required to report to labor offices for potential work assignments. Exempted were: (1) men and women in public service; (2) men and women fully employed in agriculture; (3) women with one child under school age or two children under fourteen living with them at home; and (4) students in recognized schools. Added shortly afterwards to the list of those excluded from the call-up were all men or women in police or federal labor service, independent employers with more than five employees, and the clergy.[38]

The measures to release men and women for war-related service were predicated on the assumption that a large group of industries and business activities could be curtailed or liquidated. No longer were signs, jewelry, musical instruments, cleaning apparatus, or luxury wares to be produced. The production of furniture, garden materials, rugs, linoleum, tobacco wares, flowers, and art objects could be reduced. Automobile agencies, shops selling luxury porcelains and ceramics, candy shops, perfume stores, specialty stores for jewelry, gold, and silver wares, and shops selling stamps could be closed. Beauty parlors were to stop giving permanent waves although they could still engage in hair cutting and washing. Businesses devoted to the production of surgical instruments, household wares, iron and steel, paper wares, shoes, drugs, and chemicals were to be preserved. Shops for the repair of clocks, radios, sewing machines, office machines, bicycles, and shoes were also exempt from the regulations. All bars and entertainment spots were to be closed, as were all guest homes and inns not absolutely necessary for the war effort.[39]

Later definitions of government policy indicated that the main hope for increasing domestic labor resources centered on putting more women to work in the armaments industries. But concern for negative popular reaction was apparent. Widows and lone married women were the first to be called, but those who had been widowed in the war were given special consideration. Work assignments were to be appropriate—well-educated women were not to be used in menial positions. East workers were often moved to less desirable work so that those Germans who were called up would not have to take on the worst kinds of positions. Calling up men and women who worked less than forty-eight hours a week, as the regulations prescribed, should be done carefully—many of them might already be working at capacity.[40]

In spite of the ideological admonition in the last directive to go to work with a fresh spirit, there was in these directives a considerable reflection of the fact that party leaders knew that the public spirit was no longer as "fresh" as they may have wished. Criticisms varied. In farming areas, there was a negative reaction to the setting of forty-five as the top age for calling women to work. Women on the farms, said the critics, continued to labor into their sixties.[41] There was also criticism of Goebbels's performance at the Sportpalast. His speech, some critics said, had been too excited and had made it clear that Germany was in a real crisis. Others noted sourly that if his ten questions had been answered by secret ballot, the responses might have been very different.[42] And in spite of the note of supposed equality, some observers complained that "certain persons" still traveled to the health spas. Moreover, the party's major cultural agency, Kraft durch Freude ("strength through joy"), originally founded to bring culture to the workers, was sending too many people around for unnecessary entertainment when the motif should be serious work. The KdF people worked a couple of hours a day and could use the rest of their time for their own enjoyment.[43]

These latter criticisms underscored one of the most obvious shortcomings in the party's drive for total war. Too many party functionaries were exempt. The directives themselves gave party leaders down to the level of county leaders (Kreisleiters) the right to designate party employees as exempt because of their party service.[44] Early efforts for "streamlining" party activities centered on a variety of less significant agencies that were to cease their activities and release the buildings and funds that they held to the party's central treasury and their personnel to possible war-related activities. Included were the agency for the care of war victims, the Federal League of the German Family, the Federal League of German Officials, the Federal Colonial League, and the main office for educators and teachers. Other agencies were to join the list of those closed down at a later point with a considerable increase in the power of the party's central treasury probably a more significant consequence than any realization of personnel for needed war duties. But the continued overextension of the party bureaucracy was strikingly underscored in an article that appeared in the *Völkischer Beobachter* in this period. Dealing with the incorporation of the Austrian province of Lower Styria into the Reich, the article noted that 37,422 officials were working to bring this area of 2,800 square miles and half a million people into the German "family."[45] Nazi bureaucracy was never really trimmed of the "excess fat" involved.

Through the period that followed, there were many indications that the efforts to bring more women into the work force yielded unsatisfactory results. One labor recruiter noted that many of the women eligible to work were tied to their homes and were not available in the factory areas where there was the greatest need.[46] Many women simply failed to report as required, and many of those who reported were left without assignments.[47] In Augsburg, potential gains were lost through anti-Semitic actions—when fifty-four Jewish women were taken from service in a balloon factory there, a whole division of the factory was put out of production.[48] Women of the better classes sought to avoid manual labor and when some of them came in as supervisors, they aroused the hostility of the existing women workers, who felt they did not need more administrators.[49] Even Goebbels realized that the labor offices were finding it impossible to cope with the problem of employing the women.[50] There was also continued criticism of party wives or other influential people who still kept maids and escaped work completely.[51] Party efforts to obtain more work from the women continued until the end of the war, but the party never escaped its original deification of the role of women as mothers and homebodies. A party proclamation that women working in the factories were acting as "mothers of the nation they are seeking to preserve" was too artificial to evoke enthusiasm.[52]

The real increase in the German labor force in 1943 came not with the recruitment of native Germans but with increased foreign labor. Although Fritz Sauckel claimed that 1,205,000 German workers had been recruited by the beginning of May, 800,000 of these were women working part time. In that same period, almost 850,000 foreign workers were recruited, and by the end of the year the number stood at 1,427,680. By this time, however, Sauckel was encountering increased resistance from areas in both the East and the West.[53]

Within Germany there were conflicting trends in respect to the treatment of foreign workers. On the one hand, attempts were made to ameliorate their working conditions so that they could produce more goods. Arrangements were made for the care of pregnant women workers, the "simple but hygienic" provision for the birth and later care of their children.[54] A clothing allowance (half of that available to German mothers) was to be allotted to Polish or Eastern mothers of suckling infants and some milk allowance was provided.[55] Arrangements for the free-time recreation of French, Walloon, and Flemish workers were also sanctioned—they could even rent a hall, decorate it, get musical instruments, and so forth.[56] This privilege was, of course, not available to Poles and East workers, but even they were now permitted in the interest of higher production to see movies, in barracks with wooden seats.[57]

The propaganda justification for these changes came with a lengthy declaration by Sauckel pointing out that foreign workers had achieved 65 to 100 percent of the output of German workers and that it was necessary in this time of crisis to treat them fairly. Germany should seek, he said, to show that it was free of "the shameless and indescribably brutal and unworthy methods" of "the plutocratic-Jewish, capitalist world master," which had oppressed its workers in order to secure Germany's destruction.[58] But many Germans regarded the lightening of controls over foreign workers, especially those who were prisoners of war, as dangerous and undesirable. A labor leader in Regensburg reported problems with the discipline of Soviet POW's. What was required, he said, was severe punishment, with weapons if needed, for infractions of discipline.[59] Foreign workers were blamed for an increase in the criminal statistics of robbery and murder.[60] And a secret order from Field Marshal Keitel set a tone completely different from the supposed lightening of controls by prescribing very rigid arrangements for inspections, transfer of prisoners, and the use of guard dogs against the escape of officer prisoners of war in German camps.[61]

However, the major German criticisms centered on the tendency of foreign workers not to recognize German superiority and of some Germans to forget to insist on their own prerogatives. The consorting of German women with French POW's and even with Polish workers continued.[62] The French POW's, said one report, were visited by their wives and wandered about in a free and easy fashion. The East workers not only made free use of public places on Sunday but strolled around after nightfall. And foreign workers no longer yielded place in the streetcars to German women. There was, said one Nazi critic, "an over-objective feeling of justice and equality" that led some to say in respect to a recalcitrant foreign worker holding onto his streetcar seat, "He's also tired from his work," and even to oppose the efforts of "a good party comrade" to clear seats for German women.[63] A German judicial official, reporting similar actions on the part of the Dutch workers in the area of Cologne and "fresh" remarks by Polish workers to German girls, said all of this left the public with the feeling "that they were in some ways no longer the master in their own house."[64]

The concept of total war was never fully realized. Difficulties were encountered in the effort to close unnecessary concerns and party offices. The Auslandsinstitut in Stuttgart was preserved, although its service (it was to provide contact with Nazi organizations abroad) in time of war was not clear.[65] The party's cultural activities continued—"The heart and spirit of our compatriots still require strengthening and support," wrote Bormann.[66] The Kraft durch Freude office in Strassburg arranged a series of short lectures on the radio on the general topic of the better oral use of the German language.[67] Party speakers continued to make their rounds. Alfred Rosenberg spoke in Nuremberg—the church bells rang in honor of the Nazi "Antichrist."[68] Goebbels learned that women were traveling from one Gau to another for beauty treatments and thought that "perhaps one must not be too strict about them [closing the beauty parlors]."[69]

During the period that followed, the execution of the total war measures never became evenly effective throughout the Reich. Some Gauleiters sought to preserve local businesses that were supposed to be closed down.[70] Beauty parlors continued in spite of prohibitions. Bars reopened as restaurants. The vacation resorts still found customers, especially among those associated with the state. Sicherheitsdienst observers complained that these violations of policy indicated that the state did not have the authority needed to execute its own orders.[71] Most significantly, this late move for the complete regimentation of the economy never obtained the moral lift that would have been required to give it full effectiveness. Goebbels's propaganda to some observers carried the impression that the war was lost and speakers at forty-four plant assemblies in Strassburg found their audiences universally unenthusiastic.[72] On the other hand, no government, even a totalitarian one, can achieve 100 percent control. The seriousness of the war was now clear. The old enthusiasm may have been missing, but devotion to work continued and production did rise, even through the increasing trauma of the bombing attacks that followed.

But the shadows were falling now—the era of optimism had ended. The big department stores in the major cities were closed, and in each city and town the long line of closed and boarded-up shops darkened the streets. The last of the luxury restaurants in Berlin ceased business. No longer was it possible for "important" people to savor the gourmet foods and elegant service of Horcher's restaurant or to enjoy on occasion a coupon-free meal of game or poultry. Hamburg, Berlin, Munich, all had lost their *Glanz*, their "shine."[73] Normal vacation periods tended to disappear. Special bonuses were offered to those who worked during the Easter period and train travel during that time was rigidly curtailed.[74] The shortage of paper led to the reduction of the number of newspapers, and people in the smaller towns found that the regional journal that had replaced their local newspaper carried no news of their affairs.[75] No paper could be used for birth and death notices of the army or of similar organizations or by civilians.[76]

The euphoria of good nourishment that had surrounded the Christmas season of 1942 faded rapidly during the early part of 1943. The mixture of one-third barley meal with two-thirds wheat for bread-making not only occasioned criticism of the taste of the bread but even incidents of sickness.[77] In Nuremberg's old market, where there once had been a profusion of stands and all sorts of fruits and vegetables, four peddlers displayed plenty of turnips to sell (as in World War I), but the better vegetables were only to be obtained "under the table" at high prices.[78] The Nazi food authorities issued special instructions for the careful storing and preservation of potatoes, indicating concern for the availability of this staple.[79] On February 26, 1943, butter was replaced with margarine in the food rations, cushioned by a special distribution of 625 grams of cheese.[80] And on March 9, Goebbels reluctantly acceded to a cut in the meat ration. As he said, not every cow in the Ukraine could be taken from the farming families there—even the Bolsheviks had left one cow per family.[81]

Savings of gas and electricity were ordered and the means of obtaining them were often capricious.[82] Thus a burned-out one-hundred-watt bulb could only be exchanged for a sixty-watt one, but a twenty-five-watt bulb could be traded for a forty-watt bulb for the kitchen if the housewife sewed there. Stairwells of apartment houses could not be lighted and people stumbled and fell going to work.[83] People who had homes under construction were required to complete them as simply as possible, including the bath facilities. New construction for those who had lost homes by bombing was to be of the barracks type and old houses were sometimes divided to make space for those who had lost their homes. Offices for government agencies were to be established in the closed-up shops rather than through new construction.[84] A new rumor repeated earlier predictions that excess clothing in private hands would be confiscated. One woman, hearing that those who owned more than three dresses would be deprived of the surplus, dared the authorities to try it. If they sought to take away what she had carefully saved over the years, she would spit on "the whole band."[85] But five southern Gaus found in April that they would have to divide among the many who needed them an allotment of only 1,649 rubber overshoes and 600 sandals.[86]

In the midst of the gloom, people searched for some relief by filling the movie houses, although the program was not so palatable.[87] Perhaps the worst selection was in Berlin, where sixty theaters were showing either "The Eternal Jew" or "The Jew Süss," propaganda films preparing for Goebbels's anti-Jewish action, discussed below.[88] Concerts and plays helped. Even after the air raids, the Residenztheater in Munich was performing Shakespeare's "As You Like It."[89] And sport still had the support of the regime as a means of preserving the race and teaching character, although sport contests were to be limited to local and "neighborly" contests (within one-hundred kilometers of the home town).[90] Large crowds still watched the Westphalian and Lower Rhine soccer teams battle to a 1-1 tie.[91] Even lectures helped relieve the boredom. Ulrich von Hassell reported that he spoke to 1,500 people in Cologne in spite of four daytime air-raid alarms.[92] And an early spring after a moderately severe winter helped boost morale a little—one could decorate pictures of sons at the front or perhaps of those who had sacrificed their lives for their country with a few yellow tulips or white hyacinths.[93]

But bombings at home became both more frequent and more accurate in this period of total warfare. Raids in January and February had not proven extremely destructive. Raids on Cologne and Nuremberg did more damage to surrounding areas than to the cities themselves.[94] Crowds in Berlin still watched the show and danced during a raid, but this was soon to change.[95] Already, youths of fifteen and sixteen began to man the antiaircraft guns.[96] And the lack of accuracy of antiaircraft fire was ridiculed in the story of a soldier who was condemned to death and given the choice of the means of execution. He chose death by antiaircraft fire. So they put him in a tower, surrounded it with three antiaircraft batteries, and began firing. Three weeks later the tower still had not been hit, but when they went to recover the soldier, they found that he had died of starvation.[97]

But both the number and the severity of the air raids greatly increased in March and April of 1943. This move was not specifically designed as a response to the total war proclamations of Goebbels. Rather, it was the consequence of the growing strength of the British R.A.F. bomber command and an intensification of the effort to wreak havoc on Germany's major production area of the Ruhr and on the capital, Berlin. The raids were made more effective by the use of more advanced radar and guidance techniques, which allowed the more accurate bombing of German cities (but not of specific installations within them) in spite of the strong fighter defense based on the radar installations of the German Kammhuber line. The H_2S apparatus, which provided a radar scan showing quite accurately the outline of a city and its buildings, was first used operationally with Hamburg as a target on January 30, 1943, and "oboe," which provided accurate guidance to British attackers by radio beams from England, was used on the night of March 5/6, 1943, with Essen as the target.[98]

The latter raid began a series of forty-three major raids between March and July of 1943 against Aachen, Krefeld, Duisburg, Oberhausen, Dortmund, Essen, Gelsenkirchen, Mülheim, Wuppertal, Düsseldorf, Cologne, and Münster, along with Kiel, Rostock, Stettin, Berlin, Nuremberg, Frankfurt, Stuttgart, and Munich.[99] Essen suffered two raids in March, two in April. Berlin and Duisburg were attacked three times. Attacks on neighboring cities triggered alarms and sometimes a share of the bombs. By May 1943, the authorities in Duisburg had counted 161 air raids and 623 alarms.[100] Gradually cities outside the normal target areas received a bombing visit. Augsburg came under its first, light attack on the night of April 17, 1943.[101]

Only the most eastern cities of Germany were exempt from these raids. The rest of Germany experienced constant anxiety. No one knew what city was to be the next British target. Mathilde Wolff-Mönckeberg in Hamburg wrote: "No one beds down for sleep these days. We sit stiffly on hard chairs, ready to jump up at a moment's notice, and superficial conversation barely hides the inner tension."[102] Ursula von Kardorff took part in the line of those passing water buckets in Berlin after the raid of March 2, writing that 1,700 fires had been started in the city.[103] Goebbels began the long line of diary entries expressing his concern over the raids. The temporary alliance he had formed with Göring, as noted below, began to shake, particularly with the news that Göring sat in his home on the Obersalzberg in the midst of these renewed bombings.[104] A little later, Goebbels expressed his assurance that Hitler would not "let air warfare continue in a slipshod way as hitherto."[105] But Goebbels's solution to the problem of these attacks was the concept of retaliation, which was to form his major propaganda motif during the rest of the war. When Munich was bombed on March 10, Goebbels expressed his concern: "If the English are in a position night after night to attack some German city, one can easily figure out how Germany will look after three months of such bombardments unless we take effective countermeasures."[106]

The British, by this time, were discovering that fire was a more effective bombing weapon than explosives. The magnesium stick bombs were accompanied by liquid incendiary bombs containing a mixture of gasoline, rubber, and viscous material, or of oil, liquid asphalt, and magnesium—a kind of synthetic lava that was more difficult to extinguish.[107] The refinements in the period that followed included mixing these incendiary bombs with small explosive devices that rendered early efforts to extinguish them futile and dangerous. Although the real holocausts were yet to come, the bombing raids of March and April already began to leave a trail of fire and destruction that engendered horror and fear. Goebbels thought for a time of stationing fire wardens on the roofs of buildings in order to direct the rapid employment of fire-fighting crews but then rejected the idea for fear of losing too many men.[108] The propaganda minister visited Essen after the great raid on that city on the night of April 3/4, 1943, and found complete destruction "in many places." "Sometimes," he admitted, "one would like to avert one's eyes and not see all this devastation."[109]

Fritz Nadler, during the raid on Nuremberg on the night of March 8, 1943, rode his bicycle about the city, seeing the clouds of smoke and a fire mountain "like Vesuvius" in the worst-hit places. As in many cities during the air raids, water supplies to counteract the fire had run out. Suffering most serious damage was the Nuremberg flea market, where old spectacles with gold frames but no glasses had once been sold, along with medieval furniture and old paintings. But for anti-Nazis, there were still some elements of humor. The entry door of the SS barracks had been blown off by a bomb, causing many deaths in the barracks. In the midst of destruction, the fire had left intact a placard for the last Kraft durch Freude play production—"Breakfast at Midnight"—a weird concept of a dramatic performance in this time of severe rationing and area bombing.[110] Erich Kuby, who visited Munich after it was raided in March, found that the physical destruction did not bother him that much. Buildings could be rebuilt. But how was society to be reconstructed with the kind of human material he saw about him?[111]

And Ruth Andreas-Friedrich complained that people in Germany had no idea that what they were suffering was the consequence of their own actions, that Coventry, Dunkirk, and the cruelty to the Jews had made this kind of response inevitable.[112]

But some people did begin to tie their suffering to the Nazis. The parents of a young antiaircraft gun helper killed in the raid on Nuremberg buried their son alone, without the Nazi uniforms and the "dying for the Führer" accompaniments.[113] The "Heil, Hitler" greeting began to lose much of its customary usage.[114] News reports were strictly controlled—"The people of Essen remained steadfast" reported a newspaper in Dortmund;[115] "a city [Munich] remained steadfast" said a local paper[116]—the same words were supplied for both newspapers. No local reports came from Nuremberg for several days after the bombing, but a nearby town reported that the people of Nuremberg "are life-loving but at the same time hard people, who are not lightly bowed down" and paid homage to their "iron spirit."[117]

The bureaucracy, of course, continued to deal with defense problems. Special directives for fighting the new phosphorus bombs, which clung to buildings and streets, were issued, along with warnings that they polluted streams, manure in the fields, or standing crops if they fell in these places.[118] Air-raid wardens were directed to care for the houses entrusted to them during the raids; afterwards might be too late.[119] Telephones, typewriters, and other office equipment were to be placed on the floors of offices when personnel left as some protection against air-raid damage.[120] The task of providing additional air-raid shelters and protective measures was placed in the hands of the Air Force Ministry, which was to take the lead in developing an expanded air-raid shelter program. Special attention was to be given to enrolling the population in self-help projects as much as possible.[121]

Reports of bombings, as noted above, had to emphasize the brave and determined attitude of the population, not the damages and losses.[122] And, in line with this, a new civilian medal for those who engaged in brave action during air raids was created. Those killed or injured were now to have the same designation in official reports as was given to soldiers—"wounded" or "fallen."[123]

Perhaps Berliners were most aware of the connection suggested above between the English air raids and the treatment of the Jews. In his diaries, Goebbels dealt with the actions against the Jews in Berlin in an inconsistent way. One of the party's strongest anti-Semites, he had initiated the expulsion of the Jews from Berlin in early March.

But many, he complained, slipped through "our hands" because they were warned by the "better circles, especially the intellectuals" (later he said "the industrialists"). But he promised not to rest "until the capital of the Reich, at least, has become free of Jews."[124] Then came the air raid on the night of March 1/2, and he found it unfortunate that the SD had chosen the very moment when Berliners were dealing with the consequences of the raid for continuing with the evacuation of the Jews. There had, he said, been incidents at a Jewish home for the aged where a large number of people had taken the part of the Jews, and a little later he noted other incidents involving Jews who were married to Gentiles that caused "a terrific commotion, especially in artistic circles, since these privileged marriages are still prevalent among actors."[125]

Contrary to Goebbels's portrayal that the protest against the anti-Jewish actions came from the better classes, Ursula von Kardorff pictured working-class women as being involved—standing up to the SS men armed with fixed bayonets and steel helmets to drag out terrified men, women, and children and taunting them with the charge that they should be at the front. One old lady of eighty-five who would have been evacuated by stretcher escaped that fate by taking vironal. Von Kardorff thought that the ordinary people were more concerned than the better classes.[126] Most Jews, of course, disappeared at night—Andreas-Friedrich found that the Jewish friends her family had been hiding had simply vanished.[127] Sigmund Graff, who was visiting in Berlin, found nothing but anti-Semitic films in the theaters, and when he saw the SS gathering together sixty to eighty Jews to take them away, with their friends and neighbors in tears, he reproached himself but turned aside and made no protest.[128] Similar scenes occurred in other German cities in this same period. By the end of March, 360 Jews had been removed from the area of Augsburg—most were gone by April 10, but a number committed suicide to avoid the evacuation.[129] Of the 9,000 Jews in Munich some 3,500 had left before the war, another 3,000 were deported during the war, and, as of May 1, 1943, only 483 remained in the city. The persecutions still continued—only three months before the end of the war, the last Jew in Göggingen opened his veins to escape the action of the Gestapo.[130]

Meanwhile, the government added new regulations for Mischlinge—those of mixed Jewish and Gentile blood. Second-grade Mischlinge could be admitted to the universities if there were no objections in respect to their political or moral background. But they could not study agriculture or veterinary medicine, could enroll in pharmacy courses only with the approval of the minister of the interior and the leader of the party chancellery. Strangely enough, they were permitted to take courses in medicine and dentistry if their political background was approved.[131] If party members married wives or husbands who had previously been married to Jews, they were expelled from the party.[132] Business entrepeneurs who had Jewish wives were not allowed to supervise apprentices.[133] And complex arrangements were established for the custody of children of mixed marriages where divorce occurred—the degree of Jewish blood and appearance determined whether custody fell to the Jewish or German parent.[134]

Stalingrad also initiated the period when the special courts and penalties for political opponents lost all measure and even the appearance of normal justice. Friedrich Reck-Malleczewen wrote of the summary courts presided over by "sadistic and bloodthirsty Nazi Jacobins," whose verdicts read "liquidate and expropriate." Eleven guillotines, he said, were operated in Germany. A seventy-four-year-old bank director from Stuttgart lost his head for talking to another old man on the train about the war going badly. In Munich, in a trial which Reck-Malleczewen attended, a sixty-four-year-old doctor, given eight years in prison on the testimony of his young, blonde Nazi housekeeper, was not allowed to speak in his own defense—the judge threatened to punch him "in the snoot" if he tried to continue with his "baloney."[135] And it was also in Munich that the Scholls were tried. Their arrest had followed a reckless distribution of pamphlets through the halls of the university and even from the tower of one of the buildings. Their last pamphlet denounced the sacrifice of Germany's youth at Stalingrad for "the low power-instincts of a party clique," declared that the rest of Germany's young people were threatened with the same fate, and called for a day of settlement with "the most abominable tyranny the German people had ever suffered."[136] The Scholls, too, sat in a courtroom run by a "Nazi Jacobin," the infamous Roland Freisler, once a Communist but now a fanatical Nazi who presided over the treason trials in 1944.[137] Although they made no effort to deny their responsibility for the pamphlets, Sophie Scholl replied to Freisler's insults in kind: "You know as well as we that the war is lost. Why are you so cowardly that you don't want to admit it?"[138] Less than a week after their arrest, Hans and Sophie Scholl and their ally Christopher Probst met death by the guillotine. But for the Scholls, said Reck- Malleczewen, the motto "He who knows how to die can never be enslaved" *was* valid. Still, he estimated that in Berlin sixteen others and in Vienna twenty others were beheaded each week—not all, of course, as clearly heroes or heroines as the Scholls.[139] The trials of the Scholls' co-conspirators came early in April. Philosophy Professor Kurt Haber became one of the martyrs, also dying by guillotine and leaving his widow and children without support, since all his personal rights had been revoked. The final insult to his memory came as the state rendered to his widow a bill of 3,000 marks for wear and tear on the guillotine.[140]

Even before the appearance of the White Rose movement, German officials had been greatly concerned with evidence of widespread youth disenchantment with the Nazi regime. This took the form of organized youth "cliques" or "blisters" or "bands," some of which had been discovered even before the war. But the number and activities of these groups had greatly increased during the war period. By 1942, "youth criminality" had become a major concern of police and judicial officials.[141] In the earlier period, the activities of these groups appear to have emphasized a somewhat unpolitical revolt against party discipline and work assignments. Even in the face of the British "terror" bombing, the motifs of the movement were a love of British and American swing music and dancing, the adoption of clothing and hair styles (long, "hangman's locks" for the men) that rejected military discipline and regimentation, and the following of a life style that emphasized "bumming around," free of work obligations, and ignoring commonly accepted moral standards. Sometimes the cliques set up private dance festivals where the bands played "ever wilder things" and the dancers gyrated with the long hair flying and the legs swinging "in wild ecstasy." Members of the groups greeted one another in English with "Swing-Boy," "Swing-Girl," or "Old-Hot-Boy." By the end of 1942, police reports were detailing the activities of these cliques, who often slept in tents outside the towns or in the hay stacks of the farmers. And, as one police report related, "often the young people of both sexes slept and bathed together completely in the nude."[142] Promiscuous sex was common. In Frankfurt, a police examination of young women in prison there found that of 152 prisoners, 150 had already lost their virginity.[143] The groups adopted adventurous-sounding titles and costumes. Many employed the Austrian edelweiss symbol, adding to it the term "pirates" and wearing short leather pants and boots as well as that flower, which signified a search for freedom.[144] Sometimes the leader of the band gave the group his name. Thus, in Munich, there was a "Charlie Blister"—using the English form of the leader's first name (Karl) and placing the name on the pullover sweaters they wore as a kind of uniform.[145] A mulatto who led a group in Hannover designated his followers the "Al Capone Band."[146]

In spite of severe action by the police in the Düsseldorf area and in Hamburg, these groups continued to be a source of concern to the authorities throughout the remainder of the war. Although critical of Nazi discipline and hostile to the party's youth organizations (a favorite activity was waylaying and beating up members of the Hitler Youth), their basic thrust before 1943 was not strongly political. The search for personal freedom, efforts to avoid military service (some used chemical injections for this purpose) and to avoid work, the excitement and profit of ordinary theft, freer sex relations, and forgetfulness of the monotony of war and a regimented society were the motives behind the movement. There is no evidence that the sacrifices of the White Rose group had an effect on the movement, but during the remainder of the war, the anti-Nazi tone did become stronger in spite of police efforts to destroy the cliques. Their open criticism of the party and its leaders continued to arouse fear that the party was losing its control over the German youth.

There was also renewed concern by the party in respect to the activities of the churches. One observer reported that "with the increasing severity of the war the churches have a flood such as never before. The situation today is such that the preacher no longer chases the people, but rather the opposite, the people come to the preacher. The great majority of the youth are confirmed; in the notices for most funeral processions the holding of a church service is indicated, even for the fallen of the Waffen SS, indeed even for those of the personal guard [of Hitler, the *Leibstandarte*]. . . . There is no sense in our ignoring these facts. We must reckon with this still more in the future, since the newly awakened church interest extends so deeply into the circle of our followers that we cannot look the other way."[147] And a Protestant preacher reported that when he descended by parachute into Stalingrad to bring comfort to the soldiers, he found the quest for the scriptures so strong among the soldiers that the Bibles he had brought had to be torn into sections to take care of the demand.[148]

Party agencies sought to counter this return to religion. The Ahnenerbe Office (for racial heritage) of the SS set up guidelines for "life festivals" that would replace the old church-style celebrations. Birth, marriage, and death were to be returned to the old Germanic social rituals.[149] A Sicherheitsdienst agent reported that a clearer understanding of the Nazi term *gottgläubig* (believing in God, but not in the churches) was needed. With the growing concern for the afterlife, the *Jenseits*, the party needed to explain that this term involved the discovery of god within oneself and to show the growth that could thus be realized. The falsity of the historical and biological foundation of established religions had to be demonstrated and the churches' use of heaven and hell as weapons had to be undercut.[150]

Goebbels, for his part, felt that "the bothersome church question must rest for the duration of the war" and indicated Hitler's approval of this position.[151] Although this view was reflected in one of Bormann's secret directives, which told party leaders to avoid conflicts with the churches—"Every petty, needle-stick policy must be avoided"—the indications are clear that Bormann himself and many other party leaders were not in agreement with this decision.[152] Alfred Rosenberg, perhaps the most virulent antireligious leader of the Nazis, sent out a special note to Nazi agencies, requesting additional information on the gains of the churches. His major propaganda office suggested countermeasures on the part of the party: increased meetings and discussions led by politically secure families to cut down on the erosion signified by these church gains; a reduction of the role of party officials in carrying death notices, which allowed the preacher to come in afterwards as a consoling element; a study by the party of church funeral processions so that party funerals could be made more impressive; a development of party death notices that would be as impressive as those of the churches; and a closer supervision of church festivals.[153]

Party agencies also continued activities that tended to undermine church influence. Agencies were established within the various Gaus to provide marriage advisement and assistance. In Württemberg, the head of this new office, established on March 1, 1943, was the man who had earlier been responsible for the deaths of those counted as mentally ill.[154] The activities of racial-political offices also continued. And propaganda leading some fanatical girls to have illegitimate children for Hitler had its successes.[155] The increasing influence of Martin Bormann in the party leadership was to render meaningless Goebbels's idea of going softly in respect to church matters. Party observers still counted more leaving the churches than returning in spite of the decline in these numbers. The monetary cost of making moves in either direction was relatively high.[156] Party regulations were also established that required persons in hospitals who wished religious consolation to ask for it—the clergy could not simply visit hospitals to see the sick without a prior invitation.[157]

Above all, it was vital for the party to increase its activities of explanation and assurance. The reestablishment of *Sprechabende*, evening meetings of small groups to discuss affairs and gain renewed confidence, was suggested. These were not, however, to be occasions for irrelevant discussions of war leadership, foreign policy, or church affairs—the fiery words of a speaker were more vital than endless debates.[158] School activities became more propagandized. "Live-in" schools (*Heimschulen*) were established. Replacing religious schools, they provided an opportunity for the establishment of the principles of military order and a strong emphasis on Nazi ideology.[159] Party leaders attended workdays to strengthen their convictions. In 1942, 128,409 such meetings took place, with 27,763,044 attending, and although Bormann sought to cut down on travel for such meetings, they continued on a more regional and local basis.[160]

But Nazi propaganda continued to face new challenges. There was evidence of a loss of faith in Germany's Italian allies with reports of cowardice on the eastern front.[161] Nazi propaganda still strove to emphasize "the inextinguishable brotherhood in arms" of Italians and Germans, but it was clear that German faith in Italian military aid was minimal.[162] The German "America experts" Colin Ross and Adolf Halfeld began to travel broadly in Germany and abroad to counter fears of the power of this enemy.[163] Two copies of the book by A.E. Johann (Wollschläger), *Das Land ohne Herz, eine Reise ins unbekannte Amerika* (*The Land without a Heart: A Trip into Unknown America*), were supplied to Gau leaders, with five hundred copies of this tract available for every Gau in Germany. The reader, said Bormann in his circular to Gau leaders, would see the frivolous superficiality of Americans and the destruction of all human and cultural values by the anonymous and rootless powers of capitalism.[164] And Dr. Erwin Stranik reported that Roosevelt was pretending to be the friend of Negroes in the United States because he needed them to help fight the war, but after it was over, he "will let his dog bite them again."[165]

The party suffered from a deadly fear of unfavorable public opinion. Sicherheitsdienst reports indicated for the first time some disenchantment with the Führer himself. His speech of March 21 was criticized as "almost passionless," "delivered in a monotone," and rhetorically poor.[166] A recent study indicates that Stalingrad marked the beginning of a progressive decline in the "Hitler Mythos."[167] But the party apparatus still required him as the symbol of overall authority, and party propaganda never varied from its motif of confidence and trust in the Führer. The only real danger lay with the only force able to overthrow the regime, the military. Hitler plied the marshals well with funds—von Kluge received a quarter of a million Reichsmarks for his sixtieth birthday; Keitel, a similar sum on another occasion; and Milch, half a million.[168] But March of 1943 saw two military efforts at assassination failing because of circumstantial factors.[169] The tragedy of the vain pursuit of an unattainable victory continued. The time clock marking the many signs of a coming defeat moved inexorably toward midnight.

4. Bombing Achieves Holocaust

The four months from May through August of 1943 were marked by a series of major setbacks for Germany's war efforts both at home and on the battle fronts. They began on May 12 and 13 as the German armies in North Africa surrendered to the British. The radio report from the famed and once victorious Africa Corps read: "Munition exhausted. Weapons and war materials destroyed. The German Africa Corps has fought as ordered until it is no longer capable of fighting. The German Africa Corps must be born again! Heia Safari!"[1]

The "desert fox," Field Marshal Erwin Rommel, had been called home prior to the end of the fighting. Some Germans speculated that the news of his "illness" circulated two months after the actual recall was just an excuse to save him from the fate of Field Marshal Paulus at Stalingrad.[2] The term *Tunisgrad* began to circulate for this second defeat, but there was none of the deep pathos associated with the tragedy in Russia.[3] The number of those taken prisoner, some 130,000 German soldiers, was larger than that of those captured by the Russians, but there was not the same last desperate (senseless) fighting as in Stalingrad, and reports circulated that the Germans accepted the end of their desert hardships with relief, even cheerfully.[4] At least there were letters home from these prisoners. POW's in Canada wrote that things there went "exceptionally well" and that they were "especially well fed."[5] There was not the cold, heart-wrenching silence that covered the fate of those who had fallen into the hands of the Russians.[6]

The defeat in Tunis was followed by Allied attacks on the Italian islands of Pantelleria and Lampedusa and Allied landings in Sicily on July 10. Mussolini fell from power on July 24, and by August 17, the German and Italian forces had given up the struggle in Sicily and evacuated to the Italian mainland. And to many Germans, especially those in southern Germany, it seemed likely that the road northward into the homeland would be covered quickly.[7]

Meanwhile a quiet period on the eastern front was broken with the opening of Hitler's planned *Fall Zitadelle* (Operation Citadel), designed to breach Soviet tank forces in the Ukraine and create a new dynamism for the German forces stalled since Stalingrad. The great tank battle around the city of Kursk began on July 4. By the twelfth, the Russians were in control of the battlefield. The new German *Panther* tanks had proved faulty and Soviet defensive strategy had foiled the German plans for a new offensive. Although Soviet losses were more serious than German losses, the Soviets' recovery was rapid—their operational tanks on July 5 numbered 3,800; by July 13, they had shrunk to less than 1,500; but by August 3, they were back to 2,750.[8] Citadel was to be the last great German drive on the eastern front. From this point on, it was the Russians who seized the initiative, who began to push the Germans out of hard-won gains, and who moved grimly westward towards the German homeland. Citadel symbolized a coming defeat—the only hope was for a stabilization of the front, not for great victories.

The news from the battle fronts weighed heavily on the home front. But those at home confronted increasing peril from bombing raids that became more numerous, attacked new as well as old targets, and wreaked ever more havoc and destruction. The months of May and June of 1943 were a shocking prelude to the even more shocking catastrophe visited upon Hamburg in July. In sixteen major raids, the British dropped over 24,000 tons of bombs on German cities, most of them within the industrial zone along the Rhine and Ruhr rivers. In each of these raids, an average of 1,500 tons was dropped. But these cold figures give little comprehension of the destructive combination of thousands of incendiary bombs and hundreds of enormous explosive bombs and land mines that blasted whole city streets into ruins. Dortmund, in two visits, came under 3,500 tons of bombs; Düsseldorf, in two raids, suffered almost 4,000 tons. Bochum, in two raids, was hit with 2,500 tons and Cologne in two visits, received 2,200 tons. Duisburg, Essen, Wuppertal, Emden,

Oberhausen, Krefeld, Mülheim, Gelsenkirchen, Kiel, and Bremen were also attacked during this two-month period.[9]

In this "battle of the Ruhr," many of the cities were close enough that the inhabitants of one city could see the raids taking place in neighboring cities. Josef Fischer watched the destruction of Wuppertal exactly a year after the thousand-bomber raid on his own city, Cologne. Two days later, he traveled there to see the results—"an ash heap around which the ruins of the houses provide the background scenery." In the streets, he wrote, there was total silence except when another stone dropped from the wall of a house. A new phase in the bombing war had been opened, Fischer thought—the total destruction of a city.[10] And to his nagging self-questioning of how he might protect his own home in his own city, water, he decided, was the answer. Every floor of his home was loaded with water, in cans, tubs, the bath tub, everything possible, and sand, stone, and cement were placed in the cellar to repair damages there.[11]

Goebbels was still the only major Nazi leader brave enough to visit the devastated cities. He visited Dortmund, where he found the destruction "virtually total." The raid on that city on the night of May 23/24 was, he thought, probably the worst ever directed against a German city (over 2,000 tons of bombs had been dropped).[12] Again Goebbels expressed his concern for the survival of Germany under these circumstances. The only bright spot he could find was the fairly "respectable" number of planes shot down.[13] The only difficulty with this was that canny Germans multiplied the number of planes destroyed by ten to get the probable number of enemy planes involved in a raid, and the result did not help to boost popular morale.[14] The rumors of heavy death tolls were supported by army reports that changed the earlier phrasing "the population suffered losses" to "the population suffered heavy losses." Figures of 15,000 deaths in Dortmund, 17,000 in Düsseldorf, and 27,000 in Wuppertal circulated.[15] Adding to the horror of these numbers were stories of people turned into living torches by the phosphorus bombs, of others getting stuck in the hot asphalt of the streets, and of many throwing themselves into the nearby rivers only to find that the fire rekindled when they emerged into the air.[16]

The spectacular and partially successful British raids on the Eder, Sorpe, and Möhne dams in the same period (May 16/17, 1943) resulted in some flooding in the Ruhr valley and caused great temporary concern. Complete success would have resulted in considerable loss of life as well as a major reduction of production.[17]

The obvious possibility that other dams might be breached added to the worries of the population. But neither the raids on the cities nor those on the dams produced the loss of life that was anticipated by the attackers and rumored among the victims. The total wartime losses of the three cities named above were far below the estimates current at the time: Dortmund 6,341; Düsseldorf 5,863; and Wuppertal 7,150.[18] The relatively modest losses underscore the success of the air-raid shelters provided, the effectiveness of the instructions for air-raid precautions, and, most of all, the courage and determination of the people themselves.

The personal accounts of bombing raids by the pilots concerned far outnumber the personal accounts written by the bombed. Perhaps the best of the relatively rare accounts by the victims is that of Josef Fischer, an inhabitant of the city of Cologne, who remained in that heavily bombed city until the very end of the war. On June 17, the city received its first attack of this period, a mild one since the weather was bad, most planes were recalled, and some of the bombs were simply dumped into the fields around the city. A modest death toll of 146 was scored from those bombs that were dropped, including 80 women and 34 children. But only 25,000 of the previous 250,000 homes were left undisturbed and streetcar service was completely disrupted. By now, food for those bombed out was reduced largely to potatoes. Ration cards were given out for products no longer obtainable. Placards and handbills warned the population that in the event of being buried in the next raid, one should knock on the walls with some hard object or even scratch with one's fingernails. The rescue crews were now provided with listening devices that could detect these sounds, and efforts to get attention by shouting or calling simply used up the available oxygen too rapidly. Fischer found himself a chisel which he placed in his cellar. This would allow him to take apart the cellar walls. He also heeded the advice of having rags and water cans with covers placed there so that in the event of close strikes one could breathe through moistened rags to filter out the dust and dirt.[19]

The test of these preparations was not long in coming. On the night of June 28/29, 1943, Cologne suffered under another raid.[20] This time the weather did not save the city. Five hundred forty British planes dropped 1,614 tons of bombs. The antiaircraft guns kept up an unceasing fire. Around Fischer in his cellar fell explosive bombs in an unbroken series, producing the succession of pressure-suction-pressure-suction that became familiar to Germans during the bombings. Fire bombs fell on the grounds about the house. Those in the cellar should have left the shelter to extinguish the fires that were probably starting overhead, but exploding bombs prevented it. They waited fearfully in their shelter. Only by sound could they distinguish what was occurring—every bomb had its own peculiar sound. If there was a rustle like a flock of doves flying up, it was a bundle of small stick bombs breaking apart, with each stick finding its own target. If there was a short, sharp explosion, it was a 12-kilogram fire bomb, which could spread fire eighty meters in all directions. If it was like a bucket of water splashing in the street, it was a 14-kilogram liquid fire bomb, which could spread liquid rubber and benzine fifty meters around the impact area. If it plumped down like a wet sack, it was a fire canister holding twenty liters of benzol, somewhat cruder but as effective as benzine. If it cracked like an explosive bomb as it hit, it was either a 106-kilogram bomb that threw out rags soaked with benzine or heavy oil or a 112-kilogram fire bomb, which covered nearby houses with a thousand "cow-cakes" of benzol and rubber. And there were still, of course, the explosive bombs and mines, which tore out the doors and windows to provide air to feed the flames and surpassed the effects of an earthquake, so that those in the cellar thought of themselves as perched in the heart of a volcano.

In the midst of all this destruction, a sound came from the cellar of Fischer's neighbor. A hole was opened in the wall between the houses. When they were asked what was wrong, the neighbors answered that the cellar stairs were on fire and that the fire was in the cellar itself already. The hole was opened wider—women, children, a soldier, a civilian, suitcases, a cradle with a crying baby made their way through the aperture. One great suitcase fell open to reveal only a woman's black straw hat and a jar of marmalade—its owner was undoubtedly mentally unsound. A woman was crying because her husband was still next door but refused to leave the remnants of his home. Soon they discovered that the fire next door would shortly set afire a coal supply there—the oxygen supply in both cellars would be rapidly used up. The old man had to come over so that the hole could be closed. Eventually, they persuaded the recalcitrant old fellow to give up his lost home. The piece of sheet iron that Fischer had stored for such purposes was placed over the hole and covered with sand. The soldier, almost a civilian since he had left his rifle and knapsack next door, told them it was better in Russia than here.

The sound of falling bombs ceased. They crept above, fighting smoke and dust to extinguish the fires there. Fischer's use of flame retardant had helped to save much of his house. But no door could be opened without a fearsome in-pouring of heat. Every house in the neighborhood was burning. Every window, every corner, every tree, every bush was lit in the colors of the flames—sometimes yellow, sometimes red, sometimes white. At six in the morning, the fire storm came. The air was sucked in from the surrounding areas to feed the flames until they soared to the clouds. Seventy or eighty people were now in this one cellar. All waited to see whether the fire would die down or bring them death. Fischer moved his little family into a supply cellar where the air was better. He and others fought the fires in the house and waited. By noon, the fires had died down. One by one, the people in the cellar picked up their most cherished possessions and trudged off to seek new homes—probably, thought Fischer, in the surrounding area but not in Cologne itself.

Those in the cellar had survived. But many others had not been so lucky. Hundreds of scarcely recognizable remains, merely identified by fragments and by the location of the bodies, were laid out in great halls and tagged for the information of anxious relatives or the always-needed public records. Some had died in fearful fashion. The body of a pregnant woman was found on the sidewalk outside a hospital. In the midst of the bombing, she had given birth before reaching the hospital, but both mother and newborn infant were consumed by the flames. In sixty minutes of bombing, the lives of 3,460 people were snuffed out and 400,000 people lost their homes. But the army distributed bread, fat, sausage, and milk. For the weary survivors, life went on. And many people in Cologne still wanted to stay "at home."

In the margins of this story, there is still the note of active Nazi organization, sometimes successful, sometimes not. There are the air-raid regulations, written, says Fischer, by a man working in the daylight, sitting quietly at his desk in a clean and comfortable room—regulations that make no sense when put into practice in the darkness of the night with the heat of the flames all around. There is the fire-retarding treatment, which does work. There are the fire fighters called in from an area one hundred kilometers around Cologne, but refusing to help until the proper orders come and sleeping while the fires burn merrily around them. There is the distribution of supplies, which helps to soften the harshness of events. And there is the careful collection and labeling of the bones of the dead.

Two of the rare diaries of the war period present cogent appreciations of the popular mood in this time of trial. Gottfried Benn wrote that "the situation becomes ever more enigmatic; it is in the long run only mythologically to be experienced and understood, if one wants to try to deal with it."[21] And in similar fashion, Horst Lange confided in his diary: "How much is everything placed in question! Every plan of life and every kind of tie [to the past]." But he added that one could always begin again and that "the people are astoundingly calm.—One endures everything; one would even endure the end of the world calmly, I believe, so weary is one already."[22]

There were, undoubtedly, some Germans who still believed in the magic weapons of which Goebbels spoke, closer to reality than the little propaganda minister knew, or in the possible success of that last desperate effort of the marathon runner who might break the tape before his rivals. But the great masses carried on because there was nothing to do but to carry on and in the hope that somehow they would be among those who survived. *Überleben* (survival) became the motif of life—not to be burned up in a firestorm, killed on the battle front, or executed by a dying regime. In sorrow, in weariness, in dull anxiety about the future, one continued to farm, to make guns and tanks and planes, to search for food, to "party" if one had a chance, to sit in the air raid shelters as the bombs landed ever closer, to listen to the foreign radio broadcasts even if this was dangerous because they told more about what was taking place than the official reports of the regime did, to hold on to what possessions one could as the fragility of ownership became ever more apparent, and, most of all, to survive—not to see the glorious new world pictured by the Nazis but to take on the future, however it might come. In this attitude, there was both courage and resignation, morale and lack of morale. Where Benn wrote that the period could only be understood "mythologically," one might, perhaps, substitute the word "primordially," with emotions, objectives, hopes, and fears reduced to the most elementary expression.

There was, indeed, in the bombing of Hamburg much of the "mythological" or "primordial" although the British planners of the attacks gave the operation the biblical designation "Gomorrah." The stated objective, "to *destroy* Hamburg," carries one back to the days of the Greeks and the Romans and the destruction of Troy and Carthage, except that instead of the Roman Senator Cato demanding the eradication of Carthage, this time it was the British commander of the Royal Air Force Bomber Command, Sir Arthur Harris, who set in motion on May 27, 1943, "the process of elimination" of Germany's second largest city.[23] Harris was, of course, doing no more than what Hitler himself had threatened in respect to British cities on September 4, 1940. In his speech at the Sportpalast in Berlin in that more optimistic period, he had promised that the German Luftwaffe would reply to British air attacks every night in increasing measure and that it would "eradicate their cities."[24] But that a British general should follow in the footsteps of the Führer was not greatly to his honor, and that he could accompany this move with the use of a biblical title that suggested that he was the omnipotent God Almighty raining down fire and sulfur on the evil inhabitants of a modern Gomorrah underscores a megalomaniac character. There is in any war that blighting of sensibilities that allows those on the battle front to fire bullets against the enemy that may kill or simply maim, to send cannon shells that tear at the viscerals or lop off the foe's arms or legs, and to direct the flame thrower that engulfs the enemy tank and sends its occupants screaming in agony from its ovenlike interior. But to contemplate the blanketing of a great city of well over one million inhabitants with explosive and fire in order to destroy thousands (in planning conception, hundreds of thousands) of women and children along with the male soldiers or armament workers who might be there was a return to the most primitive conceptions of warfare.

To a considerable degree, the British were prisoners of the weapons they possessed and of the exigencies of the war they were fighting. Unable as yet to attack Germany by land, with the fighting in Italy still far from the German borders, and with the German submarines now virtually eliminated from the scene, the British had only one way to bring the war home to Germany—from the air. To do this more effectively, they had built more and better bombers and constructed larger and more effective bombs. To justify these expenditures, to maintain morale at home, and (they hoped) to sabotage the morale of the enemy, the bombers had to destroy more houses, buildings, and factories and kill more of the enemy. For this purpose, the "destruction" of a city would provide a clear symbol of the effectiveness of the weapons employed. Hamburg lent itself well to this objective—as Harris stated at the time, "I had always wanted to have a real dead set at Hamburg. It was the second biggest city in Germany and I wanted to make a tremendous show."[25]

As this quotation indicates, it was the size of Hamburg that governed Harris's plan more than the status of the city as a producer of submarines or its role as Germany's major seaport. A little later, Harris was to look to Germany's largest city, Berlin, as a goal and to suggest optimistically that "we can wreck Berlin from end to end if the U.S.A.A.F. will come in on it. It will cost between us 400-500 aircraft. It will cost Germany the war."[26] By this time, he was also keeping account of the effects of aerial bombardment in terms of the degree of destruction of the cities bombed and the number of persons killed. "Total destruction" was to answer Germany's concept of "total war."

Hamburg, of course, fulfilled several other qualifications attached to target goals at this particular stage of aerial warfare. By careful planning, it could be reached without an excessively lengthy flight over German-held territory. Its location on the coast and the easily recognizable water areas in and about the city would facilitate the identification of target areas. And portions of the city lent themselves to the effective use of the bombing weapon that had increasingly demonstrated its destructive capacity—fire. There was, of course, contrary to what some inhabitants of the city had hoped, no consideration of the fact that the city had once been a stronghold of anti-Nazi Social Democrats or that it had had significant business and commercial relationships with both England and the United States.

Tactically, too, the planning for the raids on the city provided an opportunity for significant trials of new procedures. First of all, the raids were to be accompanied by the first use of "Window," the dropping of thousands of pieces of tin foil colored black on one side to produce "snow" on the German radar, thus confusing those directing opposing fighter planes seeking to intercept the bombers and rendering ineffective the radar-directed German antiaircraft batteries. Secondly, the target-marking procedures were greatly improved with the "pathfinders," who located and marked the aiming point with red indicators and who were provided with a back-up force which renewed these target indicators with green flares dropped at specified intervals. Instructions were also given that those planes that came in later should overshoot the markers by two seconds, a device intended to prevent the customary "creep back" of the bombs from the targeted area that had occurred in previous raids because of the tendency of bomber crews to try to get rid of their bombs as soon as possible when they were in areas heavily protected by antiaircraft fire.[27]

Finally, Hamburg was to be the target of the largest concentration of British bombers since the thousand-bomber raid on Cologne. The plans called for repeated attacks on the city with the American Eighth Air Force now operative from English airfields cooperating with the British night raids through follow-up daytime missions.

These plans were to eventuate in seven air raids on Hamburg, beginning with the British night raid in the early morning hours of Sunday, July 25, 1943, followed by two American daylight raids on the same day and on Monday, July 26, a British harassing raid with light mosquito bombers on the night of Tuesday, July 27, followed by the most damaging British raid on the night of Wednesday, July 28, and two more British night raids on Friday, July 30, and Tuesday, August 3.

These raids were not the first launched against the city on the Elbe. The official records of Hamburg's police chief counted the raid of July 25 as the 138th raid on the city.[28] The city had been included among the ninety-four places in Germany designated as those in most danger of enemy air attacks.[29] Its organization and planning for air-raid defenses, although by no means fully adequate, were better than those of many German cities. Although the construction of the bunker- or tower-type shelters that offered protection against the direct or near hit of high explosive bombs had lagged behind needs, every inhabitant of the city had access before the July raids to at least the kind of shelter that protected against the flying fragments of bombs or of buildings struck by bombs. Where private cellars were to be employed, connections to adjoining cellars had been provided, equipped with heavy iron doors allowing escape in two directions and the sealing off of damaged sections. Air-raid services, fire-fighting forces, special repair crews, and first-aid services had been well planned and equipped. The only problems arising in these areas resulted from the intrusion into these functions of party agencies acting with more arrogance than efficiency.[30]

Even before the war, fire-fighting experts in Hamburg had realized the dangers of prospective fire bombing for German cities.[31] The early wartime bombing had spurred efforts to secure new equipment. By the time of the July bombings, the city had 305 new fire engines, 935 portable power pumps, 49 fire boats, and 312 kilometers of fire hose—enough to have reached from Hamburg to Berlin.[32] Efforts had been made, as elsewhere, to clear the attics of old furniture and other burnable materials, but often this resulted in the storing of this kind of property in empty stores used as a kind of warehouse, which created a whole new and perhaps more dangerous fire hazard.[33] Moreover, Hamburg fire authorities had discovered from earlier raids that the small, four-pound stick bombs, which the British used in large numbers, did not simply lodge in the upper stories as had been anticipated. Planning procedures had called for those in the cellar air-raid shelters to check periodically for fires in the upper stories and extinguish them before they could set the house or building completely on fire. However, experience showed that these small fire bombs fell with such force that they could often penetrate several stories.[34] Moreover, the British had adopted the practice of fitting a portion of these stick bombs with an explosive charge, which made the prescribed "self-help" measures to extinguish them increasingly perilous.[35] These relatively cheap weapons were overall probably the most effective bombing weapon employed in World War II prior to the development of the atom bomb.

The British raid on the night of July 24 was a severe one. It came just after midnight, hence early on the Sunday morning of July 25. Seven hundred forty of the original 791 bombers leaving England arrived over the target. The dropping of "window," the strips of foil designed to confuse enemy radar, proved very effective in diminishing the accuracy of enemy fighter activity and of the antiaircraft defense of the city. There was the customary inaccuracy of the pathfinder "markers," who laid the target indicators for the main body of bombers, but these were not so severe as they had been in some of the earlier raids. Although only 306 of the bombers released their bombs within a three-mile radius of the goal, the heavy loads of bombs were concentrated in a closely built-up section of the inner city and adjacent areas. They caused, as a consequence, fires of unprecedented size and scope. Even the late-arriving bombers, which tended to drop their bombs before reaching the main target area, created much havoc in the northwestern sections of the city.[36]

In spite of all the preparations, the city's fire-fighting forces were challenged beyond their capabilities. In many places, the extinction of the fires was made more difficult by the fact that supplies of coal and coke, stored for the coming winter months, caught fire. The central police station burned down, but the command center in its underground bunker survived. The streets were filled with rubble, and fire engines could not traverse them. Those that tried lost their tires and some were caught in the bombing. Gas, water, and electricity lines were damaged. Water for the fire services had to be brought from storage basins or open waterways. Although help was brought in from Lübeck, Kiel, and Berlin, the Hamburg firefighters for the first time found themselves unable to extinguish the fires by nightfall on the day of the attack. At 4:15 on the morning of July 26, the weary fire chief was summoned out of bed to the headquarters of the chief SS officer of the city to explain his incompetence in not having put out the fires and was told that all fires had to be out by noon of that day. Although the fires had not learned to *Sieg Heil!*, the firemen were able to curtail open flames by that Monday evening, in spite of the two American daylight raids that took place on Sunday afternoon and Monday morning.[37] Both of these attacks concentrated on the harbor area. The first destroyed an unfinished ocean liner, the *Vaterland*, which was being used for lumber storage, and both raids damaged docks and business establishments in the harbor area. As in several later American daylight raids, a considerable number of planes were lost in the operations, but the mere fact that the enemy could venture to attack in broad daylight had a significantly depressing effect on German morale.[38]

But the recovery in Hamburg from the first raid was relatively rapid. Free editions, combining the efforts of the local newspapers, were distributed on Sunday. Special three-day food rations were made available along with 50 grams of real bean coffee, 10 extra cigarettes, 125 grams of sweets, and half a bottle of spirits to calm the nerves of the survivors. The news reports paid more heed to the fall of Mussolini than to the raid on Hamburg. Orders were issued forbidding workers to leave the city, but some had already begun to seek safer havens.[39]

On Tuesday, six British mosquito bombers engaged in a few "bites" over Hamburg, doing little damage but demonstrating their virtual invulnerability from the German defenses. Perhaps they also warned the people of Hamburg that it was not over yet. The water tanks were full. The fire hoses were back in order. The people who remained in the city went to the best air-raid shelters possible, filling them beyond reasonable capacity. Thousands had already decided that security lay somewhere else than in Hamburg.[40] All of their apprehensions became justified on the night of Wednesday, July 28, the "firestorm night," when Hamburg suffered the most devastating raid inflicted on any German city.[41]

The horrors of this raid have been retold many times. One major German study and two English ones have appeared within the last five years. What occurred quickly became a matter of myth as well as fact. The memories of the hundreds of thousands who survived were barely sampled. Rumors had as much effect both at home and abroad as did the official reports.

There were almost the same number of British planes involved as on the early morning of July 25. Seven hundred twenty-two bombers arrived over the city. There was the same marking procedure—the targeted point was somewhat east and south of the point that had been laid down for the first attack. There was a little less "creep back" of the bombs from the target area this time. A slightly higher percentage of planes dropped their bombs within the three-mile circumference around the aiming point. The weight of the bombs dropped was approximately the same as in the first raid.[42] But this time, the results were far more catastrophic. Partly this was due to the more accurate bombing, partly to the atmospheric conditions, which converted what might have been an ordinary firestorm into a much more severe one. The days prior to these raids had been part of a long period of hot, dry weather. The temperatures during the first part of July had risen as high as 90° (32°C) in the shade. Night temperatures also remained abnormally high. The moisture content of the air on this particular night was as low as 30 percent. Remnants of smoke and dust from the earlier bombings tended to preserve ground temperatures. At the same time a low-pressure area lay north of Hamburg along the coastline, in close proximity to the high-pressure area that had covered the city.

Any fire-bombing raid tended to create rapidly rising heat drafts. In many bombed cities these created firestorms of varying intensity. But the unusual climatic conditions in Hamburg created very abnormal circumstances. As the incendiary bombs fell, the heated air rose much more rapidly than usual—the smoke rose to observable heights of four to five miles. The air brought in from the areas surrounding the major fires attained cyclonic force. Ground-level Hamburg became the fire pan of a gigantic oven. The heat level in large portions of the city reached completely unbearable heights.[43] The fires were fed from the previously existing rubble and the new damage done by the explosive bombs that accompanied the incendiaries. The winds tended to change direction quickly, sometimes completely reversing themselves, so that the extinguishing of fires in one area could be foiled by a new rush of flame from a totally different starting point. Moreover, the rapidity of the spread of the firestorm meant that the firefighters' efforts had to be mostly devoted to extricating people from the most seriously affected areas rather than to combating the raging flames.

Death laid grisly hands upon thousands of Hamburgers during this night. Some died softly, smothered by carbon monoxide within the air-raid cellars. Some died in agony, caught in the streets as the fires raged like banshees among the fleeing. Women found the thin summer dresses they wore aflame and tore them off as they ran. Some of them stumbled alive into the air-raid shelters—a completely naked woman in the advanced stages of pregnancy lurched through the door of one of the main fire department shelters and shortly afterwards delivered her child in the bunker. Other naked women lay among the dead on the streets, seemingly untouched by the flames but dying from the effects of the excessive heat. There were stories of the shrinking and mummification of those who died, of the horrible distortion of male sexual organs by the heat, of the reddened or browned faces of the victims. Condemned as rumors at the time, these accounts were verified by official police reports.[44] Thus the oft-repeated stories of demented Hamburgers carrying bodies of deceased relatives in their suitcases—a man with the corpse of his wife and daughter,[45] a woman with the mummified body of her daughter,[46] or other women with the heads of their dead children[47]—gain some substance, together with the reports of autopsy efforts that could not pierce the skin of some dead bodies without the use of a saw or bone-cutters.[48] There were, of course, gross exaggerations. The common story that the asphalt of the streets melted and entrapped fleeing persons, in the most extreme form leaving them so engulfed that relatives came to place pillows under their heads and to feed the slowly dying captives until police bullets ended their misery, finds no factual support.[49] On the other hand, there seems to be ample evidence that phosphorus bombs were more heavily employed than the British were willing to admit.[50]

No brief resume can suggest the conduct of the Hamburgers during this enormous catastrophe. The confrontation of death measures personal not collective character. There were heroes and nonheroes. There were those who died of carbon monoxide or heat exhaustion in their shelters when a dash to safety might have been possible. There were the heroes: the firemen who made perilous journeys through the fire-ravaged areas to help the escape of those trapped within them and the civilians who kept their heads when others were losing them and led or sometimes forced their fellows to move from certain death to security. The enormous courage necessary for those who sought to move through the streets ravaged by the cruel winds of the firestorm stands above and apart from any consideration of the political philosophy of those involved. There is no evidence that the heroes were Nazis giving their all for the sake of the Führer. On the other hand, there is no evidence that those who placed themselves in peril to save friends, neighbors, or unknown helpless women and children were non-Nazis or anti-Nazis. There was much evidence of panic—not surprising in view of the nature of events—and of irresolute apathy and surrender to fate. But any evidence of widespread disorder or rioting seems totally lacking.[51] Basic discipline was apparently upheld, although the firestorm night spurred an increasing evacuation of the city.

But the British had not completed their work with the firestorm night. Two nights later, on Friday, July 30, over seven hundred bombers again attacked the city. The area of main destruction completed a semihemispheric devastation of the city's center.[52] The Barmbek area was set aflame, but this time there was no great firestorm. Nevertheless, town authorities at the time believed that the raid was even more intense than the previous one. One of the most tragic episodes of the bombing occurred on this night as the exit from the public air-raid shelter of the building housing the great Karstadt department store was blocked and 370 persons died of carbon monoxide poisoning.[53] In this raid, it was also demonstrated that even the great tower bunkers, supposedly secure against direct hits, were not completely safe—a heavy explosive bomb penetrated the bunker in the Wielandstrasse, but miraculously only two women were killed while the other two thousand occupants emerged frightened but unhurt.[54]

Over the weekend, the British gave the Hamburgers a rest while they blasted Remscheid and Düsseldorf. But on the night of Monday, August 2, 740 bombers again started for Hamburg. Perhaps the Almighty felt Gomorrah had gone far enough. Thunderstorms prevented the arrival of more than half of the planes and rendered the dropping of bombs by those that did arrive scattered and uncertain. The state opera building was hit, but the food supplies stored in its foyer were saved. Otherwise the loss of buildings and of people was relatively small.[55] By this time, a large part of the population had sought refuge outside the city. It took a while for them to return. They had no way of knowing that for the British their "Battle of Hamburg" was over.

Hamburg was the most serious victim of this hot summer of 1943. But other German cities suffered too. Cologne continued to be a frequent target of British attacks, but the cathedral, although damaged, survived and the railroad station still served its purpose.[56] The Währd section of Nuremberg was twice blanketed with bombing "carpets," and those beneath them suffered under the phosphorus bombs with the same scenes as those in Hamburg of naked people who had torn off the clothing affected by the phosphorus and crowds of people black with dirt and sweat as they sought escape from the fire areas. For those who suffered, the only semicomic relief came when the Gauleiter Karl Holz started his speech for the funeral of those who had lost their lives in this raid and was interrupted by a new alarm so that he had to talk of the "final victory" while the bombers flew over the city towards nearby Regensburg.[57]

The cities of the Ruhr were also repeated targets—along with Remscheid and Düsseldorf, named above, Duisburg, Essen, Gelsenkirchen, Wuppertal, and Leverkusen. There was even a kind of competition for the accolade of "worst-bombed city." The mayor of Duisburg pointed out in a memorandum that his city had, as early as September 1942, suffered a loss of 98.2 percent of its dwelling places whereas Cologne had only had 50 percent damaged.[58] Berlin, the capital, was not yet a significant competitor for such dubious honors. It was not until late in August that its days of trial began.

The American strategy of daylight bombing received several severe shocks during this period. The raid by the "Flying Fortresses" and "Liberators" on Schweinfurt on August 17 was far from successful—60 of the 376 planes that started for the attack were lost because of the German antiaircraft and fighter attacks, and many of the bombs fell outside the target area. This was a prelude to an even more serious setback two months later on October 14.[59] But the records indicate that the flight of a great mass of American bombers across Germany in broad daylight had an enormous impact on German public opinion. Many Germans who saw this fleet of American planes above them waved cheerfully to the pilots, assuming that they had to be German planes.[60] And another mission, much too costly at this point, the U.S. B-24 attack on the Rumanian oil fields at Ploesti on August 1, was still a harbinger of the dangers implicit in the U.S. partnership with the British—the German people knew, according to an observer, how vital these oil fields were.[61] Only the German children profited by the American air raids. The steel gasoline canisters they dropped were gathered up by the youngsters, cut in half, and used for boats on ponds and streams.[62] But the British, too, paid a heavy but worthwhile price for one of their raids. Although their attack on the night of August 17/18 on the German rocket installations at Peenemünde cost a loss of forty bombers, the operation forced a fatal postponement of the development of the V-1 and V-2 weapons designed for vengeance against the English. These not-so-secret vengeance weapons were delayed an entire year in production.[63]

Beneath the bombs, Germany became a seething anthill of people on the move. The numbers of evacuees from the larger cities multiplied enormously. Women and children, the aged, and the feeble were encouraged to leave the endangered cities. Everywhere, they were seen carrying packsacks on their backs and whatever family treasures they could manage to take with them. The Jews, wrote one anti-Nazi, were getting some revenge now, although these refugees were not going to extermination camps.[64] Places for their reception were designated by the government, special trains provided, and public welfare agencies of the party were entrusted with their reception and the provision of housing.[65]

Unavoidably, inordinate difficulties were attached to this vast internal movement of people. If the evacuees could find some place of refuge with relatives or close acquaintances, difficulties were manageable. Even then life could be trying. In spite of comfortable housing, good meals, and quiet nights in good beds, Mathilde Wolff-Mönckeberg complained about the hostess's rules requiring her guests to take off their shoes before entering the house and to refrain from smoking indoors and about her propensity to decide which of her guests she would deign to talk with. It was not long before Frau Wolff-Mönckeberg and her husband were back in bomb-torn Hamburg.[66] But for many other evacuees, things were much worse. They were quartered in parts of Germany where the style of life was much different from that at home. Food was differently prepared and sometimes seemed less adequate than what they had had at home. Their quarters were often narrow and uncomfortable because they were crowding into areas where there was not that much extra room. They had not been able to carry the necessary household equipment, so they had to use the cooking utensils of the hostess if they tried to prepare their own food.[67] Many came to feel that those who lived in the less-bombed areas of Germany did not realize the real consequences of the air raids. Reports came back to their home cities that the evacuated women were called "bombing women" and treated so unfairly that they would prefer to go back and live in the ruins. The newspapers, said the evacuees, ought to portray the effects of the raids more fully so that those who gave them shelter would better appreciate their reasons for having to accept shelter from strangers.[68]

The hosts, of course, resented this enormous invasion of outsiders. They complained that many of the women did nothing but sit around, instead of helping with the housework or the farming. Although they were duly impressed by the horror stories of the raids, they did not feel that their past hardships justified these women in ruining the daily lives of the host families. Since these evacuated women did not have to work, they could afford to stand in line for hours and buy up available food supplies. Some of them, with a number of children, were entitled by their "Muki cards" (ration cards for mother and child) to go to the front of the food lines and buy what they wanted. The visitors always seemed to have plenty of money, so they were also blamed for the rising prices of food. And they were always complaining and demanding special privileges and attention. Some went even further. One report from Munich accused evacuees from Hamburg of stealing eggs and killing chickens and related the story of one woman who took down her farmer-host's curtains to make a dress for her daughter. There were also assertions that the morality of many of these visitors was not above reproach.[69]

Obviously, the mood reports tended to exaggerate the level of complaints. Many of the hundreds of thousands who left the bomb-damaged cities during this summer must have rejoiced at the feeling of security and the freedom from the continuing air-raid alarms. Christobel Bielenberg discovered that the accommodations her family was supposed to have in the little town of Rohrbach were completely unsuitable, but she managed to get one of the private rooms of the local innkeeper, so that she and her family remained there comfortably for the rest of the war, helping with the chores and making friends with the local residents.[70] Erich Kuby and his wife lived on a farm—he worked, she paid pension, all went well, and the food was much better than they would have had in the city.[71] But many of the evacuees did return when they were able to, seeking even in the ruined remnants of their homes some sense of identity from the past.

Many people in the bombing zones were concerned about their school-age children, who were evacuated separately from their parents (the whole school, teachers and children, was moved as a unit). Some of these children were sent a long way from home. Those in Nuremberg and some other parts of southern Germany, for example, were sent into the Czechoslovak protectorate, where they were endangered by future Russian drives. And, of course, there were stories that the children were not treated well, had insufficient food, suffered from sickness and attacks of lice and scabies, and so forth. In some areas, the parents threatened the use of force to keep their children at home.[72]

There is no doubt that the ever more devastating bombing greatly increased the nervousness, fear, and depression of the Germans.[73] The process of evacuation spread, especially from the evacuees from Cologne and Hamburg, the horror stories of agonizing deaths. Everywhere the question was, "Will our city be next on the line?" Grim preparations had to be made. Frankfurt a. M., not yet attacked, stored up two thousand plain wooden coffins for the inevitable day.[74] There was, of course, and remained through the rest of the war, the hope and expectation of retaliation against the English. Thus, one man from Essen expressed the feelings of many when he said that "the hour of vengeance is now the only hope of the bomb victims. If this hour does not come and that still during this year, then there will be sooner or later a revolution in every great city, since the mood of the bomb victims in regard to the government is frightful. Many say that they have nothing to lose, at the most their lives, but before then other heads will roll."[75]

The anger of this man and of many others was directed at the absence of adequate fighter defense, the transfer of antiaircraft guns from the endangered cities to the eastern front, and the inadequacy of air-raid shelters.[76] Both Field Marshal Erhard Milch, the Reich director of air armament, and Albert Speer, the minister of munitions, were convinced after the effects of the bombing of Hamburg were seen that greater attention must be paid to the defense of the homeland. The key, in Milch's view, was an increase in the fighter forces defending Germany's cities even if battle-front air cover had to suffer. With an all-out production of the Messerschmitt 262 jet fighters and the V-1 flying bombs, Milch hoped to change Germany's fortunes. The complete fulfillment of his plans was to be shattered by Hitler's interference and Göring's incompetence, but fighter strength and tactics did improve in the months that followed.[77]

The public mood also turned strongly against Goebbels's propaganda approaches. Most criticized was his harping on the damage to Germany's cultural heritage, notably the attack on the cathedral at Cologne. From all over Germany came the response that it was the human losses that should be emphasized, not the material ones. "Better the cathedral at Cologne destroyed than one hundred men killed" was one trenchant comment.[78] The people, said one report, were tired of Goebbels's "club-footed fairy stories" and Göring was asleep.[79] Anger was also directed at the speech of Robert Ley, the minister of labor, who suggested that evacuation problems could easily be solved since Germany had two million vacant rooms that could be occupied. Perhaps this was true, was the response, but most of these were in the possession of the wealthy and the well-off, who were not going to share them with ordinary people.[80]

Goebbels himself was aware that many Germans were commenting on Hitler's failure to visit the scenes of the bombing and on the fact that he was not even shown on the newsreels. He was happy with his own reception in the bombing areas, but one Sicherheitsdienst report pictured him as visiting the Ruhr with a caravan of fifteen luxury cars and another said that he could only travel in an armored car through these areas.[81] When Hitler was finally shown on the newsreels in his command bunker, the shots were fuzzy and some critics suggested that close-ups were avoided for fear of showing how worn and depressed-looking he was.[82] One of the most often quoted jibes against the government in this period was the verse, usually attributed to the miners in Düsseldorf and addressed to the British bomber pilots: "Dear Tommy, please fly further on your way; spare us poor miners for today. Fly instead against those people in Berlin; they're the ones who voted Hitler in."[83]

The party, of course, continued to display the accustomed bureaucratic stance of feverish activity designed to deal with the myriad problems occasioned by the air raids. There were local collections to aid bombing victims and numerous contributions to funds set up for this purpose by Goebbels's Reich Ministry of Propaganda.[84] Party agencies sought to provide more information on how to deal with phosphorus bombs in order to reduce the fears of these weapons.[85] Efforts were made to speed up the building of additional air-raid shelters, to increase the use of fire-retardant chemicals, and to streamline the organization of air-raid protection.[86] Local party leaders were now given independent authority to issue the war service crosses that denoted heroic civilian action during air raids.[87] Party leaders sought to discourage rumors of the evacuation of party offices from Berlin and of any seizure of hospital space due to the needed shifting of party offices elsewhere.[88]

Some of the evacuees returned to their homes after the temporary cessation of raids on a particular area. Sometimes this was due simply to nostalgia for "home," frequently combined with the fear that if living quarters were left unoccupied, someone else would take them over. Cramped and crowded quarters still contained familiar belongings. The dirt and grime from smoke and soot could be removed with hard work, and flowers were still available to lighten the gloom. And often it was less strenuous to live within the ruins than to trek long distances from a place in the suburbs to work in town.[89] But both Cologne and Hamburg faced the menace of droves of vicious rats, grown strong by feeding on the corpses that were left unburied within the rubble as well as the potatoes and other food supplies lost beneath the broken buildings. A great poisoning action in Cologne disposed of many of the nasty animals, but in their nests beneath the surface they survived, procreated, and constituted a vermin army until many months after the war.[90] Percy Ernst

Schramm wrote of the rats in Hamburg, which "scurried fat and fresh on the streets," but added that even more disturbing were the flies—"great, shining green, such as no one had seen before. In clumps they rolled about on the pavement, sat on the remnants of the walls procreating with one another, and warmed themselves tired and satisfied on the splinters of the window panes. When they could no longer fly, they crept through the smallest crevices, besmirched everything, and their rustling and humming was the first thing we heard as we awoke." Only the cold wind of October made an end to these pests.[91]

Life in the ruins became a common part of the scene and one of the more popular articles, "How We Live" ("*Wie wir leben*") in *Das Reich* stood out from the usual propagandist publications for its more realistic contents.[92] Difficulties with transportation, failure of utilities, infrequency of rubbish collections, a decline in the number of food stores and inadequacy of their supplies were often a part of the scene.[93] Although propagandist, the accounts of cooperation in the bomb-ravaged cities and of a recovery of some sense of their original identity by those who returned to their homes seemed to reflect the reality of the day.[94] For most of those who lived among the ruins the bare quest for survival (*Überleben*) became the motif. As Ursula von Kardorff expressed it, "The thing is to have as many parties as possible and to make the most of one's house while it is still there."[95]

The party's mood in this period was increasingly bleak. Just below the surface lay a real sense of desperation. Fears of possible moves by the military gained substance with the formation of the National Committee for a Free Germany in the Soviet Union on July 12 and 13 and later on an allied "League of German Officers," which gained the support of Field Marshal Friedrich Paulus and General Walther von Seydlitz, who had been captured at Stalingrad.[96] The possibility that the defeatism represented by this movement might gain wider support among military leaders led to an intensification of the party efforts to improve the "political education" of the soldiers.[97] But party reports reflected a lack of real interest in many party activities and a loss of support from the youth. As one school leader expressed it, "In many villages the HJ is completely asleep. Thus it is reported from Westheim that no appeal (for support of the Hitler Youth) or anything else has taken place. The Hitler Youth exists only on paper."[98] But as Josef Fischer pointed out, the Hitler Youth were no longer free for meetings and organizational activities—they were used as antiaircraft battery helpers, trained for the fire brigades, and drafted early for the army. The war was being fought with children—"Children in the flak places, children with the fire brigades, children in the railroad gangs, children with the war service cross, children with the medal for the wounded, and children in the mass graves."[99]

New domestic shortages appeared and old ones became more serious. In this period, when the use of automobiles was almost impossible because of fuel shortages, the lack of new tires for bicycles began to cripple their use as well.[100] Straw shoes and shoes with wooden soles were produced, and soap, other cleaning materials, shoe and leather polish were delivered only in exchange for the wrappings of the last purchase.[101] Newspapers gave directions for ways to put up food without canning jars—dried beans, frozen peas.[102] Men's suits had long been virtually irreplaceable (except as replacement for clothes lost by bomb damage), but even party officers now suffered from the shortage—new uniforms were available only for those from the rank of Ortsgruppenleiter (town leader) up.[103]

But no stage of desperation had been reached as yet. Late in the fourth year of the war, the party chancellery could report that during the last clothing collection they had amassed 33,000 men's suits, 401,000 men's jackets, 362,000 pairs of trousers, and almost half a million hats along with 302,000 women's dresses and 16,500,000 pairs of shoes.[104] The Nazi welfare agency indicated to the headquarters of Gau Baden that it could provide all kinds of children's furniture—2,000 chairs, 90 semicircular tables, 220 square ones, 150 beds, 320 clothing chests, as well as cots for small children, toy chests, and much more.[105] And a tile factory in Württemberg was still trying to find a proper way to dispose of some 20 million building stones and 15 million roof tiles it had on hand.[106]

There were various reports of food shortages, but the complaints reflected difficulties in getting preferred foods rather than actual overall shortages. In this time, when fruits and vegetables should have been more easily obtainable, reports from parts of Germany complained that their area did not get its proper share of foods or that, for example, only white cabbage was available.[107] Obviously, some items were being held out of normal distribution. The black market flourished. Sometimes goods were brought in from occupied Holland and sold at inflated prices—a kilogram of country butter at sixty to seventy marks, a kilogram of food oil at eighty to one hundred marks.[108] The practice of "hamstering," of going out into the countryside to buy produce, continued. A verse of the day ran,

"He who goes out to hamster in an auto, goes into the Brown House [of the party in Munich]; he who goes out to hamster in any other way, goes into the jail house; he who doesn't hamster, goes into the funeral house."[109] But, contrary to the verse, in the midst of transportation difficulties and the likelihood of the rapid spoilage of fruits and vegetables, the party recommended against picayunish punishment of small offenders.[110] Party leaders did, of course, get their special perquisites. When Rosenberg made a visit to Strassburg to make a speech, he got a "thank you" present of 100 bottles of champagne and 150 bottles of first-quality wine.[111]

The party also continued its efforts to get the "voluntary" aid of evacuees in the harvesting of crops.[112] But this obviously had little effect, and farmers continued to be heavily dependent on the labor of foreign workers. Their help was so vital that they gained new perquisites, sometimes by threat, sometimes by good will. One report related that the death of the exiled Polish Prime Minister Sikorski found farmers in Swabia sharing the unhappiness of their Polish farm workers.[113] Another, undoubtedly exaggerated, report described the actions of Polish farm workers in Bavaria who received, at the evening meal, potato salad, a serving of green salad, as much bread as they wanted, beer, and two eggs but complained that the Poles who worked for the man's neighbor got five eggs. The neighbor was warned of the unwisdom of his generosity, but the observer thought he probably kept on in the same fashion.[114] These reports were, of course, colored by the fact that their writers believed that foreign workers were being "coddled." A more realistic view of the life of a Polish farm worker set forth by a young Polish girl working on a middle Germany farm finds little evidence of German "coddling." She could not find much sympathy with her fussy and mean-minded mistress's "ranting about the innocent people who were dying in the bombings."[115]

But there was, indeed, pressure during this period to get German supervisors to deal more reasonably with their foreign workers. This effort was, of course, not prompted by humanitarian feelings but by a concern for maintaining production and obtaining new recruits for German factories. The East workers (those from the Ukraine and Baltic areas of Russia) were regarded as capable of high-level production if treated properly. But the party was well aware that efforts to improve their conditions in Germany were not getting much compliance. There was a move to divide the East workers into two classes. Class 1, those who did poorly, would wear their OST (for East) insignia on their breast. Class 2, those who performed satisfactorily, could wear their OST on their left arm.[116] Some of the East workers were also allowed to take furloughs from their work and did so without serious incidents.[117]

This was not true of French workers, however. Many of the French civilian workers went off on furlough and failed to return. Even when they came back, they were often late. With train transportation slow and uncertain in this period, this was understandable. Of all the foreign workers, the French were most welcomed in Germany. They played ball and often went swimming with the German children and still made their conquests of the German women, who often came by the factories when the shifts changed to pick up their friends. But the government suggested contact with recruiters in France in respect to those who failed to come back and also an investigation of factory conditions to make sure they had not been mistreated.[118]

But there remained concern and fear for all the workers from the East. New reports said that German women were being made the target of "fresh" and suggestive comments from the foreigners.[119] In Linz, the East workers and Poles wrote letters home suggesting the coming defeat of Germany. The women workers rubbed mustard oil into their skin to get out of work and the East workers took over the inns and sometimes danced in the streets to the music of hand harmonicas. The watch personnel were afraid and kept out of sight. The Czechs took advantage of the situation to have sexual relations in the parks with the women East workers while the German youngsters watched, enthralled at the performance. Some of the workers even went to the camps of the East women workers and had intercourse through the barbed-wire fences.[120]

The records reveal even more concern in respect to prisoners of war. A report from Halle detailed the efforts of Soviet prisoners of war to avoid work. One of them working on the railroad put his hand under a passing train and let it be cut off—he was homesick, he said, and did not want to work in Germany any more. Others working for a mining company ate carbide, rock salt, or spoiled beets to make themselves sick. Many of those who ate carbide died as a result. When the carbide was locked up, the POW's used rock salt and steam to make sores, added sunflower seeds to create pus, and so forth. There were even incidents of strikes that had to be broken up.[121] It must, of course, be admitted that in this same period the Germans were completely unable to get any accurate information about the fate of their soldiers captured in Russia.[122]

The fear of the large number of foreign workers and prisoners of war was responsible for one of the famous party controversies of the period as Karl Wahl, the Gauleiter of Swabia, began, on July 15, to set up a "Heimatschutztruppe" (home guard) as a safeguard against a possible uprising. This action aroused the anger of Heinrich Himmler, who declared that such a step lay within the prerogatives of the police authorities. The growing power of the Gauleiters in this period is underscored by the fact that Wahl could continue his plans until Himmler threatened his arrest late in the year.[123] Wahl's plans, of course, anticipated the establishment of the Volkssturm in 1944.

Another new thrust of the regime during this period was directed against habitual criminals. Minister of Justice Thierack continued his efforts to harden the hearts of the judges, demanding the death penalty for these people. It was not fair, he proclaimed, for good men to die at the front and these criminals to survive at home. These "parasites on the body of the people," most of whom derived from "asocial, sick, or degenerate ancestors," had to be removed so that after victory the nation would no longer be troubled by "asocial criminals."[124]

In the midst of the turmoil of war, the government continued to devote much attention to the entertainment of the populace. The Mecklenburg State Theater still spent almost one and one half million marks for the 504 presentations it produced during the year, with light operettas such as Walter Kollo's "Wie einst im Mai" ("As It Was Once in May") and Franz Lehar's "Merry Widow" attracting the largest interest.[125] Kraft durch Freude, the Nazi cultural organization, continued to be active. For the coming fall and winter, it planned 175 musical events and 720 theater presentations for Mecklenburg.[126] The Bayreuth Festival plays were performed with plaudits for their quality in the midst of war.[127] And Ulrich von Hassell during this period saw in Ebenhausen the performance of Calderón de la Barca's play "La vida es sueña," "Life Is a Dream."[128] Movies, of course, continued to be the major source of entertainment for the largest number of people. Light stories, one called "Women Are No Angels" and another entitled "Journey into Adventure," reflected the mood of the people, the quest for escape, not the heavy tragedies sometimes shown.[129] One movie shown in Prague with the title "Moods of Love" had unexpected consequences. When it portrayed a German who was coming back to Hamburg from America after five years absence and his relatives told him. "You will be astounded how Hamburg has changed," the Czech spectators were unkind enough to break into laughter.[130]

Although the Reich propaganda ministry dispensed almost

2,700 marks from its budget for more books on America—"Gold Dollar," "America at War," "A Profile Sharply Drawn," "Land without Heart," and "Babbitt,"[131]—the tastes of the people looked for the familiar and the nostalgic. Josef Fischer wrote that "only illusion remains. It is to be bought for one mark, fifty (pfennigs). At the New Market. In hundreds they stand in line and buy at a little wooden shed a fairy tale book, and carry it home as carefully as a treasure, read the stories of the Brothers Grimm, cry and laugh as they do, and are as children again."[132]

Grumbling, mumbling, complaining, no longer full of the joy of living, no longer expecting a quick victory, even increasingly dubious of any victory, crouching in fear under the bombs, working to exhaustion in the factories or on the farms, the Germans continued their daily tasks and daily duties. A movie, a concert, an extra pair of eggs or some fresh fruit, some fresh flowers on the table, a party with the last remnants of some long-saved liquor, all of these provided some relief from the humdrum desperation of war. This time was, as Gottfried Benn wrote on August 7, 1943, "the day when summer ends.—For it is a time of finality; a new beginning from the start is not possible even if one remains alive in a country in which there is not and will not be one piece of cloth, one pair of bootlaces, or one bucket more. Astounding everything, but above all astounding until my last moment of life: this people!"[133]

5. A Joyless Victory

The fall and early winter of 1943 were marked by unusually cold weather. The cold of the weather was matched by the chill affecting German morale in this period. Before the year was out, the chill of the weather forced a cutback in the most vital part of German food rations—potatoes. This brought a further decline of the morale, which had already fallen with the desertion of Germany by its closest ally, Fascist Italy, and the continuance of the heavy bombing of its cities, accompanied by an increasing appearance of U.S. Flying Fortresses traversing the German skies in broad daylight. It was an ironic aspect of this period that for the first time since the beginning of the bombing of the German homeland, its Luftwaffe defenders were wreaking enough havoc on the invading planes to threaten their continued effectiveness.

The British date the "Battle of Berlin," the intensive attack on that city by the Royal Air Force, as having taken place from November 18, 1943, to March 24, 1944. But the heavy British attacks on that city began early in September, with raids on September 1 and 4, which dropped well over 2,200 tons of bombs. In the period thereafter, prior to the beginning of the intensive raids on Berlin, the British bombed Munich, Düsseldorf, Mannheim, Ludwigshafen, Hannover, Bochum, Hagen, Kassel, Leipzig, Nuremberg, and Stuttgart. Some of these cities were attacked a second time after the beginning of the raids on Berlin, and Frankfurt was added to the list of targets late in the year.

In spite of the cooperation of the U.S. Eighth Air Force in the bombing of Germany, the British made no real changes in their strategy or operational objectives. Sir Arthur Harris still believed firmly that the Germans could be defeated from the air by the area bombing that his forces were carrying out. In a memorandum to Winston Churchill on November 3, 1943, Harris listed nineteen German cities which he regarded as "virtually destroyed," nineteen more which he labeled "seriously damaged," and nine which were "damaged." He anticipated that before the completion of his program of destruction, "more than half completed already," Germany would collapse.[1]

Harris's assumptions were faulty. Within the "virtually destroyed" cities that he listed, life went on. Damages to factories were repaired more quickly than the Allies had expected. Streetcar service was restored. Utility services were reestablished. People who had fled returned. Additional air-raid shelters were built. Additional antiaircraft defenses were provided. The Allied air forces were made painfully aware of their misjudgments during this period as they encountered not less fighter opposition but more. New intelligence estimates provided early in November of 1943 warned the British and Americans that during the following month they would confront 800 single-engine and 760 twin-engine fighters on the western front and an even larger combination of these planes by the following April.[2] Obviously, the previous heavy bombing had not succeeded in reducing the German productive capacity.

The American Air Force tactics in this period proved particularly vulnerable to German fighter attacks. The assumption that the "Flying Fortresses" (and later the "Liberators") could defend themselves against enemy fighter attacks was one of the most serious errors of the Second World War. It was based on the belief that these impressive four-engine bombers, which carried ten to thirteen machine guns each, could fly in formations of staggered groups of eight so that each group had over a hundred machine gunners to ward off enemy attack. But German fighters, much faster than the lumbering bombers, were often armed with cannons or rockets, which made it possible for them to attack out of range of the machine guns, and the disruption of formations because of engine failure or damage from German antiaircraft fire provided an opportunity for fighters to destroy the bombers piecemeal. The most serious losses suffered by the U.S. Eighth Air Force came on October 14, 1943, when 291 bombers attacked the German city of Schweinfurt for the second time. The earlier raid on August 17, it will be recalled, had cost the Americans sixty planes. This repeat raid added another 60 planes shot down in Germany, 17 lost on the way, and 121 damaged.[3]

But British bombing also suffered increasing losses in this period. The development of "wild boar" tactics allowed the German fighter planes to gather in concentrated fashion to intercept the British bombers at the target area, where they could be seen from above outlined over the glare of the searchlights. The British use of "Window" aided the Germans in determining the target area, since the tin foil strips were dropped just before the attack and the concentration of "blips" on the German radar indicated where the bombers were. The fighters attacked independently from below aided by the blindness of the British bombers from the rear, a tactic that was later exploited by the German "slanting music" (*Schräge Musik*), marked by the use of cannons mounted in an inclined upward position. Additionally, during this period, the "tame boars," night fighters following control from the radar stations, were directed into positions where they might intercept the British bomber stream on its way into or out of the Reich.[4]

Furthermore, Berlin was to prove a much more difficult target than Hamburg had been. Large and sprawling, with more broad avenues, more buildings of brick and stone, and less clearly recognizable physical features than Hamburg, Berlin was not so easily "wrecked from end to end" as Air Marshal Harris had anticipated. No great firestorm swept through its streets, although its travail was marked by broad avenues of rubble. But government offices remained in the city, and Hitler passed the later period of the war there.

By the end of 1943, the Luftwaffe had won a victory of sorts. The losses of both the British and American air forces were so heavy that both considered the situation catastrophic—only the provision of fighter-plane escorts for the bombers could reduce these devastating losses. For a time, the skies over Germany seemed to be again in the command of the Luftwaffe. But this "victory" was not apparent to the Germans themselves. The battles of the German night fighters against the British bombers were not visible to the German public. The Germans could not, as the British had done in the earlier period of the war, watch the dogfights of their fighters against the enemy invaders and cheer as the bombers fell burning from the skies. By this time, those under the bombs had learned the necessity of hurrying to the air-raid shelters as actual attacks began. And the

British losses did not prevent the dropping of bomb loads running as high as 2,350 tons in a single raid.

The practice of bombing and rebombing the same cities continued. Hannover was attacked four times during the months of September and October; Mannheim/Ludwigshafen and Munich twice; Düsseldorf once in September and a second time in early November. The first U.S. air raid in this period was against Stuttgart, with later attacks against Bremen/Vegesack, Gotha, Danzig, and Münster before the disastrous Schweinfurt raid noted above.

Measured by the German reactions, the Schweinfurt raid was by no means a complete failure. The appearance of the American bombers flying in broad daylight across a large section of Germany had a tremendous psychological impact. This was heightened by the effects of the bombing, which revealed that even the larger edifices of the factories could be so deeply penetrated by the bombs that the cellars of the factories were no longer secure. The workers were no longer willing to stay inside the factories during the raids and promptly headed for the nearby bunkers when the sirens sounded. This, of course, occasioned the loss of labor time and concerned party officials.[5] Relocation of some of the ball bearing plants in Schweinfurt to other German cities was not always easily accomplished. The inhabitants of Würzburg, for example, protested plans to move industries there for fear this would endanger their homes as well as the many hospitals of the city.[6] Many of those who saw the damage in Schweinfurt felt that the reports denying serious setbacks to production could not be believed.[7] The party in Schweinfurt also aroused serious criticism outside as well as within the city because of the mayor's insistence on burying those killed in a mass grave rather than releasing the bodies to the families concerned because, he said, only by creating this dramatic funeral monument could later generations be made aware of the enormity of the tragedy that had occurred there.[8]

The bombings caused continuing protest and concern all across Germany. "They are the talk of the day and weigh like a nightmare on the whole population," read one of the mood reports. Many Germans felt that the war had to be ended or all of Germany's cities would be destroyed. For many women the idea of having children under these circumstances was criminal—their fathers would fall in battle and their mothers under the rubble of the cities, and even if the children themselves did not meet an agonizing death in the bombing, they might well be left orphans, subject to the uncertain hazards of fate. Many women probably followed the reported example of one mother who remade her maternity gown into a street dress because she felt that she would have no need for the former while the war was on.[9]

Some of the clergy saw God's hand in the bombings. They were the punishment of God, preached a clergyman in Schwärzelbach in southern Germany.[10] And another clergyman in northern Germany agreed, writing a hymn that castigated the existing regime: "The truth is now suppressed, will no one hear the truth? The lies are beautifully decorated, one helps them often by adding an oath [that they are true]; thereby God's word is despised; the truth is also scornfully ridiculed, one honors the lies." And these verses filled the pews of the preacher's church in Neustrelitz.[11] In Nuremberg, a "miracle" of God left the statue of the savior untouched in a bombed-out cemetery chapel and crowds came to see it—the party was unhappy that it was not a picture of Hitler that was left to catch the marveling eyes of the people.[12]

On the other hand, it seems clear that the bombings tended to draw people together in a community of striving against adversity, ignoring politics. The comments by Goebbels on his reception in the various heavily bombed cities seem genuine not propagandist. Here was a representative of the regime making a clear demonstration of concern and sympathy. But Goebbels himself displayed surprise that in the midst of the ruins people came up to him, slapped him on the back, and offered gratitude for his speeches. Obviously, they shared his anger at the enemy and welcomed his promise of vengeance.[13] Christabel Bielenberg, by no means a Nazi, summed up her feelings after the bombings of Berlin. "The bombs fell indiscriminately on Nazis and anti-Nazis, on women and children and works of art, on dogs and pet canaries." And she learned that "that barrage from the air which mutilated, suffocated, burned, and destroyed, did not so much breed fear and a desire to bow before the storm, but rather a certain fatalistic cussedness, a dogged, determination to survive and, if possible, help others to survive, whatever their politics, whatever their creed.[14]

Another Berliner, Ruth Andreas-Friedrich, an anti-Nazi activist, wrote that the British could not understand why the Germans worked so hard to restore their cities and attributed it to support for Hitler. But it had nothing to do with that, she said.

We repair because we must repair. Because we couldn't live another day longer if one forbade us the repairing. If they destroy our living room, we move into the kitchen. If they knock the kitchen apart, we move over into the hallway. If only we can stay "at home." The smallest corner of "at home" is better than any palace in some strange place. For this reason all who have been driven out of the city by the bombs return home someday. They sense among the stone blocks their destroyed houses. They work with shovel and broom, with hammer, pliers, and pick-axes. Until one day over the bombed out foundations a new "at home" exists. A Robinson-Crusoe lodge perhaps. But still "at home." The last thing one saves from a burning house is a pillow because it is the last piece of "at home."[15]

Some of the German cities that were attacked suffered more severely than others because of poor air-raid preparations. Goebbels felt that the damage in Kassel after the raid of October 4 was increased by the neglect of the Gauleiter there, Karl Weinrich.[16] Sicherheitsdienst reports from Halle warned about a potential tragedy there because local authorities failed to insist on attendance at air-raid protection lessons, to require the cutting of emergency exits between cellars, and to enforce obedience to air-raid alarms instead of allowing women with baby buggies to continue to stroll in the city park after the siren had sounded.[17] The party did, indeed, intensify its drive to stress air-raid discipline—especially the absolute necessity of "self-help" in combating fires before the professional firefighters came. In some areas, people had begun to get rooms in the country to sleep in at night and to come back in to work during the day when it was safer. But this, of course, left their city dwellings unattended during the bombings. The Gauleiters were directed to organize measures for fire protection with more energy than they had shown in the past.[18] It was suggested that fire-watch crews might be formed to stay in the larger public buildings in order to take early action.[19] Procedures for the treatment of phosphorus burns were prescribed. The procedure involved prompt removal of the poisonous substance with water and perhaps rubbing the area with sand and the use of procain or lorocain for pain. The use of chloride of lime and losantin (a bleaching powder preparation) was not approved—these were to be saved in case of need for chemical warfare defense.[20] The party should give all possible aid during air raids, stated one directive, and another suggested that the private air-raid bunkers of party leaders should at least be opened up to servants and neighbors.[21] As a means of promoting greater popular efforts in air-raid defense, the distribution of war service crosses for meritorious action during air raids was to be speeded up by placing in the hands of the Gauleiters an allotment of these badges, which they could award on their own authority (although they had to supply after the award a justification of their action in quadruplicate). The crosses were to be available to women as well as to men, but women were limited to a quota of 5 percent of the total![22]

Yet there was the beginning of concern for the financial drain of air-raid relief measures, and a secret party directive stressed that war damage claims had to be carefully checked. If possible, damages were to be compensated only in the most modest way. The tendency to pay excessive monetary claims threatened inflation and financial deficits.[23] There was still a combination of 3,500 glaziers who were able to provide 2,500 square meters of glass a day for bomb-damaged areas, but they were now providing service only for the kitchen and one other room of each dwelling.[24] Greater caution was also being exercised in the distribution of ration cards (those for clothing were not to be given out until four days after the evacuation from a bombed-out area so that authorities could see what really remained available to bomb victims) and limits were placed on special food distributions.[25]

At the same time, measures were taken to increase the number of workers in the antiaircraft batteries, including the potential drafting of youths over fifteen and the requirement that factory workers assist on their free time.[26] This continued the exposure of very young boys to the hardships of life with these flak outfits, the handling of the heavy shells, the danger of exploding bombs, the roughness of a soldier's life without being soldiers. Directives spoke of the continuance of education, of sheltering the boys from the dangers of sex and drugs, and of proper care and feeding. But there was no way in which boys of this age could measure up fully to the responsibilities placed upon them.[27] On the other hand, there were, by this time, 33,000 antiaircraft cannons to be manned in the Reich, and the regular armies were fully occupied in Italy and in Russia. The party remained concerned about its public image. The Kreisleiter of Bremen reported that conversations in the air-raid bunkers underscored the need for the party to preserve its contacts with the people and to make them aware of its continued concern for their welfare.[28] There was a suggestion that films should be shown in the bunkers during air raids, perhaps with a speech of a party leader accompanying them.[29] Efforts were made to extend the work of the NSKK, the Nazi party organization of truck drivers, which aided in the movement of furniture and other possessions of those who lost their homes in the bombing.[30] The effectiveness of the activities of this agency is underscored in the reports of this period from Stuttgart.[31]

Berlin had been well prepared for the air raids that were inflicted on it from November 19, 1943, on. Although not all of the bunkers that had been planned were completed, there were still 65,000 places with beds in the city's center. The subways were not regarded as secure air-raid shelters, but many people did take refuge in them. The roofs of the houses had been treated with lime or a carbide slime to retard burning and allow effective "self-help." An excellent command center for directing the air-raid protection efforts had been established in the high bunker at the corner of the Karl and Schumann streets. Air-raid preparation had been conducted so as to reach the largest number of people possible. Thus, on eight different Sundays in 1943, demonstrations on the sport fields of the city had proved that the phosphorus bombs used by the British were not as dangerous as commonly believed. The initial flare, it was shown, did not ignite everything it touched and scooping off those parts that were damaged allowed the remainder to be easily extinguished.[32]

But the size and scope and long continuance of the attacks launched against it meant that Berlin, regardless of all efforts, was seriously damaged. Both the official records and the private accounts of its citizens emphasize the "toughness" of the Berliners, the devotion of those carrying on governmental tasks there to the accomplishment of their duties, and the determination in spite of all hardships to preserve some of the joy of life that had once been a characteristic of the inhabitants of Germany's largest city. Already on the cold morning following the first great attack, the workers of Berlin tramped through its rubble-filled streets to carry on their daily tasks.[33] From Goebbels, the Gauleiter, on down to very modest offices, those who served in the government had to assess both their private and public losses. The Reich Chancellery was seriously damaged. Goebbels was as concerned with its injuries as with those to his official domestic residence (for which he clearly had fewer sentimental attachments).[34] Rosenberg's offices in Berlin were destroyed with all the archives stored in them.[35] The House of the German Press suffered damage in the first two attacks but was quickly repaired and all the archives and typewriters saved.[36] Large sections of the German Opera House were destroyed, but the side theaters, rear theaters, costume rooms, and rooms in its service building offered some chance for resumption of its activities.[37] The ladies responsible for the work of the Berlin headquarters of the Foreign Office of the German Dozentenschaft, which entertained foreign academic visitors to Germany, lost their headquarters building but worked from private homes while repairs were made and window panes restored ("almost senseless to replace them but with this kind of cold one can't sit without window panes"). Reestablishing routine and hunting up foreign visitors in this period involved real difficulties—a cross-city trip, which normally took half an hour, now required two to three or more hours.[38]

Again, as usual, the raids carried with them the unusual outcomes determined by chance. During the raid of November 26, a high explosive bomb blew the heavy iron door off the building in which Ursula von Kardorff's apartment was located. But a ninety-six-year-old man, who had stayed in bed on the first floor of the building, was rescued without injury. At the same time a public air-raid shelter in Kurfürsten Street was struck by a bomb and all the inhabitants burned to death. The corpses were unrecognizable—"all quite black."[39] Horst Lange told the story of an actress saved from the bombs on one occasion by the instincts of a stray dog she had picked up and on another by the simple fact that she had bent over her pocketbook to find her glasses while riding home on a suburban train—the other occupants were badly cut by flying glass from a bomb dropping close to the tracks.[40] In another case, a young but determined woman led a whole group of refugees through a long maze of cellars before they finally came to safety.[41] And in still another story a blind caretaker in an apartment house, who had been secretly sabotaging the elevator, now used his wiles to climb on top of it and toss away the incendiary bomb that might have set the whole building on fire.[42]

Life was precarious and no one could prejudge his end. In Berlin, as well as elsewhere, many of the bombs that fell failed to explode. Some were set to detonate later. Some were duds. Those that failed to explode had to be defused. Josef Fischer told of a police expert in Cologne who had been lucky in dealing with fifty of these unexploded bombs, but as his steel saw pierced the steel mantle of the fifty-first, a 350-kilogram explosive bomb, his luck ran out and nothing was left to bury. And in that city, neglected by the big bombers while Berlin was being bombed, the British Mosquitos still buzzed over its buildings like the insects whose name they carried and dropped the few bombs they carried without the sirens having given warning—four seconds still determined life or death there.[43]

Hitler, however, had much more to deal with than the air raids in these declining months of 1943. In September, the Italians surrendered to the Western Allies, Great Britain and the United States. This was not totally unexpected. German intelligence had indicated after Mussolini's fall that Badoglio's ties to Germany were not to be trusted. Although waiting for the formal decision of the Italians to act, the Germans had prepared all measures to take over

Italian military positions, supplies, and weapons. A new Fascist government was established under Alessandro Pavolini on September 9 but placed under Mussolini when the latter was rescued from the Gran Sasso on September 12 in the brilliant operation headed by SS Lt. Col. Otto Skorzeny. The Germans took over full control of military operations in southern Italy and treated Italy as an occupied territory throughout the remainder of the war. The British and American operations in the Salerno area began on September 9, but the advance from that area was to prove slow and difficult.[44]

For some Germans, the Italian surrender came as a shock. But there was little concern for the loss of Italian military power—the average German had little regard for the Italian contribution to the war effort. There were frequent references to the renewal of confidence provided by Hitler's speech and the freeing of Mussolini.[45] Hitler's prestige among the women remained strong. As one housewife expressed her feelings, "The Führer meets one blow after the other, but he never lets himself be beaten and he is always on guard."[46] Nevertheless, these events still weakened many people's belief in an eventual victory and some opponents said that "one is gone now; the other will disappear too some day."[47]

The matter was a difficult one for the German authorities to handle. The lengthy explanation of Mussolini's fall and Italy's surrender prepared by the German Foreign Office was distributed to party leaders with a "top security" classification (*geheime Reichssache*), and it blamed the old institutions (the king), Badoglio's ambitions, and some of the great industrialists.[48] But when Goebbels, in a speech early in October, said that Italy had been led by a "treacherous king," that for the Germans "kings occur only in fairy stories and operettas" because Germany was "a republican leadership-state," party critics wondered whether this did not have a bad effect in Japan and Rumania, both of which had monarchs.[49]

The latent tone of hostility to Italians per se now tended to become much more open. That they were cowardly, lazy, and sluggish could be stated, although government directives tried to direct the best possible treatment of Italian prisoners of war and civilian workers coming to Germany, with an especial concern for providing them with adequate shelter in camps in view of the colder climate.[50] Soldiers still fighting with the Germans, ordered another directive, were to be treated mildly—small kindnesses would win respect. Those working with Italians were not to expect German military discipline, to refrain from nasty comments on Italian fighting ability, to let them prepare their food in Italian style, and to permit them to hold religious services.[51] But by October 26, Ursula von Kardorff wrote that "the first of the Italian prisoners have appeared here—poor freezing creatures, in their tattered uniforms, it hurts me to look at them. What a contrast to yesterday's allies, who used to sweep through the streets in government cars, dressed up to the nines and glittering with gold lace!"[52] And by the end of the year, the Italian workers in Hamburg were cleaning away the refuse, "but first they try to find something to still their hunger, chewing ancient potato and apple peel." They were labeled members of the "Badoglio Clique," too lazy to work, and Germans were not supposed to speak to them.[53]

In Russia, too, the fall marked the very perceptible beginning of German retreats from the territory won with blood and suffering. Before the end of the year, the Dnieper River had been reached and crossed by the Russians, and German troops were cut off in the Crimea. The threat of losing the Ukraine and valuable food and mineral supplies became increasingly clear. The Germans followed the news from Russia with greater concern than that from Italy, but both received less attention than the air raids, which were, of course, of more direct concern at home.[54] But worrisome popular comments began to come to the attention of the Sicherheitsdienst that a victory of the Bolksheviks might not be all that bad—"With the Russians it's not at all as bad as it is always being said. They are only people like us. So many Russians still work here who make an ordinary impression."[55] "Let the Russians come," said Ursula von Kardorff's concierge, "that's what I say. They wouldn't do anything to little people like me and at least the war would be over."[56] And German workers did not feel that a Soviet victory would bother them so much—"We didn't have much before and will not have much then," said one. "We have worked until now and will continue to work," said another. And others thought the English and Americans would not let Bolshevism take over Europe.[57]

But there is no doubt that the German propaganda connecting the Jews and Bolshevism still had its effect.[58] Perhaps there was an effort to tie all Germans to the fear of Jewish revenge for their treatment of the Jews and of Bolshevik revenge for the harsh handling of Soviet prisoners of war. Certainly during this period, the Gauleiters were made specifically aware that the state was engaged in a "final solution" of the Jewish problem and glimpses of the truth came to the general public.[59] And although mood reports always pictured the German soldier as stabilizing the morale at home, there is no doubt that the accounts of the growing brutality of the war in the East tended to add more than propagandist fervor to the fear of Bolshevism.[60] The apprehension of the frightfulness that would follow the end of the war was to increase through the remaining days of the war.

Perhaps it was concern for the popular morale that led Hitler to make, for the first time in many months, a major radio address directed to the German people. The speech came as a surprise to Goebbels, who had not anticipated that Hitler would leave the direction of the war in the East to attend the party's annual meeting in Munich on November 8. Wolfgang Domarus, who gathered Hitler's speeches together after the war, believed that Hitler's attendance was only an excuse for a vacation with Eva Braun.[61] Regardless of his reasons, Hitler presented the first long address dealing with the whole complex of the war since the beginning of the serious air raids.[62] Germany, said the Führer, had begun the war with the enemy only 150 kilometers from Berlin. Now the enemy was still 1,000 kilometers from the German borders. The Germans faced the hardest fighting in the East that they had yet had to confront, but at least it was far from the homeland. And in Italy, the British and Americans would have no easy victory. For the first time, Hitler also dealt at length with the bombing war, calling "the hundreds of thousands of bombed-out people the avant guard of revenge." He spoke of his pain at the sacrifice of women and children and promised the rebuilding of Germany's cities "more beautiful than ever before . . . within two or three years of the end of the war." And he assured his listeners that "the hour of vengeance will come."

Germany, he declared, would never surrender. The party remained firm—"I read every week at least three or four times that I have either had a nervous breakdown, or I have fired my friend Göring and Göring has gone to Sweden, or again Göring has replaced me, then the army has replaced the party, then in reverse fashion the party has replaced the army . . . and then again the generals have made a revolution against me, and then that I have arrested the generals and had them locked up." But one thing, he said, was certain—"that I shall lose my nerve is completely excluded." As for defeatists, Hitler said, he could not imagine anyone really believing that any profit would come to Germany from the victory of the Allies. He would not hesitate, he warned, to give over to death "some hundreds of the criminals at home" who might work for such a consequence. It would be much easier for him to condemn these traitors at home than to send brave soldiers to their death on the battlefield. And in one of his final statements Hitler told those who talked to him of religion, "I, too, am religious and in fact deeply religious inwardly, and I believe that providence weighs men and that he who can not withstand the testing of providence but breaks on it is not fated for greater things." He declared that Germany had withstood its tests and said, "I bow in gratitude to the Almighty that he has blessed us in this way and that he has not sent us more difficult tests, the war on German soil, but rather that he has allowed us to succeed in carrying out successfully this fight against a world of superior forces far beyond the boundaries of the Reich."

Hitler's speech was effective. His voice still carried conviction, although those who were accustomed to Hitler's earlier long tirades were surprised at the shortness of the speech. Many listeners reported that Hitler's assurance of the coming of the vengeance weapons was much more believable than earlier party notices. There were, of course, complaints that little attention had been given to the eastern front and some ironic comments on Hitler's new-found religion—"Necessity has taught the Führer to pray" or "Apparently even the old Nazis can't get along without God." And the classic put-down came from a farmer when he was asked if the Führer had not spoken well: "It must be going badly in the East."[63]

Even before Hitler's speech, the party's drive against defeatism had increased. A report from Schwerin in September had noted that people were more cautious in their conversation since "today the head sits right wobbly on one's shoulders."[64] Now in the aftermath of Hitler's speech, Thierack increased his pressure to get the proper penalties from his judges. There was a considerable discrepancy between the penalties assessed by the special courts and those handed out by the regular ones. In the special courts, even a diary entry could bring a death penalty or a verse that made fun of the political leaders or an honest statement that victory was impossible and Hitler should resign before everyone burned to death.[65] But a regular court assigned only a year's imprisonment to a former officer from World War I, who now served as a work supervisor in a large firm, when he predicted that Germany would soon be defending itself on the Brenner Pass and behind the Elbe and said that all the government leaders were incompetent—Göring a morphine addict, Goebbels a syphilitic, Hitler a hysterical and choleric person, and Keitel an old aunt who had been called the regimental aunt when he commanded a regiment in Fulda. A verse by a stenographer got her only two years in jail as she wrote (rudely translated):

> He who rules with true Russian art
> Has his hair cut in a French part.
> His mustache in the English style is shorn
> He himself was not even in Germany born.
> He taught the Roman greeting to us,
> With our women for many children he makes a fuss,
> Although for producing one, he's not one who can,
> That is in Germany the leading man.

Undoubtedly, many of the milder penalties were upgraded when reviewed. But many of the regular court justices complained that the severity of the punishments often prevented people from denouncing wrongdoers who might otherwise have received a more reasonable penalty—it ought to be possible, said one, to distinguish between real saboteurs and those who were just engaging in "dumb gossip."[66]

The party's mood of sweetness and light in respect to care for foreign workers and prisoners of war also began to darken. The major emphasis of the period was directed towards more disciplinary controls over both foreign workers and prisoners of war. Reports came from all over the Reich that the prisoners of war, especially Soviet prisoners of war, were being treated too laxly, especially since German prisoners of war were being handled so harshly in the Soviet Union. New directives played down the need of being so careful in respect to the health of these prisoners and a full use of their labor was to be required. The use of weapons was authorized in case of mutiny or "passive resistance."[67]

Directives also prescribed decent treatment for foreign workers but directed that a line was to be drawn between them and Germans. These foreign workers were not to share sleeping or eating arrangements with Germans, and Poles or East workers were not to take care of German children.[68] The party was to cooperate with the SS in rounding up foreign workers who left their workplaces after air raids and returning them to those workplaces.[69] The German Labor Front was to curtail its propaganda activities among the foreign workers. The only real task in respect to them was to get the most work possible from them and keep them peaceful. But reports came in that the Poles were openly showing their happiness that things were going so badly for Germany and that groups of them in the Tucheler Heide (in the occupied area of Poland south of Danzig) were increasingly engaging in raids and robberies that the police could not control.[70] Some of them were removing the "P's" from their jackets so they could get better jobs and go to the movies. This was difficult to control—one official suggested that "P" holes be cut in their jackets so that they would have to have the letter to cover them.[71] In the Protectorate, the Czechs were quieter and more reserved in their *Schadenfreude* over Germany's troubles, but there was a marked decline in the use of German by those who knew it.[72] There were reports of sabotage by foreign workers in the armament factories, sometimes aided by German workers who had been Social Democrats.[73]

But there was still some evidence of sympathy for these inadequately clothed East workers—one warm-hearted German left anonymously a package for "der Olga," a Ukrainian farm worker in Swabia, with an undercoat, a blouse and aprons, and a warm head scarf.[74] And there were indeed some Germans who became more than friends with foreign prisoners of war or workers. A woman in Schwäbisch Hall got six months in jail for giving a wounded Canadian pilot a bouquet.[75] Thierack's letters dealt in some detail with the problem of Germans consorting with prisoners of war. Prisoners of war, said the minister of justice, should not eat at the table with Germans, as was often allowed by German farmers. They were not to be counted as members of the household but still to be treated as enemies—after all they might well have killed Germans. On the other hand, mere acts of friendship such as washing their clothing, engaging in conversation about their personal interests, and taking care of them when they were sick were not punishable. The judgment of the relationship of women to these prisoners was more difficult. An occasional accompaniment of a POW, joint photographs, or declarations of love were not juridically punishable, although these were usually the last steps before sexual intercourse, which was subject to severe penalty, or to aiding in plans for escape of sabotage, which was subject to the severest penalties.[76] In wartime Germany, falling in love with the enemy could cost a woman her head.

There was, of course, in this period an enormous sense of urgency for the production of munitions, of more tanks, or fighter planes, of "vengeance weapons," which weighed heavily on the feelings of government authorities and affected their attitude towards foreign workers. This was the period when many of them were moved into cold and damp underground factories to evade the bombings. The sense of desperation warped normal standards of human decency. This was the period when Himmler told his SS followers that if he used Russian women and children to dig antitank ditches and they died on the job, this was of no concern "because if the antitank ditch is not dug, German soldiers will die, and they are the sons of German mothers. They are our blood."[77] In similar vein a Sicherheitsdienst report dealing with unhealable East workers who were taking up German hospital rooms suggested that "a *final and radical* solution" would have to be found to put them out of the way "through a medical means of assistance."[78] And Erhard Milch, the commander of the Luftwaffe fighter arm, when he learned that production in his aircraft factories was threatened by agitation among the foreign workers, said harsh action must be taken against "this foreign scum." "If, for instance, there is a meeting at X, an officer with a couple of men, or a lieutenant with thirty troops, must appear in the factory and let fly with their machine guns into the mob. The object is to lay out as many people as possible, if mutinies break out."[79]

By this time Albert Speer had finally arrived at his most impressive title as minister of armaments and war production. The awarding of this title was later labeled by one of Speer's lieutenants, Hans Kehrl, as the "Magna Charta of the War Economy."[80] But the high-sounding title was not always attended by the kind of power it implied. Speer fought a continuing war with the Gauleiters, who clung to their authority within their regional territories and tended to become increasingly self-sufficient during the late years of the war, with Bormann who resented any central authority not under his control, and with other ministries that resented his efforts for overall planning. There were also difficulties with subordinates, for Nazi personal ambition found no fault in sabotaging superiors to get ahead. And Hitler's freaks of judgment were apt to throw off well laid plans.[81] The story of Hitler's efforts to convert the Messerschmitt 262 jet fighter into a bomber is well known. In December of 1943 the Führer learned that only 1,200 flame throwers a month were being produced. In anticipation of the Allied landings in Europe, he now ordered that three times as many be made—with twenty or thirty thousand of these available, he could never be surprised in the West.[82] In Speer's postwar judgment the autumn of 1943 marked the beginning of his own downhill movement in influence in spite of the new position he held.[83] Goebbels's "total war" objective was, as a consequence, never fully achieved.

Although Speer complained of the inefficacy of his efforts to cut the production of consumer goods, he did accomplish much. The shortages that began to appear in desperate measure during this period bear witness to the enormous emphasis on armament production. Except for a measured distribution to bomb-damaged persons, new clothing became virtually unobtainable. New leather shoes were reported in very short supply.[84] In respect to both clothing and shoes the emphasis grew ever sharper on the repair of existing items. In some areas, a special office for the maintenance and repair of all items was set up.[85] Essen created a series of new shoe stores and shoe repair places after the air raids it suffered in the spring.[86] The Reich clothing office let people use their stamps to buy cloth pieces at 0.8 meters by 1 meter for repair. Some people made dresses by putting these small pieces together. Others bought them without using them—but at least they had received something for their stamps![87] School children again collected bones, paper, cardboard, and textiles of all sorts.[88] Paper began to be in serious shortage. People could not find envelopes for their letters and even government agents complained that they were not getting some of the reports they had formerly received.[89] There were shortages of electrical fuses and light bulbs.[90] The head of the Ahnenerbe office of the SS had to issue a warning that those employees taking home light bulbs or office materials would be prosecuted.[91]

Coal was short and regulations that required apartment renters to maintain a winter temperature of 18°C (64°F) were suspended.[92] Light usage was to be reduced as much as possible. Special "minute lights" were to be placed in the stairwells of apartment houses, giving late comers enough time to get up the stairs without falling but avoiding all-night burning.[93] In some areas soap was short.[94] Finer qualities disappeared, and obtaining a cake of shaving soap in Cologne required four hours of form filling and standing in line.[95] The trivial often disappeared completely. With a sudden urge for prewar luxury, Ursula von Kardorff searched for new earrings in ten shops in Berlin without success. Later, she got three pairs—one from Budapest, one from Paris, and one from Rome, supplied by friends who had found a less stringent regimen in those cities.[96]

But more vitally, the fall of 1943 marked the beginning of really serious cuts in rations.[97] In August, the rations for bread, general foodstuffs, meat, and potatoes all declined. Even the egg ration, which had earlier in the year allowed five eggs per ration period, now fell to one. The decline of the meat ration was aggravated by the absence of any fish ration. In September, there was a further cut in general foodstuffs as well as a cut in the cheese ration. Some improvement came in the bread ration in the following period, but also a further decline in the cheese ration. By December, there was a more marked recovery in the rations of bread and general foodstuffs but still another drop in the potato ration. For many Germans, the hateful barley grits had to become a replacement for both potatoes and meat.[98]

Although these ration cuts did not bring a fall below reasonable levels for nourishment, they did increase the sense of malaise. They were accompanied by temporary shortages, which meant that some foods were not available for several weeks at a time. There were complaints of the unavailability of some fruits. Many of these were still heavily imported from abroad. Until the defection of Italy, there were plentiful supplies of oranges and lemons, but these were cut off completely during the later part of the year.[99] Berries and cherries were obtainable if one had something to trade for them.[100] In areas where fruit was abundant, some bakers used it to bake fruit cakes, which they could sell for a higher price than a regular bread and which also qualified for white bread stamps.[101]

The increase of the bread ration that accompanied the reduction of the meat ration produced disappointment and disgust. One observer noted that it allowed each person two more rolls per week.[102] Nor was the fact that white bread was available well received. Families who bought it consumed it so rapidly that they exhausted their bread rations before the end of the ration period. Workers much preferred the heavier black bread and would have preferred a mixture of wheat and rye grains.[103]

But the most serious problem arising late in 1943 was an unexpectedly short crop of potatoes, probably occasioned by the excessive rain and early cold weather during the later part of the growing period. This threatened the most respected staple in the German diet and aroused government efforts to seek out all supplies available and to ensure careful storage.[104] It also hampered the preparation of food in the factory kitchens, where the main dish was a prepared stew. One of the groups to suffer most, with a decline of work productivity as a consequence, included the East workers in the factories.[105]

The food problems were accentuated by the continued growth of the black market. In November, a goose sold for 150 marks or more.[106] Farmers were lured by the profit motive. A duck required as much feed for raising as a pig, which brought more meat, but the duck brought more money.[107] As for those who were buying, perhaps the prices were not all that important. Many people felt that if they did not spend their money, the government would take it over in the form of taxes or a confiscation of savings, especially if they could be characterized as war profits.[108]

All of these difficulties were compounded by the existence of so many people on the move. To the thousands of evacuees from the Ruhr and Hamburg were added thousands from Berlin, many of whom had left before the beginning of the heaviest raids. The problem of finding places for new evacuees became ever more severe. The number of evacuees was so large that the regime was stymied in finding fundamental solutions for the problems involved. The efforts to complete emergency housing in the heavily bombed areas were made more difficult by material shortages occasioned by the all-out efforts for armaments production. The plans of the Reich Labor Service for these temporary homes were simple enough, diagrams in the newspapers resembling primitive versions of wartime Quonset huts in the United States.[109] But even these simple, barracklike sheds proved beyond the capabilities of Speer's genius in the midst of the drive for weapons. Hitler, in discussing the problem, talked about constructing one million ten-by twelve-foot homes—it is, he said, "immaterial whether they are of wood, concrete, or prefabricated slabs. I am thinking in terms of mud huts or at worst just holes in the ground covered with planks." These were to have no lavatories, no gas, water, or electricity. Fittings were to be primitive—two benches, a table, a cupboard, and nails to hang clothing on. He thought of these "homes" as scattered around towns and villages on individual plots under trees if possible.[110] But very few of these auxiliary homes were ever built.

The party's concern for popular morale increased as the year moved towards its end. There were reports of members leaving the party, of party officers displaying less than adequate leadership, of the party's loss of its hold on the youth, and of party members involved in actions contrary to wartime regulations.[111] Goebbels had begun emphasizing the unwavering belief in victory in his "Thirty War Articles for the German Nation" published in *Das Reich* on September 26, 1943. His proclamation that "war demands from us all a total surrender to it and its duties" was to be continually repeated in the period following, as was the threat of beheading for those who "through treachery and unfaithfulness fall upon the rear of the fighting front."[112] These approaches were, as has been noted, emphasized in Hitler's speech at the party anniversary in November.

Each party organization sought to justify its work in this year of the tenth anniversary of the party's acquisition of power. The German Labor Front stressed the advances it had brought for German workers in contrast to Bolshevism, which did not really care for the workers' problems, and set out a new appeal to the "creative German youth."[113] The Nazi Welfare Organization (*Nationalsozialistisches*

Volkswohlfahrtsamt) proclaimed its accomplishments in "Ten Years' Socialism of the Deed."[114] In proper propaganda style, the agency pointed to 15.5 million members, 28,000 help stations for "mother and child" work, 3.6 million youths sent for vacations in the country, and 3,465 educational institutions.[115] But behind the scenes, the war service of the party was not always a shining example to the public. Bormann still regarded party leaders as engaged in work too important to allow them to be drafted. Late in December, he worked out a secret arrangement with the army by which party officials born in 1901 or later might be given a six months period of service on the front lines after which they would be returned to party duties.[116] And the mania for meetings failed to impress some critics—what was really needed was not "promises and fantasy" but "facts."[117]

The whole tone of party speeches, meetings, and activities of the party during this period was a defensive one. It was as if they said to themselves, "We must redouble our efforts because we are losing the support of the people." The artificial efforts at self-confidence carried little conviction. Doubts of the future extended strongly into the ranks of the workers, and although there were references in party directives for appeals to their patriotism and efforts to train new foremen, including some non-German supervisors, the motif was strongly on punishment for breaches of labor discipline: loss of pay for extra time, weekend work, loss of pay for vacations, the cancellation of bonuses, or exclusion from social welfare payments, such as help for marriage, housing, and care of children.[118]

But fines and punishment could not well be employed against the many thousands of women who complained, criticized, and often disobeyed party regulations during this period. A Sicherheitsdienst report of November 18, 1943, detailed the woes and tribulations of women with unusual perception and frankness.[119] Women, especially the younger women, said the report, no longer showed much interest in the events of the war, ignoring the newsreels at the movies and not listening to the radio reports unless they had close relations involved in the fighting. Many women, continued the report, saw with sorrow that the basis for mutual understanding in their marriage was beginning to suffer because of the long duration of the war. The long periods of separation, broken by brief furloughs, the changes in the living arrangements because of total war, and the great demands of the day tended to weaken their commitment to soldier husbands. And front-line soldiers often showed little understanding for the shortages that war had brought at home and the daily problems that confronted their wives. As a consequence, the marriage partners grew away from each other and the furlough periods became times of arguments instead of pleasure. As a result, women tended more than men to criticize the measures of the party and its leading personalities, although they still remained loyal to the Führer and blamed difficulties on the fact that he did not know all that was going on. But their most serious concerns related to daily problems—the shortage of potatoes and vegetables. Many had sleepless nights because they did not know what they would put on the table the next day. Shopping for food was difficult—the butcher was closed on Monday, the baker on Tuesday, the other merchants on Wednesday, and individual merchants at various times. When they arrived at the shops, they found rude proprietors no longer interested in the well-being or good feelings of their customers. And one of the greatest worries of the women was the fate of their school-age children, who had been evacuated away from their parents. Some worried about religious influences—Protestant mothers did not want their children engulfed in the religious practices in Catholic regions. Others were concerned for the children's health.

The life of the women in the evacuation areas was full of annoyances. Most found shelter in little villages and rural areas under the most primitive circumstances. The evacuees had to cook in the same kitchen with the quartering hostesses, and there was fussing back and forth if either had something better than the other. To get their needed ration cards, evacuees were pushed from one authority to another—from burgomaster to Ortsgruppenleiter, to Landrat, to Kreisleiter, to the Kreis representative of the welfare agency, and perhaps back again. Buying food meant leaving the children alone while the mother slogged through wind and weather, ice and snow, to the shops, kilometers from their quarters. These problems were aggravated by the nagging fear that their homes left behind might be taken over by someone else and permanently lost. As a result, many evacuees and their children returned to the cities, determined to stay with husband and children, regardless of government orders. Efforts to force them to go back to the evacuation areas met with massive resistance defying threats of withholding food rations from them—"They can send us to Russia or aim machine guns at us so it will all be over." The people of the cities, noted a report, wanted more great bunkers built, more help in building shelters for their own security, more efforts to make at least temporary repairs of the houses, and more use of the extra room still held by some of the better circles so that the workers and their families could remain together regardless of the bombings. The husbands agreed with their wives's feelings. One said, "As long as I am at the factory, I don't think about things, but when I come home at night, I have the horrors. Then I miss my wife and the laughter of the children." And he wept unashamedly.

As the Christmas of this fifth year approached, the party faced the same problem that returned with each Yuletide season—how could some lift of morale be provided without accentuating the religious element; how could Christmas be made merry but not excessively Christian? As in previous years, the Hitler Youth and some work groups in the factories were urged to make toys for the children. One set of directives stated that these were to be toys reflecting German traditions and the home (horses, woodpeckers, wagons, and jumping jacks); or toys reflecting healthy manhood or womanhood, such as dolls, baby beds, scales, doll furniture, stoves, simple building sets; or toys reflecting the experiences of the homeland or the technical experience of the century (railroads, ships, autos, trucks), or war toys, although those firing projectiles were to be avoided. Not desired were toys that had a droll appearance, such as American Mickey Mouse characters, children with big heads or rolling eyes, "sweetish little Negroes," dwarfs, joking figures such as jumping jacks of Churchill or Stalin, or sentimental figures of hit personalities like Lili Marlene. Waste materials were to be used as much as possible and poisonous paints avoided.[120] These fanciful guidelines did not reflect reality. With many of the Hitler Youth involved in antiaircraft service, the production of toys appears to have been much smaller than anticipated—one party official seeking three hundred toys for five children's homes came up empty handed.[121]

Arrangements were to be made for the visits of parents at the evacuation schools (not vice versa, for fear that the children would not return) and for the distribution of sweets, marzipan, hazelnuts, fresh and dried fruits, and baked goods, as well as a government gift to each child in the form of a savings book with a deposit of three marks indicated. One hundred twenty special trains were to aid in this process. Teachers were to stay with the schools—their relatives could come to visit, too. Extra free time was to be provided for Christmas decorations at these schools, and there was to be no interference with the attendance at church services.[122]

Some regular Christmas music, such as "Holy Night," was also allowed for Christmas celebrations for the wounded in lazarets and rest houses, although Nazi music was to predominate.[123] The party also tried in other ways to promulgate a Nazi Christmas, for instance through the publication of a "Volkisch and Homeland Political Christmas Brochure" of ninety-six pages, 10,000 copies costing the propaganda office in Neustadt 4,000 Reichsmarks; arrangements for proper books for Christmas gifts for the Waffen SS from a Berlin publisher; monetary gifts for school sisters of the Nazi Welfare Agency; and a combination of Christmas trees, traveling bars, and SS placards for Christmas celebrations of the party in Freiburg, preceded by practice sessions to give the singing of the old party fighting songs more oomph than they had had recently.[124] And special efforts were made to recruit party speakers for the Christmas season.[125] One party circular looked forward to a happier postwar period when Christ could be removed from the calendar so that the terms "present time reckoning" and "before the present time reckoning" would replace the before and after Christ designations.[126]

Ordinary people, however, still sought the old Christmas trees or a fir branch if they could not get a tree, regretted the party decision not to make Christmas candles available, which made it necessary for them to dig out stumps of candles from the previous year, bundled up against the cold because of inadequate heating, found that even if they were lucky enough to get a Christmas goose, it did not make much of a feast for four people, and enjoyed the special distribution of fifty grams of real coffee or the quarter of a liter of brandy and fifty cigarettes that were distributed.[127]

This was portrayed by the party as the "Christmas of the brave hearts," but Germans wondered fearfully what the next one would be like. Far too many of them, for Nazi tastes, still sought the solace of the churches, which still had plenty of candles and still sought to reach out to their members.[128] But Horst Lange wondered whether mankind could even have begun to comprehend the message of the angels of "peace on earth to men of good will," if they had proclaimed it that day. For nothing but evil lay about him and man no longer distinguished between good and evil. Worse still, since there was no longer a heaven, or gods, or angels, "the power of becoming godlike, which dwells in mankind itself, is dead and lost."[129]

6. Life Goes On

On January 1, 1944, Hitler's customary New Year's greeting to the German people repeated much of what he had said at the party's meeting in Munich in November. Again there was the reference to the loss of homes, public buildings, and cultural monuments and of the lives of women and children who perished in the bombings (in that order). Again there was the promise of the rapid rebuilding of the cities after the war. Only through victory, he emphasized, could those who had suffered losses hope to have them made good. 1944, he said, would bring great demands for all Germans, but this time, unlike the situation in 1918, Germany's leadership was resolute and determined to prosecute the war with "the utmost fanaticism."[1]

His greeting to the army on the same day pointed to the defensive successes in Italy and promised success for the efforts in the east, although admitting that the coming year would be a very difficult one.[2] At the end of the month, a radio message from his headquarters in East Prussia, addressed both to the soldiers at the front and to "the fighters in the homeland," promised again, as in November, the reward of the Almighty for enduring the hardships of the coming year. "No matter how much the storm against our fortress may howl and rage, in the end it will, as does every storm, abate one day, and out of the dark clouds the sun will come forth to shine on those who, steadfastly and unflinchingly remaining true to their faith, have fulfilled their duty. Therefore, the greater the sorrows of today may be, just so more significantly will the Almighty at that time weigh, judge, and reward those who against a world of foes held high their flag in faithful hands and marched forward undismayed."[3] And Hitler's promises of a hard year were quickly realized. In spite of German defensive efforts, the bombing war took on new dimensions of frequency and severity. The threats on the eastern front increased. And the hardships of war in terms of food and material shortages began to press ever more severely on the home front.

The score card for the air war over Germany during the first four months of 1944 gave plus scores to both sides. The German fighter planes continued to take a heavy toll of Allied bombers. In spite of the bombing, the figures of German aircraft production rose. The inhabitants of heavily bombed cities continued to repair their damages and to carry on their daily activities. On the other hand, the Allied bombers were increasingly accompanied by strong fighter escorts, which reaped a healthy harvest from the opposing German fighters. The ever larger contribution of the U.S. Air Forces to the bombing operations added daytime raids to the British nightly incursions, creating a twenty-four-hour pressure on German defenses. A large group of smaller and middle-sized cities joined the lengthy list of those already bombed, most of them largely because of the location of aircraft factories in or near them. And the presence of so many Allied fighter planes over Germany added the perils of ordinary strafing to those of the bombs. But, most importantly, although the bombing did not immediately reduce aircraft production, it did add hardships to the increasing problems of maintaining the raw materials needed and of transporting raw materials and finished parts to and from the factories now scattered across the German countryside. In this period, the loss of German fighters in their conflicts with the Allied fighter planes also reduced to less than adequate figures the number of well-trained and experienced pilots available during the critical months that followed.

The trauma of the hail of bombs in the homeland was accompanied by continuing bad news from the battle fronts. By the middle of January, heavy Soviet offensives were being launched into the Ukraine and Crimean areas. In spite of valiant defensive actions by the German armies, Soviet forces moved relentlessly forward. In some areas, new German catastrophes like that at Stalingrad loomed on the horizon. Fifty-four thousand German troops were surrounded near Tscherkassy—thirty thousand were later freed and returned to the German lines. Hitler insisted on the holding of the Crimea, which almost resulted in a catastrophe. Shut-in troops there and at Odessa had to be evacuated later, partly by sea. The winter Soviet offensive was broadened in the spring and Soviet forces rewon one city after another in that region. By the end of April, the Soviet armies were already into territory that had been Polish before the war.

Meanwhile, the strong defense of Italy by the German forces there provided one area of great satisfaction for those at home. The rapid movement of Allied forces up through the peninsula that had been so much feared at the time of Mussolini's fall and the surrender of Italy did not occur. The battle of the Allied forces from Salerno northward had been very difficult. Heavy fighting in the area of Monte Cassino still blocked British advances. The Allied landing at Anzio on January 22 did not break the stalemate south of Rome. Although the Germans' strong efforts to dislodge the bridgehead failed, the Allies also failed to exploit the second landing as an effective means of pushing forward towards Rome. Although the situation in Italy was, therefore, not a cause of serious worry, it did not provide reason for rejoicing either. And the events there cast doubt on the German propaganda claims that the impending invasion of France by the Western Allies would be unsuccessful.

The bombing war continued to be the primary focus of attention for the Germans at home. For those in the great cities, the frequency of raids began to convert the experience of living under the bombs almost into a routine, although each new raid carried new perils by virtue of new bombs and new bombing techniques. Those in smaller places had their first taste of the terror that their countrymen in the big cities had experienced during the last three years. The appearance of large numbers of American bombers by day added to the horror of nighttime attacks. The Germans were impressed by the Americans' perfect formations (adopted for the vain efforts at defense against fighter attacks) and the rapidity with which bombs were dropped in the "carpet" pattern. But they soon came to realize that the British bombers carried the larger and more destructive bombs. In this period, according to Josef Fischer, the British began to use a bomb between the size of a land mine and an ordinary explosive bomb (probably the 4,000-pound explosive bomb), which had an even more serious effect than the mines. The latter were in light casings and, when they exploded, exerted pressure over a large area. This was a regular bomb that tended to penetrate more deeply before exploding. The most noticeable effect of this bomb was the force of the vacuum or suction created by the explosion. It will be recalled that all of the explosive bombs exerted first a pressure outwards and then, as the blast effect passed over a particular area, a suction effect. The suction in this case was so strong that it penetrated the slightest crevices of the air-raid shelters and literally pulled the hair of the women present aloft, so that the words, "their hair stood on end" became a physical description not a literary expression.[4]

In spite of Cologne's already long "road of sorrow," one-half million people still lived in the city, many of them simply sleeping in the bunkers at night and going to work in the daytime. A bride and groom were married in a bunker and then rode on a bicycle to their honeymoon refuge across the city. The air-raid warning system became useless with the constant threatening of the city as bombers moved to many other destinations in Germany. People listened to the plane trackers on the radio to know when the raids were really meant for Cologne. After the Fischers had gone to their shelter, their little dachshund provided a second warning. When his sharp ears caught the sound of the coming bombs, he wet the floor and rolled in fear.

After air raids, emergency first-aid stations tried to handle the multitude of lesser complaints quickly. Many people helped themselves—Fischer and 130 of his neighbors worked together to add to the security of their own air-raid shelter, carrying dirt, stones, and sand from wherever they could find them to bolster up the sides and top of their refuge. By the end of this period, Cologne could no longer count on the help of hundreds from outside the city as had been true in the earlier raids. The evacuation of those trapped in air-raid shelters had to be carried out by mechanical means, often with the danger of completely burying those trapped below.

In Berlin, a dozen new attacks joined those begun in November. The city was still a difficult target, requiring a long flight to the goal, and was always heavily defended by antiaircraft fire and usually by strong fighter forces as well. Each raid took a heavy toll on the attackers and only too frequently the bombs fell more than three miles from the aiming point.[5] Neither the factories located in the city nor the government offices there were fatally damaged. The bureaucrats continued to find some place from which to carry out their assigned roles, and the people of the city ruefully watched the loss of more and more of their apartments, but somehow most of them stayed in the city. The use of heavier bombs made the great tower bunkers more popular. Hundreds crouched along the winding staircases that led ever higher into the structures—most people thought the lower floors were "safer." Even anti-Nazis now used the opprobrious "they," which designated those who threatened their peaceful existence, for the British enemy pilots as well as the German secret police and the Gestapo. But if Ursula von Kardorff's diary reflects a reasonable sampling of the scene in Berlin, many of those who were stuck in the city danced on the edge of the volcano, looking for anything that might relieve the dullness and tensions of daily life.[6] The long, cold, and sunless winter finally moved to an end by April, but the bombings did not. The city continued to be the prime target of air raids until the end of the war. But among Berliners, as the Sicherheitsdienst reports frankly said, "the majority of our people are also firmly of the opinion that we must endure all difficulties and 'set one's teeth.' One does it because one must and because there is nothing else to do."[7]

In Hamburg, half a year after its great catastrophe, life had returned to some semblance of normality. Traffic in the main streets had been restored. Many of those who had left the city had returned. Someway, somewhere, they had found shelter, however primitive, in order to be back "at home." People were, of course, not "optimistic" and "happy." Most assumed that new raids would come and previous experience engendered almost universal fear. There were shortages and surly officials dealing with the public. The only real hope lay with the prospect of vengeance, which was "dressed up with mystical dimensions."[8]

For some German cities, the hazards of the air raids were affected by strange tricks of fortune. Stuttgart, which had not been seriously attacked before 1944, suffered twenty-five attacks in the period following. The loss of life here was relatively light because of the earlier evacuation of women and children. The heaviest raid of this period, that of the night of March 15, in which 865 British bombers dropped over three thousand tons of bombs, the highest record until then, should have obliterated the city. But the target point was incorrectly set some seven miles southwest of the city and most of the bombs fell in forests or in open spaces outside the city or in its suburbs. Stuttgart's time of greatest sorrow was reserved for the months of July and September.[9]

Nuremberg, too, was fortunate during this period. The British raid against this city on the night of March 30/31, 1944, became one of the most serious catastrophes in the entire history of Allied bombings. Ninety-five of 795 bombers sent to attack this city deep within German territory were shot down by fighters or antiaircraft guns; 71 more were seriously damaged and 12 were wrecked during forced landings. Poor planning, bad bombing weather (cloudless skies and side winds on the way to the target), and a cloud-covered target played havoc with the bombing efforts. Few bombs landed within the city. Some planes bombed Schweinfurt instead of Nuremberg. The most damage was done to several little towns miles to the east of Nuremberg.[10]

But these mishaps should not be taken to indicate that all of the British night raids were ineffective. Even smaller cities began to suffer the devastation that had been visited upon the larger ones. Although Friedrichshafen had a population of only 28,000 people, it was the center of airplane and tank factories and of the construction of some parts for the V-2 weapons. On the night of April 27, 1944, it was half destroyed— 15.3 cubic meters of rubble were left behind for each inhabitant.[11]

Artificial fogging, which rotted the washings on the clothes lines, failed to save Augsburg from its fate. On the night of February 25, 1944, 50 land mines, 2,400 explosive bombs, and 300,000 incendiaries kindled 4,400 fires, 2,000 of them classified as major fires. With below freezing temperatures, the firefighters were helpless against the flames. Ninety percent of all the losses suffered by this city during World War II came on this one night.[12]

Renewed raids on Schweinfurt did not put the roller bearing mills there out of commission, but they did occasion damage greater than is often noted. The attacks of February 4 and March 24 put 1,200 machines out of service and the total roller bearing production fell significantly from 9,269,509 in December of 1943 to 8,661,110 in January of 1944, to 7,760,446 in February, and to 6,811,900 in March.[13] Local observers doubted the truth of government reports that the local industries had not been affected—one could see, said the local Sicherheitsdienst observer, "how well the North Americans put our most important factories out of use."[14]

The "angels of death" also flew over Frankfurt. New chain bombs—four bombs chained together—were employed here, and the use of phosphorus bombs was also reported. Repeated attacks were made—on January 29, February 8 and 11, and March 2, 18, 22, and 24. The whole nucleus of the city and significant parts of the outside areas were destroyed. A third of the population left the city, one old woman carrying as her most prized possessions three umbrellas and a chamber pot. Rebellious feelings against the regime were noted, but relief trains and trucks with kettles of noodle soup, which even had pieces of meat in it, and sandwiches with butter and sausage helped the mood of the populace. Telephone and electricity service soon returned.[15]

Other cities suffered, too. Kiel took heavy damage in a raid early in January.[16] Rostock was raided, but most of the damage centered in the shipyards and the Heinkel aircraft works.[17] A small raid on Dresden on February 20 failed to stir its leaders to provide more adequate air-raid protection.[18] Complaints in respect to the poor provision of air-raid shelters there were shared by the inhabitants of Würzburg, who had protested the transfer of some of the ball bearing works from Schweinfurt to that city. But in spite of this, the parents still refused to allow their children to be evacuated into strange hands.[19] Both there and in Dresden the only bunker really secure against bombs was that of the Gauleiter. In this same period, a new secure bomb shelter was built in Munich near the Regina Palace Hotel and all party officers were instructed to stay in this hotel when visiting the city.[20] The Austrian cities of Vienna, Steyr, Wiener Neustadt, and Klagenfurt were also raided in this period. The establishment of the 15th U.S. Air Force in Italy made all of southern Germany and Austria particularly vulnerable. Raids from Italy, not very successful at this time, were also directed against the Rumanian oil fields at Ploesti.

With all of this continued bombing, the Germans at home could draw little joy or comfort from the newspaper reports of the heavy Allied bomber losses. By April, the regime was claiming that 1,234 enemy planes had been destroyed.[21] But if that figure was believed, the assumption offsetting it was that Allied production still allowed the raids to continue in spite of losses. A well-meaning suggestion from one of the many correspondents writing to Goebbels proposed sending Jews to England and the United States to carry the threat of liquidating "the some millions" of Jews in the hands of the German army if the air war was not stopped. The response suggested that "for reasons which can not be more specifically set forth, the carrying out of your suggestion must be refrained from."[22] By this time there were no longer "some millions of Jews in the hands of the army" to be used as hostages.

The most serious need at home in these days was additional housing to replace that lost in the air raids. Labor Minister Robert Ley had proposed in August of 1943 a massive building program for the homeless, but Speer had indicated that materials for such a program could not be provided.[23] By this time, the construction was being portrayed as a "self-help" procedure with major direction and aid to come through the respective Gaus or regions of Germany. Both the housing itself and the furniture for those occupying it was to be as simple as possible with the major requirements being that they should be scattered about for security against the air raids, make use of building materials nearby, have access to good drinking water, and use arable land only with special permission.[24] A promise of 1,700 Reichsmarks per home to help in this construction came from the party welfare agency.[25]

The party continued to sponsor assistance in repairing the damage within bombed cities. The agency concerned was entitled the "Expansion-Repair Service" ("Ergänzungs-Instandsetzungs-Dienst," abbreviated "Erg. I. Dienst"—the Germans, unlike the Americans, used abbreviations rather than acronyms).[26] But party services for ordinary people were matched by party demands for additional building for party activities. Early in 1944, the party treasurer forwarded a memorandum to Speer, setting forth the need for about two hundred barracks during the first half of the year with a total space requirement of 11,600 cubic meters. Among the largest items was a major building program on behalf of the party's welfare agency, particularly for day care for children.[27]

Party directives continued to deal with various aspects of the bombing war. One directive suggested that voluntary assistance in manning the antiaircraft guns could be accepted from Belgians, Bulgarians, Danes, Esthonians, Finns, Frenchmen, Dutchmen, Croatians, Latvians, Lithuanians, Rumanians, Slovaks, and Hungarians, but not from Portuguese, Swedes, Swiss, Spaniards, or Turks. As for Italians, they could be required to assume this service by virtue of an agreement with their government.[28] Police and labor-front personnel were now also made subject to this duty.[29] A new office of "flak leader" for the women helping in the antiaircraft batteries was esablished; her task was to help train the personnel, provide political leadership, and arrange for free-time amusements.[30]

The party controlled the awarding of war service crosses, and ideology determined the outcome. One Fritz James, the leader of a mining group in the area, was recommended by the Superior Mining Office in Karlsruhe for a war service cross second class without swords. He never got it. Regardless of his service, he had three strikes against him: he was observed to have dropped a twenty-mark piece in the Catholic church collection but gave only twenty pfennigs to a party welfare collection; he did not give rooms to a seventy-year-old widow until he was sure she was Catholic; and he had never attended one of the party's open assemblies in all the years since 1940.[31]

But war or no war, the party was always prepared to take on

another brave song! The air-raid wardens in Westfalia, "the land of the red earth," dramatized their dangerous work in defiant words.

Red are the flames in the houses and factories,
The fire blows over the blast furnaces.
Red is the flag to which we belong,
And red are the bombing nights.
When the air raid bunkers shudder and the street burns,
When the enemy fliers lurk above the land,
    then out of the red earth rises
    grimly the call on high,
    "Forward, you bomb fighters,
    we shall win in spite of death and terror."

Hard is the work before the blast furnaces and smelters
When the air raid warning sounds.
Hard is the fight of the soldiers in the East
And hard is the heart of Westfalians.
When the nights resound with Alarm, Alarm!
When the mother clutches her child in her arms,
    then out of the red earth rises
    grimly the call on high,
    "Forward, you bomb fighters,
    we shall win in spite of death and terror."

Hot are the hours in the trenches and shelters,
Glowing the pools of phosphorus.
Hot is the storm in the widespreading fires,
And hot the cry for revenge.
When the devils rave, and hell is set loose,
When the houses fall to ruin with the blow of the exploding bomb,
    then out of the red earth rises
    grimly the call on high,
    "Forward, you bomb fighters,
    we shall win in spite of death and terror."

True is the land and bright its seeds,
No one of us is alone.
True rings the song of sacrifice and deeds.
The land will survive and [continue to] exist.
When the first fanfare rejoices aloud,
When the peoples are united and Great Germany is freed,
    then out of the red earth rises
    glowingly the cry on high,
    "Forward, you bomb fighters,
    we won in spite of death and terror."[32]

Propagandist as the words of this song are, it did, indeed, underscore the heroism of those who faced the hardest tasks of the bombing war—seeking to extinguish the fires before the bombing had been completed, moving as swiftly as possible to the relief of those buried in the debris, and salvaging what could be saved from lost homes.

Also propagandist was Goebbels's piece published in *Das Reich* on April 16, 1944, entitled, "Life Goes On."[33] Goebbels with journalistic flavor caught the mood of resistance and solidarity with which the people of the bombed cities had faced the hardships of these raids. These trials, he said, had underscored the helpfulness of neighbors, the weakness of the talkative, and the strength of those who remained silent. He could not help it, he said, but he had never loved Berlin as much as in the aftermath of these bombings. Although transportation in the vast city had been cut off, he had seen the streams of people going by foot to their daily work: the men unshaven and smeared with the dirt of their fire fighting; the women in pants and old pullover sweaters, carrying cases with the utensils for their daily needs. He did not, he said, want to live in any other city. Berlin had shown its unity and strength against all adversity. The same thing, declared Goebbels, was true of the other bombed cities of the Reich— Cologne, Essen, Hamburg, Mannheim, Frankfurt. The enemy terror had not silenced them. "If one were to recount all the sorrow that these bombing nights have brought, one could fill whole libraries with it. But in spite of this, life goes on." After a couple of days, he wrote, there was again water, gas, and electricity. The transportation arrangements started to work again, although perhaps with blockages here and there. But these were borne with patience and often even with a kind of grim humor. Everyone got something to eat and at least an emergency roof over his or her head. From the rubble and ashes, the stove pipes rose again, sticking their noses inquisitively out of the wooden ruins. The people had learned to adapt to their problems.

But both the firefighters' song and Goebbels's essay showed a note of optimism that did not accord with the true spirit of those who had survived these bombings. The prevailing mood was one of fatalism—more than ever the quest to survive but with little faith in any fortunate end of the war.[34] One of the prominent resistance leaders in Germany, Adam von Trotz zu Solz, told a friend in this period that he could not understand the continued bombing and the emphasis on unconditional surrender that accompanied it: "I can't believe they [the British and Americans] want to create a vacuum here in the centre of Europe—a vacuum fills, and if the bombing goes on it will fill from the East."[35] Already there was reason enough to be concerned about a vacuum filling in from the East. The advances of the Soviet armies made it clear that the day of German victories on the eastern front was now past. But the mood reports carried no notes of panic. In spite of loses, the front lines were still far away from home. The press followed the line set forth in Goebbels's speech to the Reichsleiters and Gauleiters in Munich late in February. The German armies, said the propaganda minister, now had "a more favorable position on a new shortened front, which could be held under all conditions." And Goebbels assured his listeners that the Russians had not suddenly become superior soldiers and the Germans weaker ones. Rather, he said, the enemies were "armies of rats who rush obediently against our protective dam in confused packs."[36] The confidence remained, therefore, that the Russians would be stopped at a secure distance from the homeland.[37]

There were, however, hints that these comfortable feelings might be deceptive. Soldiers on furlough from the eastern front described the "withdrawals" as a regular flight and told of the demolition of whole parks of vehicles because the rapid approach of the enemy did not allow them to take the wagons and weapons with them.[38] And a soldier on furlough told Christabel Bielenberg that "if we are paid back one quarter of what we are doing in Russia and Poland, *Frau Doktor*, . . . we will suffer and we will deserve to suffer."[39] Some of the real desperation of the day was revealed in draft changes, which in January moved the number of children required to qualify a father for deferment from five up to eight and then, in March, made even fathers with eight or more children eligible for the military.[40]

The warning voices of the League of German Officers coming from the Soviet prisoner-of-war camps seem to have had little effect. The propaganda line that these officers were only traitors being "used" by the Russians carried conviction. All of the German commanders on the battle fronts, Rundstedt, Rommel, von Kleist, Busch, von Kluge, von Manstein, von Weichs, and Model signed on March 19, 1944, a common declaration that General von Seydlitz, chosen as the exemplification of all the others, should be labeled a traitor and asserted that "his person is for all times covered with shame and disgrace."[41] Although there was some hypocrisy on the part of these generals in labeling as a "traitor" a general who openly recognized what many of them knew—that the war was lost and an early end might save hardships for their country—it may also be doubted whether any negotiations with the Russians at this point could have prevented the Sovietization of Eastern Europe or the division of Germany.

By this time many German officers had given support to plans for deposing Hitler. Assassination efforts had been made but failed. Colonel Klaus Schenck von Stauffenberg, the major figure in the July 20, 1944, attempt, was already committed to action against Hitler. In February, Rommel met with the chief burgomaster of Stuttgart, Karl Strölin, in regard to possible action against Hitler, but gave a rather indecisive response.[42] Even yet there was no firm conviction on the part of the major military leaders that all was irretrievably lost, and some of them were convinced that what occurred in respect to the coming Allied invasion in the West might be more vital in determining the outcome of the war than the operations in the East.

Hitler had never fully trusted his military leaders. All of his moves to war had been opposed by some of his outstanding generals[43] and his military strategy had often been criticized as the war proceeded. By this time his suspicions had grown stronger. Undoubtedly the actions of General von Seydlitz and Field Marshal Friedrich Paulus were a proximate cause— their propagandist advocacy of German surrender because the war was lost accorded with the numerous warning advisories Hitler had received previously from his generals. And if the steadfastness of generals could not always be counted on, how much more vulnerable were the lesser officers and ordinary soldiers likely to be!

Even before the fall of 1943, the German army had had "officers for leadership in respect to military morale" (*Offiziere für wehrgeistige Führung*), who acted as a kind of National Socialist chaplains. Publications were circulated among the officers, explaining why they fought and the relationship of the war to politics, history, ideology, and art. But Goebbels, Bormann, and Hitler himself became increasingly convinced during the fall and winter of 1943 that circumstances on the eastern front had revealed a deficiency of political instruction designed to create a clear realization of Nazi standpoints and teachings. They now set up as their basic aim the creation of the "political soldier" who would be completely reliable in the eyes of the party. On January 8, 1944, Hitler issued a decree requiring the ideological training of the soldiers, involving the creation of "National Socialist Leadership Officers" (*NS-Führungsoffiziere*) all the way down to the regimental level. But the army moved slowly and reluctantly to execute this order. Not until March 14, 1944, was General Ferdinand Schörner named chief of the National Socialist leadership staff for the army (*des Heeres*) (although he remained in command position in the east and never occupied that post) and General Hermann Reinecke named to the same post for the armed forces (OKW). Reinecke did engage in planning work for recruiting these officers.[44] Some reflection of the lack of enthusiasm of the military for this new office is seen in the memoirs of Sigmund Graff, who was named a part of the leadership staff in this early period but found that it meant little—there was a fourteen-day course on *Mein Kampf* but he did not have to take it.[45]

The Air Force took the plan for National Socialist leadership officers more seriously. Its directive of March 20, 1944, required that those chosen had to be uncompromising Nazis, have an especially worthwhile personality, display outstanding service on the front, and have experience and practical abilities in National Socialist leadership and education.[46] Hitler denied that he favored political commissars but pictured his generals as acting in their place. But the events of late summer were to prove his anticipations of uncompromising obedience false and Bormann was to give renewed efforts to creating a corps of party leaders within the military ranks. All members of the general staff were required to assume positions as National Socialist leadership officers after the failure of the assassination effort in July.[47] And some fanatical Nazis were still in training camps for this duty at the end of the war.

The routine work of the party proceeded with little abatement of accustomed fervor and dedication. The parades for the day of the party takeover (January 30) still had the crowds usually taking part in that celebration. In Dortmund, the streets were thronged with party uniforms and bands.[48] In Freiburg im Breisgau, after a theater evening with Beethoven and a band concert the next night, the party held its own starlight parade singing "We march through Baden land," the Kreisleiter having prescribed *practice* beforehand—evidently the singing had previously lacked some of the desired enthusiasm.[49] In February, special arrangements were made for the tenth anniversary of the Nazi organization designated to assist "mother and child." Preparatory work by radio—lectures, children's songs, work reports—was to be accompanied by issuance of four special postage stamps and the showing of films such as "Friend of the Child," "Out of the Diary of a Community Sister," and attendance was encouraged with special rations of 125 grams of sweets and 125 grams of nuts or dried plums.[50] In March came the day of acceptance of members of the Hitler Youth and League of German Girls into full party membership with, as usual, films and singing to celebrate this event, and the celebration of Hitler's birthday in April had its normal accompaniment of "Führer weather," a good day after a period that had been cold and gloomy, with flags and decorations and parades even in the bombed-out cities—red flags waving from empty window frames and paper flags decorating the rubble, although a new picture of the Führer, which showed his physical deterioration, could not be published.[51]

But there were also signs of the party's concern for internal weaknesses. Party directives threatened punishment of those who did not give full support to the war effort.[52] Bormann conveyed to party leaders a report of the Reich Security Office on the effect of corruption, which had been revealed in the quality of cement in the Atlantic Wall, the avoidance of military service, and profiteering from war contracts.[53] Another source of party weakness also occupied Bormann's attention. He directed the dismissal from the party of those mentally ill, but left the definition uncertain. Some persons, he noted, might remain in the party who had the same symptoms as those who were expelled. The party court was to decide who should be expelled and sterilization was to follow dismissal.[54]

Party members were also warned against intervening in the cases before the special courts on behalf of the defendants. These "defilers of the people," spreaders of complaints heard on the foreign radio broadcasts, and defeatists were enemies of the people and should be cast out of the German community.[55] Those who were defense lawyers were allowed to act on behalf of the accused unless the latter were Jews, gypsies, or Poles, none of whom were entitled to a defense. But if they used their positions as defense lawyers to cloud the facts or to work for a mitigation of the sentence by painting rosy pictures (Schönfärberei) of the accused's past, they were misusing their proper role and were subject to disciplinary action.[56] What was proper was mirrored in a report from the propaganda ministry in this period that described the work of the special court of Roland Freisler, who "in a lively and very clear manner" handled his cases "in a refreshing National Socialist fashion far removed from all formally juridical thinking."[57] A few months later, Freisler was to apply his National-Socialist method to the trial of those arrested after the failure of the plot to assassinate Hitler.

The party continued its drives against Jews and the churches. Marriages of Germans and second-grade Mischlinge, although permitted by the Nuremberg racial laws, were closely controlled and carried with them the exclusion of the German partners and their children from positions in the party, state, or army and from some professions.[58] One significant party directive of this period noted that the shields in front of businesses that warned against buying from, allowing admission to, or permitting the placement of newspaper advertisements by Jews, gypsies, and Poles could now be changed. With the evacuation of Jews and gypsies, it was no longer necessary to include them on the warning shields and in respect to Poles "political objectives" would suggest "a certain reserve" in the use of shields and placards.[59] The directive mirrored a general awareness that "the Jewish problem" no longer existed within Germany.

As for the churches, harassment of various sorts continued. Arrangements were established that made it easier for soldiers to leave their churches if they wished to.[60] Evacuees were excluded from using vacant schoolrooms for church services—they could use existing church facilities regardless of denomination.[61] Church activities continued to be watched closely. In one Catholic area, party concern arose because a figure of Mary and Jesus was carried from house to house with appropriate prayers and ceremonies.[62] The pastoral letter of the Bishop of Würzburg in February found its way into the office of the Sicherheitsdienst in full text. In almost Nazi-like slogan phrases, the Bishop called for the return of the young people to Christ, of the family to Christ, and of the moral order to Christ. The people, said the Bishop, were ignoring the ten commandments and replacing them with "moral norms bound to blood and earth." "When once on the day of world judgment all of the unjustly shed blood cries to the heavens, even the righteous will tremble." And he also warned against the moral decline of the day— "the recognition and sponsorship of unmarried motherhood tears down the protective barriers of modesty. And as a consequence much evil and misery goes through the land."[63]

The activities of the Catholic church really troubled the SS observers. They worried about the number of choirs that even small town churches had, particularly because they appeared to be picking up youth support.[64] They worried about religious letters in verse sent to widows or close relatives of those who died on the battle fronts.[65] And they worried about the religious burials, which won out over those sponsored by the Nazis (somehow those who had lost relatives in the air raids were not comforted by the singing of the national anthem and the Horst Wessel song!).[66]

This was a period in which the populace at home, particularly the working-class people, faced increasing pressures. Sauckel worked for an increasing "tempo" of the workers from the beginning of the year on. If, he said, each worker performed with "fanatical will and hot love," where 1,000 rifles had been produced, 1,100 could be made, 1,000 airplanes could be increased to 1,100, and so forth.[67] But tempo alone was not enough. In March, German workers came under the so-called "*Jäger* program" for the increased production of fighter planes, which established a seventy-two-hour week for men and a sixty-hour week for women and youths. Those enrolled in this program were given special attention and special food allotments— for each person legume soup plus 30 grams of meat, 15 grams of fat, and 150 grams of bread per week. These extra rations were to be provided in the work kitchens of the factories or in special places provided for the meals. But foreign workers and prisoners of war were also required to carry the same hours of work as the Germans and received neither the extra bread nor extra meat ration given to the Germans.[68]

Little wonder that the full involvement of women in war work was never achieved. One solution suggested was to distribute some of the work of the factories into the homes of the workers. The reliability of a German worker at home, said one directive, was at least as high as that of a foreign worker in the factory. Obviously, there were some areas of production in which such work at home might be carried out successfully—a hat factory and a shoe factory in one region found it quite helpful.[69] The wife of a retired judge, Willibalt Apelt, helped to knit soldiers' trousers and mend socks with the Nazi "hyenas" of the women's organization.[70] But much of the armament production offered little opportunity for women to work at home.

On the other hand, the drive for armament production left the production of civilian goods virtually suspended. In the midst of the new air raids, with consequent demands for replacement clothing, housewares, and other needs, the special distributions to war-damaged persons no longer covered the most urgent needs. In Essen, after the great attacks of March 26 and April 27, the ration offices were able to supply 990 men's suits, 133 men's coats, 450 work suits, 375 women's coats, 972 women's dresses, and 417 night gowns—a valiant effort but far below what was required. At the same time, claim cards were issued for 97,000 pairs of street shoes, but the raids had destroyed eighty of the shoemakers' places of business, twenty of which were rebuilt by the owners by July and thirty-six of the other sixty were newly built in a later period.[71] There were also indications that replacements never had the quality of the articles that were lost. A beautiful camel's hair blanket lost in an air raid was replaced with a crude, gray, army-type blanket, and a new nightgown sometimes went to pieces in a single washing.[72] Better items were only available by swapping things on the black market. Even air-raid-damaged persons often found it possible to use their special ration cards only when they provided some material advantage to the provider.[73] As a result, farmers and meat handlers were observed to be well provided with good, new clothing, sometimes even with elegant attire. Tobacco was already to a high degree a new kind of money.[74] Party statements seeking to emphasize the idea that any kind of black-market activity, large or small, damaged the war economy had little effect.[75] Everyone sought to get some small advantage out of the few material possessions remaining after all the air raids.

A serious shortage throughout the Reich was that of streetcar wagons. Some 10,000 of these had been lost in the air raids by the end of January 1944. Although 200 of these were gathered up in the areas occupied by Germany and 80 more were to be brought up from Italy, these did not cover the needs. A special streetcar wagon building program was underway, designed to provide 1,200 new ones by the end of 1944.[76]

But of all the shortages of this period the one that most seriously depressed popular morale was the shortage of potatoes. The cold fall and long winter had drastically reduced the supply of potatoes available. From March 6 on, the ration of seven pounds per person per week was cut to four and deliveries in some areas were late and uncertain.[77] The delicious odor of potatoes frying in a little left-over fat and the satisfying effect of a filling meal with potatoes helping to eke out a stew designed to make the most of short meat rations began to be rare treats. Cuts in potato rations were compensated by a little more bread per week—150 grams, about a third of a loaf—or perhaps some rice or rye grits. This occasioned widespread griping.[78] Additionally, potato shortages were accompanied by vegetable shortages, due in part to the increased problem of transportation for the importation of vegetables from outside Germany.[79] The price of vegetables rose also. One-half kilo of cress, reported one observer, cost one Reichsmark so that a worker had to labor for one hundred minutes to buy a handful of "grass."[80]

Internally, the party sought to encourage the expansion of the "war gardens" (the German equivalent of American "victory gardens"). The work of Gauleiter Robert Wagner in Baden and Alsace was held up as an example of what could be done. In 1943, a party notice proclaimed that the number of war gardens in Baden had risen from 13,286 to 23,937 and in Alsace from 6,216 to 11,448 with eight million kilograms of vegetables produced. In 1944, admonished the directive, every available piece of land was to be used, especially in cities over 5,000.[81] There was, indeed, an effort to carry out this idea. In the city gardens of Dortmund, cauliflower plants replaced the narcissi, not as pretty but more nourishing.[82] And domestic gardeners were told that they could raise tomatoes and potatoes and use the same stake to support both plants.[83] But potatoes remained desperately short. By May, the government was directing a search of the cellars of abandoned homes for any potato stocks remaining there and placing self-suppliers under rigid controls in the use of potatoes, along with all others.[84] The women were told to cook the potatoes with the skins on to get the fullest possible food value from them.[85]

Although there was some beginning of milk shortages, the government decided in February and March of 1944 not to close off the production of ice cream. As it was a product that required a relatively small amount of labor and was not harmful to health, efforts to curtail its production were ended.[86] But by the end of April, the government was encouraging the conservation of every drop of milk available. Calves were to be fed on milk from which some of the butter fat had been removed. Cows were to be milked three times a day and every drop was to be squeezed out since what came last was richest in butter.[87] Another note of increased concern involved fertilizer. Small-animal manure was now to be collected to be used as fertilizer.[88] Special instructions were also issued for the shearing of sheep to obtain maximum results.[89]

In this time of increasing food problems, party propaganda turned again to the emphasis on the great role of the farmer in German life. Germany was, Dr. Ludolf Haase wrote, to become "a farmer's Reich." The country's turn away from its rural orientation had weakened it. Now that it had broken its narrow limits, the state could return to its rural origins. "An internal revolutionary transformation" could now be completed and the possibility of feeding more people realized.[90] This ideological mumbo jumbo was accompanied by an effort to find and preserve rural culture—old homesteads with their furniture and equipment.[91]

The food shortages noted above brought desperate conditions to many of the foreign workers in Germany, especially to the East workers. One of these East workers, who wrote back to Stuttgart after the war, told of how he and his fellows had nothing to eat in this period but spoiled potatoes and a kind of broth of turnips and were saved from starvation only by the kindness of the farmers who took pity on them when they left their camps and gave them bread, potatoes, and apples to eat and to carry back to their comrades in camp.[92] An official report from a labor official in Freiburg confirms this situation—"The food they receive in camp consists of a soup. It is mostly thin and insufficient." And on two different occasions, this labor official underscored the fact that the level of production of these workers depended on better food. "A betterment of their food is absolutely necessary or else the achievement of the East workers is imperilled."[93] In Augsburg, too, German housewives were reported to have given Russian women standing around in the market place not just a loaf of bread but also a ration card. When their actions were questioned, their response was, "The poor devils also need something to eat," and police interference was unpopular.[94] Little wonder that in some areas less sympathetic observers reported that East workers were threatening women for bread or food stamps.[95]

Germans still sought the relief from tension supplied by the movies, the theater, sport, and above all, music. In spite of all the British bombing, Shakespeare remained popular in Germany. Prof. Wolff-Mönckeberg lectured on his works to capacity crowds in the university auditorium in Hamburg.[96] The cultural organization of the party, Kraft durch Freude, continued its activities, but its stage presentations were apparently not Shakespearian. Complaints came in that bad jokes were being told in the presence of young people. In one scene, a group of women in a railroad car were discussing what they wanted from a man seeking companionship. A nice trip, a pretty home, a few nice evening gowns were mentioned. As the demands became more modest, a man's voice rose from the audience: "When you get to a bar of chocolate, I'm interested." In another scene, a housemaid getting ready to be married was asked, "Do you mean that you will have it better?"—"Not better," she answered, "but more often."[97]

Music provided the most satisfying relief from the tensions of these troubled times. In Berlin, both the German opera house and the buildings of the Berlin Philharmonic Orchestra had suffered serious damage from the air raids, but the orchestra under the direction of Wilhelm Furtwängler continued its concerts, playing some in the Prussian State Opera House, others in the city cathedral.[98] In Dortmund, the local philharmonic played Brahms and a local composer, Hubert Eckartz, and a string quartet performed works of Beethoven.[99] And in Hamburg, Mathilde Wolff-Mönckeberg and her husband "trudged through rain and storm, and even when it snowed like fury," to the music hall to hear the concerts, especially

Beethoven's sonatas. Never before, she said, had she listened to so much beautiful music.[100]

But even music could have difficulties with ideology. Richard Strauss, the composer, earned party obloquy by his refusal to accept evacuees in his nineteen-room villa in Garmisch, although performance of his works was not prohibited.[101] And harsh judgments were directed at an inoffensive object—the saxophone. The Sicherheitsdienst took serious umbrage at the remarks made about this instrument on one of the radio programs. The saxophone, complained the SS critic, was not a German instrument—it did not have the heroic tone needed for German military music. It really should not be a part of Luftwaffe bands. The infantry rejected it, as was proper. It had some utility for dance music, but even there it carried a false note suitable only for "the perverse feelings of Frenchmen and Jews." "Only a small part of the youth," concluded the observer, "who by instinct or racially is un-German, finds pleasure in the sultry, trashy tone and continued wailing of this instrument."[102]

There were, of course, even bitterer complaints by party faithfuls in respect to the music enjoyed by increasing numbers of the German youth. The origin of the youth "cliques" or "bands" has been detailed in a previous chapter. Throughout 1943, these groups of semioppositionist youth organizations had spread across many parts of Germany and by the early part of 1944 and through the summer months of that year had obtained their largest followings and presented a serious challenge to the local authorities. Never a real challenge to the Nazi regime, they were, however, a disturbing sign that the party's grasp on the youth had greatly declined from the early days when hundreds of thousands of ecstatic boys and girls had marched joyfully to the beat of the drums and raised enthusiastic faces to the figure of the Führer.

The major attraction for these youth groups continued to be the lure of swing music and "hot" dancing. Although the British and American bombs were progressively obliterating German cities, Anglo-American music, clothing styles, and dance motifs attracted a following among those young people "turned off" by the semimilitary tone of the Hitler Youth and the League of German Girls. Sometimes the groups picked up "the wild songs of the Russian steppes," but these never obtained the same popularity as those of English or American origin. Phonograph records for the latter were obviously more easily obtainable.[103]

New names for the cliques and their members appeared: "Black

Hand," "Allah Band," "The Golden 13," "Hot Club," and "the Avengers" and nicknames such as "Jonny," "Texas Jack," "Alaska Bill," "Wisky Bill," "Kamera," "Hatte," "Fatz," and "Jtz."[104] Added to the attractions of the music were the lures of relaxed sexual standards, with girls of the middle or even early teens joining the teenage youths in promiscuous sex. Often the young boys horrified staid observers by rendering pornographic verses in public.[105] Although sexual activity usually involved girls of their own age or younger, the members of a swing club in Kiel took up with a twenty-one-year-old woman with syphilis and all of them had to take the cure.[106]

Accompanying the music and life-style aberrations of the youth cliques was a distinct hostility to the regime—levied most strongly against the Hitler Youth at the outset but by this time also against Hitler himself. This is reflected in the songs of the groups, often composed by local song writers who used well-known tunes and provided new words. A few were reproduced by the police from the handwritten song books that clique members carried with them.

> In Hunker's cafe, with wine and pipe,
> We sat with one another.
> A good measure of malt and hops,
> The devil leads us on.
> Ho, where the youths sing
> And the guitars sound,
> And the girls join in,
> What can the life of Hitler give us?
> We would rather be rebels (bündisch).
> Ho, where the bowie knives gleam
> And the Hitler Youths scurry away,
> And the Navajos attack.[107]

Sometimes the songs contained a challenge, such as, "We would like to be free of Hitler," or "the Navajos fight for the freedom of the youth."[108] The words of a song from Cologne were romantically heroic.

> In Cologne many have fallen,
> In Cologne many took part,
> And the Edelweiss Pirates still fall,
> [But] the rebel youth will be free.[109]

A fragment of a song from Munich was even stronger in its oppositionist tone.

When the free word is forbidden everywhere,
And when stupidity reaps glorious harvests,
When impudently stupid helots in public office
Proclaim meaningless slogans for the people,
When justice is bent awry,
And a braggart friend brandishes his great orations,
One cannot demand from the people,
Whom one has just bamboozled, that it sing happily.
Nevertheless: we sing still!
[last phrase in English in original][110]

The clique groups were everywhere the bitter enemies of the Hitler Youth. They lurked on the streets to attack them and harassed them in their meetings. On at least one occasion, they made plans to blow up their barracks. But along with their actions against the Hitler Youth, the cliques also engaged in various forms of criminal actions, some mild, some more serious. The search for and obtaining of weapons was common. Usually this involved pistols or knives (commonly referred to as Bowie knives by the Navajo pirates), but in two cases machine guns were obtained, one from a downed American bomber. Plundering, putting nails on the railroad tracks to see the sparks fly, heating up a locomotive with the idea of taking a ride, stealing motorbikes or cars (in one case a doctor's car, in another case a Gauleiter's), making telephone calls to important people, robbing the bodies of fallen enemy pilots, and using false passes were some of the offenses noted.[111]

Police actions against the cliques proceeded in part because of their opposition character—they could be acted against as efforts to form new political parties as well as for subversive action—and in part because of outright criminality. By this time the police were taking them much more seriously and handing out good-sized jail terms as well as periods in reeducation camps or sometimes even imposing death sentences. Early in January, a law established Reich youth courts and Thierack, with his usual quest for severity, recommended terms of imprisonment without a specific time limit, with release to be determined by whether rehabilitation seemed possible.[112] The fall of the year was to bring even harsher actions.

Although the youth cliques were worrisome, they were not numerous enough to justify a judgment that at this time the youth as a whole had rejected the Nazi ideology or philosophy. They may, however, be regarded as one visible sign of the growing uncertainty of many people in respect to the validity of Goebbels's propaganda.

The "braggart friend" referred to in the youth songs assured his readers late in April that "we are still the elite people of the earth whether others will admit this or not." "We are," he continued, "a sworn community which must on our own fight our way through the darkness and the thicket and knows well that at the end golden freedom beckons." No one, Goebbels proclaimed, could have accomplished what Germany had achieved. No other nation could match the glory and honor of Germany. Any other nation would have broken on the great obstacles that had confronted it. And he stressed again his standard line of approach, that a Bolshevik victory meant the destruction of Europe as well as of Germany— that the British and the Americans were deceiving themselves in believing that the Russians could be restrained.[113]

But the reports of the Sicherheitsdienst carried many signs that the adults as well as the young people were no longer so secure in the assumption of German superiority. On the eve of the impending Allied invasion in the West, the Germans had little hope except in the often promised but not yet materialized "vengeance weapons." And the military leaders, many of them dubious of real victory ever since Stalingrad, finally began to consider seriously the possibility of overturning a regime headed towards disaster.

7. The Bombs Still Fall

During the spring months of 1944, the Germans at home became increasingly aware that an invasion of Europe by the Western Allies was imminent. German civilians talked of potential naval attacks on northern Germany or airborne assaults on Germany proper as well as the more probable assault on the coast of France or Belgium. Strangely enough, there was a note of hopeful expectation in the discussions of the coming invasion. Morale reports reflected the optimistic belief that the invasion would signal a decisive turn in the course of the war in favor of Germany.

Whether all of this optimism was genuine or whether it was a reflection of the stronger guidelines against pessimism and defeatism is debatable. But the German propaganda emphasizing the strength of the Atlantic defenses, and the snail-like pace of the British and American forces up the Italian peninsula provided grounds for a feeling that when the Western Allies met the German armies in France, they would suffer severe reverses. Moreover, German observers did not believe that the Western Allies would continue to work in a secure partnership with their Communist Allies on the East. Indeed, there was the frequently expressed feeling that if, by chance, the invasion did not come, Germany faced an unavoidable defeat occasioned by the continued poundings of Allied bombardments. There was a very real fear as the invasion got pushed back into the late spring and early summer that it might *not* come at all and the gloomy sequence of air raids would continue unabated.[1]

There was, therefore, some sense of relief when the news reports of the invasion of Normandy by British and American forces ended the suspense. The news tended to obscure the unpleasant report from Italy of the surrender of Rome on June 4, 1944.[2] And there was, indeed, a very temporary reduction of the Allied attacks on German cities. However, any temporary optimism occasioned by the news of the invasion soon faded. Expectations of the defeat of the Allied forces on the beaches, the decimation of the invasion forces by submarines, or the devastation of enemy territory by the new vengeance weapons proved fruitless. A flurry of hope occasioned by the dispatch of the first V-1's against London on June 12 and 13 soon died away as even the casual observer became aware that the numbers, accuracy, and destructive powers of this first "vengeance weapon" (the "buzz bomb," an unmanned bomb-carrying airplane) were less than anticipated and could never bring to British cities the kind of havoc that had been suffered by German cities. Soon the weapon was being called a "*Versager*" ("failure") weapon.[3] Not until September 8 were the first V-2's, genuine rocket weapons, launched against England.

Meanwhile, the Allied forces moved forward in the West. General von Rundstedt was replaced and even ordinary civilians knew that things were not going well there. The situation on the eastern front grew more menacing and there were rumors of division and disaffection within the military leadership.[4] Perhaps most depressing to Germans at home was the fact that the Allied invasion had brought little moderation of the bombing raids. Although few Germans outside the bureaucracy were aware of the crisis conditions they created, the concerted Allied bombing attacks on the oil fields in Rumania and Hungary and the synthetic oil plants in Germany during this period marked the most effective use of air power in the entire war.[5] Two hundred thirty bombers of the U.S. Fifteenth Air Force attacked the Ploesti oil fields in Rumania and oil refineries near Vienna, Bleckhamer, and Odenthal on April 5, 1944. These attacks continued through the remainder of April and into May. On May 12, 1944, one thousand bombers launched attacks against synthetic oil factories in Leuna, Brüx, Böhlen, Zeitz, and Lützendorf. In all, twenty synthetic oil works were attacked, having a total capacity of 374,000 tons of synthetic fuel per month (including 175,000 tons of flight fuel).

Speer and Hans Kehrl, his "crisis manager," obtained a conference with Hitler on May 23 and set forth the dire consequences for the German war effort if effective fighter protection was not provided to repel these attacks. It required, Kehrl was able to tell Göring, 2,000 to 2,400 antiaircraft rounds to bring down an Allied bomber and at this rate, without effective fighter defenses, the synthetic oil production would be lost to Germany. But Göring remained unconvinced and hostile to the intrusion of civilian critics into his sphere of air war strategy. Fighter protection was not provided and on May 28, the synthetic oil works in Leuna and Magdeburg were again attacked and seriously damaged. On May 29, the largest operation at Pölitz/ Stettin was severely damaged and in June, new attacks on the Rumanian fields at Ploesti and on German refineries followed. Allied aircraft also mined the Danube, making the transport of oil from Rumania and Hungary more difficult.

At the end of May 1944, under pressure from Speer and Kehrl, Hitler named Edmund Geilenberg as Reich commissioner for emergency measures for the repair of damages to industry and war production. Geilenberg gathered together 350,000 workers to deal with the damages to the synthetic oil plants and sought to move portions of the works to underground facilities. About seven hundred works of this sort were established, but their production was limited and the underground locations increased the dangers of fires and explosions. Efforts to husband the declining stocks of gasoline and aviation fuel had a very negative effect on the war effort. Fuel for the training of new pilots, especially for those who might fly the increasingly available ME 262 jet fighters, was lacking. Trucks and armored cars had to be converted to methane gas usage. Transportation of supplies and food became increasingly difficult.

The loss of the struggle for the oil refineries was the "Stalingrad" of German war production. But for most German civilians, what weighed most heavily on their spirits was the continuance and intensification of the already familiar area bombing of the cities. This was made still more disturbing by the frequent presence of fighter bombers that could strafe as well as bomb and that turned up at unexpected times in small numbers to disturb normal routines and to add to the nighttime attacks worrisome threats during the daylight hours. Smaller cities began to feel the panic effects of bombing, since they were no longer exempt from the attention of the enemy. But the old familiar targets continued to suffer. Raids on Cologne reaped new harvests of victims. The five months from May through September, Fischer wrote, were filled with crashes, explosions, dirt, hardships, and death. There were the wounded and the dead—those blown to pieces and those burned to cinders. And in this same period, the sounds of cannons were added to the now familiar explosions of the bombs.[6]

Berlin continued to be a prime target. The stories circulating in the city emphasized the vagaries of fate during the raids. A mortuary company started its crew with the funeral wreaths to take part in a burial ceremony. On the way, they were caught in an air raid at the railroad station in Treptow. Taking shelter in the station's bunker, they left the funeral wreaths outside. The bombs wrecked the bunker. The wreaths decorated their own unplanned burial.[7] Each new raid brought more destruction, but familiarity dulled the sense of terror. One pregnant woman, after escaping the destruction of the train on which she was riding by climbing a burning fence, sat four hours later in the theater as if nothing had happened.[8] Under the curve of an elevated railroad train topped by a burning train, workmen welded together the broken pieces of equipment left by an earlier raid.[9] Another story told of an old woman in a bunker who calmed those present by counting the eight blasts of the bombs that dropped nearby and explaining that each bomb cradle carried eight bombs so that with the last of these bursts the most immediate danger had passed by.[10]

Scientists suggested more accurate measures of danger. A German physicist suggested that people should carry a barometer into the bunkers so that they could measure the intensity of the bombs falling nearby.[11] But a German engineer in this period, when six-ton "earthquake" bombs were falling, warned that the concrete protection of bunkers needed to be doubled from their 1.8 meter thickness (5'9") to 3 to 5 meter thickness (10' to 16').[12]

Berlin survived its trauma, as did all the German cities, through the courage and determination of its ordinary citizens. But in all the cities, the damage continued to increase and there were fears that the enemy might extend the attacks into the open areas of the countryside. Kiel, already heavily bombed, suffered under more than 8,000 additional explosive bombs, 1,200 of which were delayed-fuse types or duds—322 unexploded bombs were successfully defused but 70 bombs detonated in the process. Some of the unexploded bombs exploded more than a week after the raid of July 23/24, 1944. By September, a city which had sheltered 300,000 inhabitants could count only 121,000 still living in its ruins. But propaganda signs proclaimed that in spite of bombs and grenades the people were still "acooking and abaking."[13] Hamburg, devastated in the catastrophic raids of July 1943, presented a picture of "muck, paper, and rotting vegetation" on the streets, accompanied by "a foul, murky smell," but anniversary raids of July employed bombs that crashed down through all the floors of the buildings they struck and shattered the roofs of air-raid bunkers.[14]

Raids on Munich broke the calm of the "premier city of the Nazi movement" and sent an endless stream of refugees down the surrounding *Autobahnen*. Many of these were old women trudging along, bearing their heavy bundles on long sticks over their shoulders.[15] A burial fete after the raid for seventeen supposed victims had an unexpected result when one of the air-raid victims "buried" turned up alive in a nearby hospital. People wondered whether all of the coffins might have been empty.[16] The *Münchener Neueste Nachrichten* blamed the bombings on the Americans and declared that the planes were piloted by black officers who were venting their hate against the white race and the centers of Western culture. But it also detailed the effectiveness of relief efforts with trains bringing in food to the stricken city—on one train alone, it declared, 30,000 warm meals and drink and clothing for those in need had arrived.[17] Joachim Günther detailed the destruction of Hannover in the raids of early August. "Ruins stand next to ruins and summer-clad people pilgrim among them as though they no longer took notice of them any more. . . . Over the ruined entry of a building in which there was formerly a movie still hangs the transparent of the last film which was played there. It reads 'The Dark Days.' For the destructions themselves there is no correspondence to a life with feelings for the visitor who is not accustomed to their view. They surpass the breadth of one's spiritual reactions and leave one almost passive." And the cemetery notices, little placards with the words "unknown female corpse," "unknown male corpse," "unknown child's corpse" seemed to reflect a lack of sensitivity unfitting for a cemetery.[18]

Stuttgart almost suffered the same tragic fate in July that Hamburg had experienced a year earlier. In four days, July 25-29, 1,690 bombers dropped their deadly cargo on the city. Some observers considered the attacks a retaliation for the German use of the V-1 weapons since some parts of these were produced in the city. But, as usual, since these were night attacks, it was mostly the center of the city and some adjacent dwelling areas that were affected. At least 5,000 explosive bombs (1,100 of them delayed-fuse explosive bombs), 240 mines, 20,000 stick and 50,000 flame-trailing bombs (many of them gliding into the center of the city from the perimeter) found their mark. But the loss of life—884 dead, 1,916 wounded, and 14 missing—was astonishingly low in view of the ferocity of the attacks. The dwelling area of this city was more broadly spread out than that of Hamburg. Several of the attacks found the bombers dispersed so that only a portion of the bombs reached the target. German night fighters harried the attackers. And, most significantly, many of the bombs dropped were of 1918 origin and failed to explode. Numbers of the liquid fire bombs were also duds and provided some lucky inhabitants with unexpected supplies of gasoline for long-unused automobiles. And the provision of air-raid shelters, dugout protections, and a very extensive underground connection of cellars saved many lives.[19]

Not that the results were not grim enough. On the night of July 26, a firestorm drove the city's leaders out of the town hall and through the streets, threatened by a rain of sparks and collapsing walls. Later raids garnered an ever increasing toll of churches and public buildings. As the raids came to an end, the mayor, Dr. Karl Strölin, summed up the end results in graphic words:

> In their half-destroyed houses, in cellars without heat and light, in the corners of the walls, often in the sinister and horrifying neighborhood of those who had been buried [in the raids] lived the people, [suffering] by [the later] grim, cold weather, in a constant struggle against the wind, against walls, partitions, and ceilings which threatened to cave in, against the penetrating rains, and not least against the ever increasing plague of rats. . . . In the midst of all this misery, all this rubble, the inhabitants lived and carried out their duties without interruption. Only some time later will one be able to judge what superhuman accomplishments were achieved in these months and years by men and women, old and young, harassed by constant alarms, bombings, and fires, poorly clad and badly fed, in the fulfillment of their professional and domestic work and in an unbroken struggle for life itself. In this last stage of the war life in these great cities affected by the bombing attacks was perhaps often more dangerous and harder than on the front.[20]

Incidents of strafing of civilians in the fields increased the feeling of anger against the pilots whose planes were lost because of German antiaircraft or fighter action.[21] In Stuttgart, some of those captured had to be protected by the police against possible lynch action.[22] In Rostock, in the midst of a violent argument between one of the Sicherheitsdienst agents of the area and the Kreisleiter over the adequacy of air-raid bunkers in the city, the Kreisleiter demonstrated his toughness to the SD agent, who brought an American pilot to his custody, by shooting him "as he sought to escape."[23] An American pilot shot down in the country area near the little town of

Rohrbach was much luckier. The mayor gave him a VIP reception with a meal of roast pork, mashed potatoes, cranberries, and dumplings topped with caramelized sugar, all served on a table covered by a spotless white table cloth.[24]

By the end of July, Bormann advised the reduction of the special rations provided after the raids and suggested efforts to limit aid to those who were directly affected by the bombings.[25] Repair of damage and help in the form of projects for additional housing became the obligation of local officials since no centralized projects for this purpose could be carried out. Materials for the relief of bomb-damaged persons were to be collected and distributed on a local basis.[26] The major contribution of Berlin to dealing with the new wave of raids was the provision of medals—a group of "purple heart" medals for those wounded in the raids: black ones for those wounded once or twice; silver for those wounded three or four times or severely in a single raid; and gold for those wounded more than four times. There was also a second group of medals for those fighting air-raid fires—bronze for twenty fighting days, silver for fifty, and gold for one hundred.[27]

The fears increased during this period that the bombing raids might involve the dropping of poison gas bombs. Efforts were made to supply the population with gas masks. These were sold to most persons for five marks per mask, with a price reduction for heads of large families and those with lower incomes.[28] The widespread discussion by German government agencies of the possibility of the use of gas warfare on the part of Germany's enemies suggests that there was more than a passing consideration of its usage by the Germans themselves. Supposedly, 200,000 phosgene bombs had been captured in France in 1940 along with 50,000 hand grenades for mustard gas, 9,800 phosgene bottles, and 11,000 adamsite candles. Gas warfare exercises on June 15, 1944, in a camp on the Lüneburger Heide were described in a war diary of the navy headquarters.[29] Had the V-weapons worked better, they might well have carried gas against the British. If so, the gas masks would have found use against the Allied retaliation and air warfare would have assumed even more fearful dimensions. Perhaps this less than cheerful note in respect to the future may have derived originally from Hitler's opponents. A pamphlet from "the preparatory revolutionary committee North," which was first circulated in Berlin but turned up in Schwerin, spoke of millions of Germans dying as "Hitler prepares for gas warfare." The pamphlet called upon the Germans to take up "terror against [the Hitler] terror" and to seize the munitions depots.[30] But one party leader in a small village in Bavaria sought to give a kinder view of Hitler's potential use of gas—the Führer had prepared "a gentle and easy death by gas" for the German people if the war went badly.[31]

But in spite of all the bombings and their attendant fears, the German population continued to eat, drink, and find some entertainment to relieve the stress of warfare. Some parts of Germany still seemed to preserve their idyllic prewar character. In Rohrbach in the Black Forest, Christabel Bielenberg lived calmly and well, food rations almost forgotten.[32] Klaus Granzow, who hailed from Pomerania in the northeastern part of Germany, found his Hitler Youth friends from the Rhineland jealous of his peaceful countryside. Even in a time of potato shortage, the Pomeranians could have potato roasts on their farms.[33] And a professional diplomat with good connections could enjoy trips to friends in the countryside by which he escaped "the horror-world in which we have our being."[34]

There was a certain irony in the fact that, during this period, much of eastern Germany, soon to be the scene of the most severe suffering of the war, was still unblemished. The foreign office of the German Professorial Organization continued its cultural activities throughout this period. The most noteworthy activity was a weekend visit of members of the agency with foreign scholars to the unblemished city of Dresden. In almost poetic fashion, the leader of this expedition, which took place in early July of 1944, reported how they arrived before the city to receive "a characteristic overall impression of the city, which most wonderfully rose out of its green surroundings in the morning sun, with its gray sandstone buildings standing out against the summer skies." The Berliners marveled at this view of a city untouched by the air raids. The visitors listened to the music of Mozart and Haydn, which created images of shining silk dresses, white powdered wigs, and gracious minuettes, and then visited the wealth of old and famous buildings, the Renaissance-style opera house, the originally Gothic castle church, the "Zwinger," once conceived as an entry hall for the castle but made into a pleasure garden, and the Frauenkirche with its gigantic stone spire. Fräulein Roth's description provided a graphic view of a city soon to become one of the most tragic victims of the enemy's bombs.[35]

But July 1944 also brought the first signs of real panic in respect to the eastern front. The Soviet offensives of the summer of 1944 were launched on June 22 with German estimates that 126 infantry divisions, 6 cavalry divisions, 45 tank brigades, 16 motorized brigades, and 4,000 aircraft were being thrown against defensive forces of 40 German divisions.[36] Within a week, Soviet forces were achieving deep incursions into German-held territory east of the former Polish borders. Names that had been learned by the Germans at home as their troops made their triumphant drive into the Soviet Union were now repeated as they were yielded back to the Russians—Witebsk, Orsche, Mogilev, Bobrushka, Minsk. By July 7, strong Soviet forces aimed their efforts toward Vilna and Brest Litovsk and by July 13, they had breached German lines near Vilna.

Now came real concern on the part of those who understood the meaning of this incursion into German preserves. "The unexpectedly rapid forward drive of the Soviets is frightening and occupies the minds [of the people] more than anything else," read one Sicherheitsdienst report. Women said they could not bear to read the battle reports—"I simply have to wait until better news comes again," said one.[37] The most serious consequences were felt in East Prussia and not revealed to the German public. A frenzied series of correspondence between the Reich propaganda ministry and its representative in Königsberg (now Kaliningrad) mirrored a near-panic situation.[38] One cause of unrest was the presence of large numbers of evacuees from Berlin, who were desperate to elude the dangers of a Russian occupation. Soldiers and officers in the region were also sending their families out of the endangered area. By July 10, plans had been made to return some five thousand families to the Reich. Fifteen trains daily were to carry an expected fifty-five thousand people into German territory, but not to Berlin itself.

German "efficiency" soon reestablished quiet. Front-line troops arrived and brought renewed confidence in the area's defenses. Deserters were rounded up and shot. And Gauleiter Erich Koch, now the Reich commissioner for the defense of this area (as were all the Gauleiters in border areas) began to put every able-bodied "man" from fifteen to sixty-three to work building the antitank ditches and town defenses, which were designed to arrest the oncoming storm of Russian troops. The return of evacuees and other refugees to German territory was portrayed not as an evacuation from East Prussia but rather as a move designed to free quarters for reinforcing troops, space for more lazarets for wounded soldiers, billets for workers on the fortifications, and shelter for refugees from areas further east.

But no general on the eastern front could regard the situation with optimism by this time. The forty weak divisions that had faced the drive westward of the Russian forces on a front stretching from the Baltic states southward through the Ukraine had suffered grievous losses in the uneven battles of June and July 1944. It was obvious to every commander that the front lines needed to be shortened and that the Army Group North, still relatively undamaged in its position along the Baltic Sea, ought to be moved southward to aid in the defense of East Prussia and Germany's eastern frontiers. But for Hitler, who had in a more favorable period been called the "greatest field marshal of all time," strategy had reduced itself to one word, "*behaupten*"—give up no territory and maintain the defense of all areas still in German hands. He even opposed the fortification of rear-line areas since this might encourage front-line troops to look backward to retreat rather than forward to reconquest. Successive field marshals, Günther von Kluge, Ernst Busch, and Walter Model, had vainly sought Hitler's approval for the consolidation and strengthening of the defense of Germany's eastern frontiers.

The mood on the western front was also pessimistic. On July 15, 1944, Rommel dispatched a telegram to Hitler, saying that "the situation grows more difficult from day to day" and ending with the words, "The troops are fighting heroically everywhere, but still the unequal struggle tends to come to an end. I must request you to draw the unavoidable consequences of this situation. As Supreme Commander of the Armies, I feel obligated to state this clearly."[39] It was just five days after this note that the well-known effort to assassinate Hitler took place.

The story of this assassination attempt of July 20, 1944, and of its consequences has been told and retold by others. Its significance remains debatable. Was Colonel Claus Schenk von Stauffenberg, who placed in his East Prussian headquarters the bomb that almost killed Hitler, a hero or a villain? A distinguished officer with an impeccable war record, he had been considered worthy of a general staff position. Yet he was a volunteer for the role of assassin, and the bomb he placed killed fellow officers while the primary target was left only moderately injured. His fellow conspirators were generals and field marshals, most of them more motivated by the hope of saving Germany from ultimate catastrophe than by a real conviction of the evil of the Nazi regime. The lack of decisiveness on the part of these officers, who had commanded thousands of men on the battlefield, made possible the liquidation of all their plans by a simple major, Otto Ernst Remer, to whom Hitler gave supreme authority over the military in Berlin.

In the aftermath of the failed plot, one of Germany's most famous generals, Heinz Guderian, assumed the position of chief of staff of the German armies, ignored the progressive arrests of large numbers of his honored colleagues, and required all members of the general staff who remained to assume the role of National Socialist leadership officers, tying together the party and the army. Throughout the remainder of the war, Guderian acted as the loyal executor of Hitler's orders even when he had sought vainly to secure their modification or change. The failure of the assassination plot initiated the darkest period of the war. Its success might not have accomplished all the conspirators had hoped for, but it did portend the possibility of a lessening of the useless sacrifice of men on the battle fronts, of some mitigation of the last desperate strokes against Jewish remnants, and, perhaps, of obtaining a negotiated peace.

The party's efforts to extend the Nazification of the military during the remainder of the war had little real success. Negative reactions followed the replacement of the military salute with the Hitler greeting. As one soldier phrased it, "That still doesn't strike me [as proper]. We are still soldiers and not S.A. men." And another complained that "the party makes a firm effort to save our souls. I regard it as unnecessary to convert us. We are Germans but we will probably never be Nazis."[40] A memorandum of the propaganda ministry in June had complained that most of the officers acting as National Socialist leadership officers were incompetent. Many, it noted, had not even read Hitler's *Mein Kampf*, let alone worked through it in a disciplined fashion, and were not prepared to deal effectively with tired soldiers. They would have to be replaced, the memo counseled, by politically reliable but warlike soldiers who would choose helpers from every company of the troops to carry the message of National Socialism by personal contact rather than by lifeless, formal meetings.[41] Schools for NS-leadership officers were established—some candidates, such as Wilhelm Prüller, were still in these at the close of the war, defying all about them as they still believed victory could be won with Nazi determination.[42]

Shortly after the assassination attempt, Hitler issued a new decree, often labeled his second proclamation of total war. Joseph Goebbels, the propaganda minister, who had always believed he was the only person capable of directing total war measures, was finally entrusted with that task.[43] But the lines of authority within the party and state still remained confused. Too many cooks still sought to provide the proper recipe for victory. Bormann remained in the strategic position as head of the Reich Chancellery and as secretary to the Führer. Göring continued to be Hitler's official second-in-command. Speer controlled the armaments industry and the production of war materials. Himmler directed Germany's replacement army as well as the police apparatus. And beneath all this centralized bureaucracy, the Gauleiters tended to become more and more regional political bosses, not always subservient to central authority and often making defense decisions without consulting the army commanders in their Gaus. As Reich defense commissioners, they could call upon police, transportation personnel, and armament directors for aid in setting up last ditch defenses.[44] The propaganda ministry still believed that the old fighters of the party could kindle the confidence of the people.[45] But in spite of uncertain lines of authority, it was clear to all party members by August 1944 that Germany was entering into a period which would test its power of endurance and in spite of rivalries there was, indeed, a valiant effort to survive.

The most notable consequence of Goebbels's new role was the closing of theaters, movies, and other centers of entertainment. Through the spring and summer, there had been complaints by party agents in respect to the quality of entertainment. A Security Service agent in Linz had found offensive a film shown in Neustrelitz called "First Love," which showed too many women undressing and included "wild jazz music" and "exotic dancing."[46] Another agent in Posen worried about the performances in Germany of a Belgian orchestra that claimed to play "international music" but was really playing American-style jazz.[47] Kraft durch Freude had run into internal bickerings, and there had long been the feeling that too many of these cultural-minded individuals were not making their proper contribution to the war effort. The head of the party's music office made snide comments about the ideological content of some of the KdF performances and many ordinary customers regarded these wartime productions as mediocre.[48]

But there was a sense of growing darkness as the theaters closed. The Bayreuth Festival barely escaped the deadline, taking place late in July. Goebbels's associates took this opportunity to obtain their last dose of good German culture.[49] The propaganda office still supplied funds for lecture and concert evenings in Vienna and, with some reluctance, agreed to the "high" fee of five hundred marks for a lecture by Heinrich von Srbik, Austria's most famous historian, who had anticipated the *Anschluss*, the Austrian-German reunion, with his writings on German unity.[50] And trains from France were still carrying into Germany a vast collection of paintings and art objects confiscated from foreign art galleries.[51] But these did not gladden the eyes of Germany's hard-pressed workers. And at the same time in Stuttgart, as elsewhere in Germany, the opera gave its last performance on July 24 and the state theater of Württemberg closed its doors two weeks later on August 8.[52] Far to the east, in Breslau, the lights of the opera house were also darkened. Opera singers, musicians, concert directors, the whole range of people who had been devoted to providing at least a brief diversion from the grim realities of war, now came face to face with the hardships of Germany's final struggle. The baton, the violin, and the playscript were exchanged for the shovel for fortifications or the rifle for military service.[53]

The last-ditch efforts at providing tank barriers, trenches, and defensive lines around the frontier cities never attracted real enthusiasm. It was too apparent even to untrained observers that these were woefully ineffective against well-trained and well-equipped enemy forces. In the final battles, only the defense of Breslau stands out as an example of some significance on the part of these amateur fortifications. In most cases, their value was mirrored in the commonly told story that they would hold up the enemy for an hour and five minutes—an hour to allow the fit of laughing by those who saw them for the first time to subside; five minutes to remove them from the scene.

Meanwhile, these fortification efforts tended to siphon away the last remnants of effective labor at a time when Germany's work force was already stretched to the breaking point. The only new conquest of Goebbels's draconian *Jäger* program was in the party offices, which were now placed on a sixty-hour week.[54] Although a party memorandum declared that party members had the same obligation to render war service as did anyone else, army proposals to place party leaders in the infantry as a means of restoring its "fighting strength" soon gained official opposition for fear that "with one blow the entire leadership corps might be sacrificed in a blood bath on the front." Furthermore, said party commentaries, if party leaders were used on the eastern front, they would be in danger of being captured, tortured, and held up as symbols of their hatred by the Bolsheviks.[55] By August, arrangements had been made for party leaders going into the army to achieve officer status quickly. Arrangements were also made for wounded war veterans, after a training session, to move into party leadership offices.[56]

On the other hand, numerous cautions were issued against excessive display at party meetings and "happy, alcohol-influenced sessions" after they were over.[57] Party members were to conduct public acts only if they were directly related to the war; officials were to live frugally; there were to be no long lines of automobiles at public meetings when fuel was short; and leather-bound reports of party accomplishments were no longer to be regarded as good form. Moreover, party activities were no longer free— obviously the party treasury was no longer as flourishing as it had once been.[58]

Although strong efforts were made to enroll more women into "honorable service" for the war effort, the consequences were negligible. Most of those enrolled in this way could provide only part-time labor and their use in the factories was difficult. Factory managers, said one report, had always taken "a very unenthusiastic attitude" in respect to the use of half-time employees.[59]

A new drive was also launched to provide "home work" for portions of the armament production. A Speer memorandum in early August of 1944 suggested a variety of jobs that might be done outside the factories—in the metal industries the cutting of small tubes, some screwing together of parts, polishing work, and so forth; in the electrical industries the winding of wire, completion of small parts, and the mounting of simple, small pieces; in the chemical industries such operations as cleaning and packing; in the clothing and textile industries the sewing of buttons, the making of arm bands, covers for steel helmets, and protective gloves, and the cutting and pressing of pieces for certain kinds of clothing. Similarly, some simpler operations for the woodworking and paper-products industries could be accomplished at home.[60] The most significant outcome of the drive was increased bureaucratic paper work. Negative reports flooded in. The Kreis office in Geldern reported on August 7, 1944, that few industries had any such work to offer. Textile and shoe concerns expressed a willingness to use home labor but warned that even their possibilities for farmed-out labor would require some special skills. One labor leader found absolutely no possibilities for home work in his area—the "merchant standpoint," he explained, "was too much in the foreground." Factory managers, he said, considered home work "unprofitable."[61]

Although there was less criticism of male workers in the reports of this period, observers noted that the seventy-two-hour week was taking an increasing physical toll of all workers.[62] There was a wider use of pep pills, mostly pervitin, although the party's health officer warned of serious consequences if it were used excessively.[63] Factory managers were empowered to exercise more severe disciplinary measures against absenteeism, but there were also reports that shortages of raw materials made the lengthened hours of labor useless so that workers were sitting at their work places with nothing to do.[64]

The party also made belated efforts to win greater cooperation on the part of foreign workers. East workers were now allowed to wear an identifying patch on their left shoulder—for Ukrainians an oval sunflower blossom.[65] Reliable foreigners working far from their homes were even allowed to use bicycles to get to work (if they could find them in this late stage of the war!).[66] Poles were propagandized as to the dangers of their homeland becoming Bolshevized.[67] Along with other foreign workers, they were made eligible for a bronze service medal adorned with a German eagle if they had performed efficiently for two years.[68] Obviously, an increase in the level of productivity of foreign workers and prisoners of war would have had a significant effect on the overall level of production. As one directive noted, if one million Soviet prisoners of war could be raised from their existing 80 percent of the standards of German workers to 100 percent, it would be the same as adding the labor of 250,000 new workers, and if 800,000 French prisoners of war could be raised from their 70 percent level to 100 percent, it would be the same as adding the labor of 240,000 new workers.[69]

But hopes of such increases were not accompanied by any real betterment of the condition of foreign workers. The obvious conclusion of the last directive was that greater pressure had to be exerted on prisoners of war by their control officers. The dark meaning of the directive was intensified by the statement that the work of these control officers should not be hampered by bureaucratic regulations.[70] And another directive of the same day indicated that all prisoners of war labeled as unfit for work should be promptly reexamined to determine the level of their recovery.[71]

At the same time, German fears of these hordes of foreign guests on German soil tended to increase. Guards of Soviet prisoners of war now carried arms loaded and ready for action.[72] Specific orders were issued that prisoners of war were not to walk on the sidewalks when Germans were there.[73] The foreigners were glad to encourage these fears. French prisoners of war joked that they were the advance parachutists of invasion forces.[74] Polish workers made it clear that they expected Germany to lose the war and taunted Germans with the story of "lists" of Germans who were to be liquidated after victory.[75] News of Polish robber bands operating on the Tucheler Heide in the northern part of occupied Poland was followed by reports that these activities had spread across a much larger part of the area.[76] The security service reported that many Poles now knew and sang "Tanjushka," the song of Tatjana, the partisan.

In the dark light of the morning hours the village lay quiet,
The icy wind blew coldly over its roofs.
On the street the Germans seized the maiden Tatjana,
And carried her into the house for her hearing.

Her eyes shown fearlessly.
They found a pistol and grenades on her.
They tried to learn more from her,
But Tatjana, the partisan, remained silent.

The evil wind bent down the branches
The hangman brought the chest and the rope.
The maiden looked for the last time to the heavens
And saw only the smoke over the roofs.

But all this could not subdue us,
For nothing more was to be understood.
In many eyes one saw the tears,
Only Tatja could see them no more.

In the dark light of the morning hours the village lay quiet,
The icy wind blew coldly over its roofs
And our farmers buried the maiden Tatjana
Near the gate.

They kept the oath not to forget the foe,
They kept the oath also not to forget Tatja,
Promised to swell the ranks of the partisans
To bring retribution to the Germans.

Let only the fame of Tatja spread further
And more maidens rise up as did she!
She has paid with her life
For her beloved country.[77]

A note of desperation highlighted Hitler's speech on July 4 at a party meeting of the economic leaders of the Third Reich called by Albert Speer. Hitler boasted of his own maintenance of "nerve" in the face of existing difficulties. He recounted a meeting with "a great financier" who had warned of possible defeat and whom he had told that Germany had survived the Romans, the Huns, the invasions of the Mongols, the Thirty Years' War, the Seven Years' War, the war of the Spanish Succession, and the World War and would also last out this one. In an apocryphal religious tone, he did admit that his state was being subjected to "the tests of the devil, of Satan, and of hell," but added that providence would favor those who fought and did not surrender—the gods, he said, loved those who asked the impossible and then obtained it.[78]

The party sought to combat criticism with propaganda, but there were increased references to Goebbels's "club-footed fairy stories."[79] As a consequence, this period was also marked by increased police and court measures against defeatism and opposition. Late in May, the party headquarters proposed the establishment of honorary members of the security police. These would be party members, not officers, who would be given the right to make "citizens' arrests" of complainers, rumor mongers, and defeatists. The total number suggested was 6,025. It was planned that they would operate largely in the cities. Berlin alone, for example, was to have 200 such special police.[80] Increasingly, pressure was exerted on the courts to hand out the severest penalties for defeatism. Guidelines for the Reich League of Jurists forbade lawyers to use improper means to get their clients off "by turning and twisting the facts and by coloring the circumstances."[81] It was obvious by this period that the "guided justice" of Minister of Justice Georg Thierack had reduced itself to an almost universal use of the death penalty.[82]

The time of terror had begun—the most fanatic party men remained in control.[83] In the multiple executions of the period, the men in Berlin's Plötzensee prison went to their death nude, except for little short pants and even these were removed before the executions to be saved for the *Spinnstoff* collections. Even in the Middle Ages, wrote one critic, those executed had been left their undergarments.[84] Late in August, all former leaders of the prewar Socialist or Communist parties were arrested, regardless of their activities during the war.[85] These arrests, added to those of military leaders, monarchists, defeatists, complainers, plunderers, and deserters served to underscore the sense of desperation pervading the regime.

In spite of the severity of court actions, the scope of losses by plundering assumed staggering proportions. A Security Service agent in Darmstadt reported that during the period from May 1943 to May 1944, losses in the Rhine-Main area by the combination of air raids and the attendant plundering included 311 million kilograms of sugar, 3.25 million kilograms of butter, almost 6 million kilograms of cheese, 27 million kilograms of flour, 3.5 million eggs, and so forth.[86] Youth crime continued to be a concern of the authorities. Breach of work contracts and thefts were the most common complaints. Many of these youth problems resulted from a lack of parental guidance. Many young people lived alone in the great cities, their parents lost in the air raids or evacuated to safer places. Hitler Youth organizations had lost their appeal.[87] The party agencies had also lost the confidence of parents. There were complaints that the leaders at the camps of the League of German Girls had advised those attending to have children out of wedlock, since, with the shortage of men, they might not find husbands.[88] And some parents strongly resisted party efforts to move their children to schools out in the countryside, where they would be under the care of the Hitler Youth.[89]

The wartime shortages became more severe daily. New clothes ceased to be available. Paper grew ever more difficult to obtain and its quality declined. Most party agencies ran out of headed paper in this period and began to exchange notes on what must be called scrap paper.[90] The existing inflation caused by declining possibilities of purchasing goods brought a fabulous price increase on items obtained on the black market. Ordinary soldiers handed out tips in restaurants amounting to two weeks' pay, and one waiter bought a country farm with the tips he obtained by "finding" bottles of Moselle wine for his customers.[91] Party collections still brought up quantities of used materials—the final accounting for the year 1943 included 26,000 tons of bones, 40,000 tons of old textiles, and 117,000 tons of old paper.[92] But even swastika flags could not be purchased without ration stamps and then only for party purposes.[93]

The most serious shortage of all was petroleum fuel and gasoline. As a result of this, only two-thirds of the long-hour *Jäger* workers could be used in the factories. The party cut its own activities. Although the supposed cut was to be 20 percent across the board in gasoline, the propaganda ministry managed to reduce its own cut to 5 percent.[94] And although there was a strong move for the conversion of cars to gas generators, a memorandum noted that this could provide only moderate relief, since few cars were capable of accepting the changes needed. The memorandum directed that only Gauleiters and higher party officials and only those SS officials above the rank of Obergruppenführer were to be authorized to drive to work. Doctors, veterinarians, and midwives were to have their rations cut by 20 percent.[95] A little later, a party directive required the use of gasoline-driven cars by every Gau to be cut by 20 percent and of Reich offices to be cut by 30 percent, and all cars with engines larger than 2.0 liters were to be put out of use entirely.[96]

Most severely affected by these cuts were the doctors. As many of them converted their cars to methane gas, the wood needed to fuel them became more difficult to obtain. Some doctors in the cities used bicycles to reach their patients. Others asked the local burgomasters or party officials to look in on patients to see how seriously ill they were before they made their own visits.[97]

Transportation problems increased. Postal deliveries were seriously hampered. In country areas, the use of horses and wagons for delivery was increased and in cities, streetcars were sometimes turned into delivery trucks.[98] People were told that they would have to make their own arrangements to get coal for heating. Some had to trek many blocks to bring home the needed fuel. Even then coal usage was to be reduced to 40 percent of the normal ration.[99] The effort to expand the use of horses for transportation of goods domestically was handicapped by the increasing use of them by the military. But the supply of horses was quite limited. An informed discussion by Security Service authorities in this period (they were, indeed, dealing rather sensibly with a broad range of domestic problems) dealt with the breeding of horses. In the eastern provinces, there had been much pride in the breeding of "warm-blooded" horses, those that had once graced the chase and the cavalry charges. But the need now was for heavier and less delicate horses that could pull wagons and materiel for the military and aid in transporting civilian goods. The report warned that the studs to provide the needed mixture between "warm" and "cold-blooded" work horses could not come from the warm-blooded group. This mixture produced offspring with weak legs, large rumps, and small heads. The cold-blooded stallion produced in the mixture a much better horse. The right mixture was about 80 percent cold and 20 percent warm, which resulted in horses that were active but also strong. But this involved problems with the government studding stations, which were over-taxed. The result was that the stud was often overstrained and no offspring were produced. The Security Service agent suggested that it was worthwhile for farmers to obtain their own studding horse and recommended that studding stations be provided with more stallions.[100]

The Security Service also reported on the problem involved in the conversion of gasoline and diesel tractors to the use of wood-gas generators.[101] The power of each tractor converted in this manner was reduced by 20 to 30 percent. Although this left the larger and more powerful tractors somewhat weaker, no great harm was done. But many of the smaller tractors were left ineffective in bad or hilly territory. Moreover, the process of conversion often proceeded at a snail's pace. Three thousand two hundred tractors in the Rhineland area were to have been converted, but of these only 87 had been started on the road to conversion for the use of wood and 104 for the use of brown coal, and of these only 60 were actually converted for the use of wood and 20 for the use of brown coal. The others were in the works, waiting for parts. After conversion, maintenance became a serious problem. There was a shortage of capable repair personnel and the different makes required different parts. One farmer reported that his wood-gas tractor had required 1,415 marks of repair work in 1,273 hours of use. His diesel tractor with 4,000 hours of use in ten years' time had required only 320 marks in repair costs.

The exposé by the Security Service of bureaucratic shortcomings in horse breeding and wood-gas tractor conversions was followed by a critical report on railroad transportation arrangements.[102] The report highlighted the insanity of some of the existing dispositions, which resulted in long hauls for goods close at hand and many empty cars rolling back and forth across the country. Thus a firm in Breslau could have obtained 10,000 kilograms of malt coffee from a firm in Silesia only 130 kilometers away, but was told that that firm's production had to go to the Government General (Poland) so that the Breslau firm had to get its coffee from a firm near Posen, 360 kilometers away. A firm in Swabia made dried carrot powder for children's food, but this had to go to a distribution center in Danzig and then come back to Nuremberg for usage there. Carpenters in Eger near Bayreuth made standard furniture, but this was sent elsewhere and the imports came from away. Eggs from the region around Garmisch-Partenkirchen were kept by the collecting agencies for months before being taken to Munich. When they returned for distribution, they were often spoiled. And poor-quality coal, which was less efficient, was transported across Germany, while good coal that would have required less transport was burned near the mines. Not noted, of course, in these criticisms was that much railroad transport was being wastefully employed for the last-minute transport of Jews to the death camps.

It is remarkable that under these circumstances the provision of food supplies did not suffer more than it apparently did. The potato shortage discussed earlier had reduced the potato ration for the normal user to eight kilograms (17.6 lbs.) per four-week ration period from March through June 1944.[103] By the end of June, the shortage had tapered off somewhat and the ration allowance returned to ten kilograms (22 lbs.) per four-week ration period through the remainder of the war. But when potato beetles threatened the crop in August, the party sought to rally school children and evacuees to aid the farmers in dealing with them.[104]

Under the bombs in Berlin. Rescue workers search the rubble for survivors.

Unless otherwise indicated, photos are from the German Information Center, New York.

No escape: the effects of the dreaded phosphorus bombs.

Firefighters in Berlin attempt to extinguish fires caused by bombings on the night of January 31, 1944. Bundesarchiv-Militärarchiv, Freiburg i. Br.

Above, fires consume Hamburg after an Allied air attack. Below, emergency first aid is set up for possible survivors after a bombing attack in Berlin. Bundesarchiv-Militärarchiv, Freiburg i. Br.

After the February 1945 firebombing of Dresden, bodies are collected and brought to the Old Market for identification and eventual incineration before being buried in mass graves. Opposite, Dresden lies in ruins.

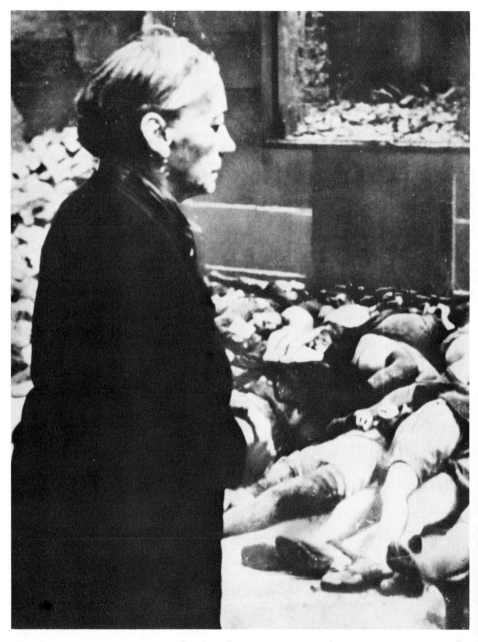

A woman searches for relatives among air raid victims.

Life goes on in Berlin at war's end, despite 75 million cubic meters of rubble in the city. Below, the Reichstag, Germany's Parliament building, was heavily damaged by both bombing attacks and sabotage and looting in the course of the war.

The city of Mainz lay in ruins on February 27, 1945, following an air attack.

The spires of Cologne Cathedral rise over a devastated city, with the wreckage of the Hohenzollern Bridge in the foreground. Consulate General of the Federal Republic of Germany, Atlanta.

By war's end the Nazis were fighting the war with children. Above, the Hitler Youth were called upon to man antiaircraft stations when they reached the age of 16. Below, captured youth await imprisonment in December 1944.

German refugees from the east fled the advancing Red Army as the war drew to a close, seeking food and shelter in the west and traveling by whatever means they could, including cattle cars (left).

Wartime refugees, joined by expellees, swelled the population of West Germany by seven million in 1945. Many, like this man in Berlin, found no roofs available.

The survivors of air raids left messages for relatives and new addresses on their bombed-out homes.

Above, the "rubble women" begin the cleanup of Berlin. In East Berlin (below), the first place cleaned was Stalinallee.

At the end of the war, Frankfurt (above) and Wesel on the Rhine (below) were ruined cities. Within a few years both had been rebuilt (opposite) with modern structures and reconstructions of historic buildings, such as the old Town Hall in Frankfurt. Frankfurt photos from Consulate General of the Federal Republic of Germany, Atlanta.

For years, many Germans, like these Berliners in 1948,
continued to live amid the ruins of war-ravaged buildings.

Complaints were made that some of the later raids were damaging grain in the outlying areas of bombed cities and towns, and instructions were issued that the largest amount possible should be salvaged. If glass or other material were embedded in it, the grain could still be placed in the carp ponds to add to fish resources and if this were not possible, it might be fed to the ducks, which could then be sent to the U-boats. The worst-damaged grain could be burned in the breweries and would be the source of a swill that was very useful for fodder. Meantime, every effort should be made to protect the harvests from the danger of air-raid fires.[105] A draft circular of the farmers' office signaled a coming shortage of fodder, which was to become increasingly severe during the remainder of the year.[106]

The Security Service agents were sympathetic with the widespread complaints about the shortage of vegetables. Newspaper articles repeating the old propaganda advice that wild daisies could be used to eke out vegetable shortages had drawn adverse criticism. That article had pictured German housewives harvesting these forest gems plentifully available and cooking both the stems and leaves with flour or potatoes. As a housewife said, "It would be better for us to rent a meadow and lead our families out to eat the grass. Then we would save coal and gasoline, and now I know why they are so strong against our raising small animals since the greens are needed for human food."[107] The Security Service agent, this time an expert on caring for gardens, noted that the prices of specialized vegetables such as potherbs were much higher than those for ordinary vegetables like leeks, so that the farmers chose to raise these "noble vegetables" rather than the ordinary ones even though their soil might not be best employed in this way.[108] On the average, the farmers got only 42 percent of the final selling price. Often they had to sell their products as second-class goods, only to find that the grocer had reclassified them as first class. All of this tended to increase the black-market sale of products by the producer directly to the consumer.

The Security Service agents also showed some sympathy with farmers in respect to insufficient deliveries.[109] Many of the arrangements for determining delivery quotas were faulty, as were the penalties for failing to meet these quotas. Thus, a farmer whose quota was high and who delivered more than was required believed that he should receive a premium for this excess since his neighbors who failed to live up to their obligations could get rich in the black market. Penalties for shortfalls were often very light. One farmer was penalized .20 RM for each egg not delivered, but he could sell one for .50 RM, so he made .30 RM through black marketeering. Another farmer with five cows was penalized for shorting his quota but did not pay and continued to ignore his quota for ten months without a penalty. These shortfalls seriously affected food supplies and severer penalties were in order.

All of these criticisms voiced by agents of Himmler's SS in respect to the management of internal affairs tended to emphasize the decline of any real spirit of self-sacrifice for the welfare of the nation. The quest of the city dweller for survival regardless of circumstances was matched by the tendency of the farmer to make whatever profits he could from his crops. "The war," wrote Horst Lange "is like a pestilence which overwhelms us and makes us sick. . . . Before all of us stands a breakdown and a dissolution which will be horrible."[110] And Willy Beer spoke of the great longing for alcohol, which brought a brief narcotization against the evils of the day. For many, he said, it was as necessary as their daily bread.[111] In the days to follow, the darkness and disillusion grew so deep that no one could raise himself or herself above the shadows.

8. Germany's Darkest Winter

September 1944 marked the beginning of Germany's sixth year at war. A deep sense of gloom lay across the country. No longer was there any relief from the hardships of overly strenuous work, the fear of the next bombing raid, the struggle to keep outworn clothing wearable, the worries about the steadily approaching enemy forces from the east and the west, and the apprehension of danger from the hordes of enemy workers and prisoners of war cramped within the shrinking frontiers. And in the midst of all this, there was the dread that a thoughtless word of pessimism might bring the vengeance of a dying regime that visited its wrath upon any civilian or soldier who breathed aloud the universally held knowledge that the sands of time were running out and midnight was about to descend on Germany's rulers.

Allied bombs rained more relentlessly than ever on German cities. Nighttime raids were followed by raids coming in the early daylight hours, raids breaking the lunch-hour calm, raids that arrived in mid-afternoon. The flying time from Allied bases into Germany was now so short that air-raid warnings no longer functioned effectively. People listened to the radio reports to follow the course of Allied flights across Germany. Multiple targets were often hit by the same initial flights, portions of the planes peeling off to attack different cities. Low-flying bombers could bring danger to the inhabitants of a city even when only a few of them were involved.

Strafing added to the perils of bombing. Every civilian now kept his air-raid pack with him at all times and took to the bunkers or cellars without delay when it became clear that his city was on the day's schedule.

The bombs fell upon old familiar targets as well as new ones, little disturbed until this time. Cologne, the site of the first thousand-bomber raid was the target of 3,700 more explosive bombs in September and even more in October. Old craters were filled with the old rubble as new bombs created new craters. People waited in the bunkers in darkness because the air pressure of the exploding bombs blew out the candles they had lit. Neighbor "Joe" said "Auf Wiedersehn" to his friend Fischer in one of these raids but never reached the air-raid cellar. A bomb destroyed his house and killed Joe, his wife, his son, and his daughter. The father brought four coffins to fetch the corpses, but the remnants of the family lay in one tin bucket in the courtyard. The four coffins remained behind, unused. The rats already in the city were joined by lice, and clean water was difficult to obtain. Cologne was hell itself.[1]

Stuttgart had new raids leaving thirty to forty thousand more inhabitants homeless. Hospitals and homes for the aged became critically short of space. New resettlements of those not working in the factories became necessary.[2] Munich suffered too, losing not only its accustomed panorama of buildings but even its familiar smells. No longer could one savor the scent of new-mown hay on summer evenings or the crisp sweetness of approaching snow. Everywhere, one was attacked by the odor of smoldering rafters, stifling rubbish, damp cellars, moldy paper, and rusted metal.[3] And Hamburg had thirty-five air-raid warnings and eight heavy bombardments in the month of October. The dash for the air-raid shelter became automatic, regardless of day or night warnings and the interruption of sleep or meals.[4]

The Ruhr area and the cities along the western frontier of Germany remained the most frequent targets. As Allied armies closed in on western Germany, new names joined the list of familiar targets. Düren, near the scene of desperate land struggles in the Hürtgen forest, was leveled. Sterkrade-Holten, Wanne-Eickel, Castrop-Rauxel, Soest, Hagen, Giessen, Jülich, Heinsberg, Homberg-Meerbeck, and Neuss joined the list of heavily bombed cities. Heilbronn suffered a firestorm in December that killed hundreds in their cellars, some buried, some burned, some dying from carbon monoxide, and others perishing in underground panic.[5] Dortmund, Düsseldorf, and Duisburg received new damage. A thousand-plane attack on Duisburg left the city in critical condition throughout the remainder of the war but later raids added almost 5,000 tons of bombs to those which had already descended upon the city.[6] Dortmund closed its doors to any outsiders after severe raids in October.[7] Düsseldorf shook under 4,500 tons of bombs, and Essen, home of the Krupp enterprises, received the astounding load of almost 12,000 tons of bombs during this four-month period.[8]

Moreover, the attacks on the synthetic oil plants and refineries continued unabated and were joined by attacks on canal and railroad facilities all across Germany.[9] The new Allied "glide bombs," which drifted into their target areas with a roaring, buzzing sound, had some of the same terror effect that had earlier been attached to the German "buzz bombs." Since they were dropped from peripheral areas, they were more difficult to judge and caught some of those in the target cities by surprise.[10] In Rüdesheim, these bombs killed seventy children in a kindergarten.[11]

But the greatest civilian concern was occasioned by raids of the "Jabos" (Jagdbomber—fighter bombers—either P 38 Lightnings or P 47 Thunderbolts and later P 51 A 36 Mustangs), which appeared suddenly over small cities as well as large, dropped a small but accurately aimed load of bombs, and strafed any convenient target, including the cattle in the fields.[12] Linnich, a village with 427 houses, was the recipient of 120 bombs on Sunday, October 8, 1944. Forty houses were destroyed, 90 badly damaged, and 180 others affected. The village afterwards presented the same rubble-filled picture as the big cities. Many of the population, shocked by the unexpected attention their village had received, fled in panic.[13]

In western Germany, the bombing was joined with the horrors of land warfare. Cannon shells and machine-gun bullets added to the destruction already wrought by bombs. Although the disastrous plan for "operation market garden" (September 17-24, 1944) failed to capture "a bridge too far" at Arnhem and thus open a path into the industrial heart of Germany,[14] the first German city, Roetgen, fell to American forces on September 12.[15] This opened a desperate conflict centering on the Rur River (in Dutch, Roer, a tributary of the Maas), one marked by stubborn and determined German resistance that was to take a heavy toll of Allied forces before they achieved a real breakthrough into the Ruhr area itself. Although Aachen was encircled and captured on October 21, the Allies fighting in this area faced the deep slime occasioned by late rains, a morass of mines, tank traps, and bunkers in the area in and around the Hürtgen forest, and the resilient defenses of German troops who had been much too soon counted as beaten and dispirited.[16] By November, the Western Allies were also moving forward on the south into Alsatian territory long disputed between Germany and France. Metz, Strassburg, and Mulhouse were taken, and in December, Haagenau and Saargemünd fell into Allied hands. A wide reach of German frontier in the south was imperiled by these operations. Allied optimism received a serious setback in December with the daring German counteroffensive planned and carried out by Hitler, the "watch on the Rhine" drive through the Ardennes forest designed to divide the Allied forces in Belgium and northern France. On December 16, a quarter of a million German troops including refurbished and reequipped armor units, supported by almost 1,800 planes, burst across weakly held American lines to attempt a drive to the sea. Deep penetration was achieved but fuel shortages and heavy air attacks once the weather had cleared stalled the German troops. In the end, the battle was lost—before the year was out, Hitler acknowledged the failure of the effort.

In retrospect, this adventurous counteroffensive of Hitler's, which became known as the Battle of the Bulge, appears to rank high among the strategic errors of the Nazi Führer. But it must be noted that, during this period, the Soviet drive into East Prussia had become stalled, their move towards Warsaw had been halted at the Vistula River, and the revolt in Warsaw of the Polish Home Army had been (in the face of Soviet inactivity) squashed by German forces. Although Soviet forces had established control in Bulgaria and Rumania and had moved into Hungary, they did not as yet, during these months, pose as direct a threat to German home territory as did the Americans and British in the West. If the Ardennes offensive of 1944 had achieved the success of Germany's earlier operation in 1940, the war on the western front would have been thrown into serious disarray. But even had it been successful, it would have been difficult to justify this profligate expenditure of tanks, planes, and men in an offensive drive at a time when the German lines were being pushed relentlessly northward in Italy, when German troops were withdrawing painfully from Greece in the south and Finland and the Baltic provinces in the north, and when it was becoming ever more apparent that the Third Reich faced a woeful preponderance of Soviet forces in the east.

Undoubtedly there were some Germans even at this late date who managed to believe that Hitler could still gain a miraculous victory, and the Battle of the Bulge provided a temporary flickering of new hope for others. But the available sources for judging morale indicate clearly that the prevailing mood was profoundly pessimistic.[17] Yet in view of the police and court action of the day, this always had to be cautiously expressed—as noted previously, a common saying was "it is better to believe in victory than to run around without one's head." But the gloom and doom of the situation marked the beginning of the end and made this Germany's darkest winter.

Evacuations from the east and west added to the sense of overcrowding in many parts of Germany. Many evacuees from Silesia came into the area of Swabia and placed serious pressure on the supply of such commodities as salt, vinegar, and baking powder.[18] By December 25, there were 590,918 requartered persons in the Gau Württemberg-Hohenzollern. A month later, the number had risen to 736,488.[19] Soldiers mixed with civilians among those who pushed in from the West. The government issued stern instructions to the Gauleiter that all of these runaway soldiers were to be picked up and held for return to military service.[20] There were also complaints that stories of Soviet atrocities carried by rear-line troops in the east were stirring up the population, who heard them second-hand from the evacuees.[21]

The evacuation of western areas under the direct threat of Allied invasion began and added new streams of people trudging toward the interior, pushing their carts loaded with basic necessities or wearily lugging heavy suitcases and baskets. The government told them to take with them serviceable clothing (for most now only remnants), a three-day supply of food, and basic tableware (enameled ware was particularly recommended). Bakers, butchers, and millers were to stay behind as long as possible and carry on their work. Often the moves were directed by SA personnel, who behaved in an arbitrary fashion towards those on the move. Efforts were made to drive cattle towards the interior and to harvest as much as possible of the vital potato crop. Special harvesting commandos for digging the potatoes were set up at some points. In all, some 246,000 people were moved out of the endangered area along with 33,000 tons of armaments, machine parts from the electrical works, and 36,500 cattle.[22]

In every little village, some brave souls stayed behind, unwilling to desert their homes or, perhaps, their cattle, pigs, cats, and rabbits. Burying themselves in the strongest cellars, they waited in fear while the shells fell closer and closer. Even short expeditions to get food or to take care of the animals might cost them their lives. Providing care for wounded German soldiers or civilians was difficult. Potatoes were normally their main staple, although sometimes cattle were killed in the fighting and more meat was available than normal. Eventually, they emerged from their shelters with the realization that for them the war was over. Often they were not allowed to return to their homes but were herded toward the rear of Allied lines to survive with considerable hardship in camps established by the enemy.[23]

For many of these Germans, this was the first personal encounter with Americans—the "Amis" of the postwar period. Sometimes this was pleasant—the children made their acquaintance with the chocolate bars and other delicacies thrown to them by the Amis. The adults discovered that American field rations, regarded as less than satisfactory by the "G.I.'s," provided a filling repast for those who were really hungry and that discarded American cigarettes were a real delight after the rationed German *Einheitszigaretten* (one-brand cigarettes). But those whose houses were occupied by the invading troops often found them ransacked and ruined when the enemy moved on and too frequently all items of value disappeared with the onward march of the soldiers.[24]

There were also problems with the children who remained behind during the hostilities. They found the ammunition lying about fascinating. Empty shells were filled with powder and lit so that they became "flame throwers," spewing out fire twenty to thirty feet. A "funny" hand grenade almost destroyed the whole group of children who found it. Many children lost arms or legs in this "fourth of July" experimentation. Little wonder that it was difficult to answer the inquiry of some parents who had left as to whether their children would be able to play in the little villages again if they returned—with such dangerous "toys" lying around in the midst of the rubble of destroyed homes.[25]

But even in areas not subject to immediate enemy attack, there was an increasing tendency for home front and battle front to become unified. And this was accompanied by ever more desperate efforts of the Nazi party to assume the responsibility for the direction of defense efforts and to suppress without mercy signs of opposition to the war effort. The nastiness and pettiness of party leadership became more and more evident as the crisis Germany confronted grew more severe and more obvious.

The role of Martin Bormann in these months also gained in significance. He virtually controlled access to Hitler so that the decisions he announced in his various circulars, directives, and information papers apparently bore Hitler's approval and support, whether or not all matters had been brought to the Führer's attention.

He dominated the party's line of communication between its central offices and the subordinate Gauleiters, Kreisleiters, and Ortsgruppenleiters. He was given the major role in the recruitment and organization of the Volkssturm, Germany's home guard. And he exerted considerable influence over the administration of justice, the determination of labor policy, and the whole complex of problems resulting from the destruction accomplished by the air raids.[26]

In his personal life, Bormann exemplified the division between the ideal of stern and selfless wartime morale that he pictured in his directives and the quite self-indulgent personal life that many of the party leaders led even in this troubled period. His wife and children were sent to the Obersalzberg area in southern Germany in the summer of 1944 and Bormann sought to keep significant wartime production out of this area even though he had already had significant housing and strong air-raid shelters built there. Trucks carried lavish food supplies for his family's needs. He also maintained a mistress from early 1944 on.[27]

But Bormann's role can be overemphasized in this closing stage of the war. Communication between the Reich headquarters and regional and local authorities grew ever more difficult. The Gauleiters and their subordinates tended more and more to determine their own courses of action. Karl Wahl wrote later that he did not have time to read all of Bormann's directives, let alone try to execute them. He just did what he regarded as right and necessary for his Gau, Swabia.[28] Other Gauleiters ignored Bormann's orders against special dispositions in respect to food or fuel.[29] The Gauleiters themselves were principally responsible for the building of fortifications, the actual raising of the Volkssturm, and the real execution of economic, social, and labor policies. Even air-raid protection was in this period transferred to party agencies, and in this area, too, the Gauleiters assumed major responsibility. There was a strong tendency on their part to revert to the earlier stage of party history when the Gauleiters had acted as the ruling lords of their party districts.

The quality of the execution of these multiple tasks depended heavily on the character and energy of the particular Gauleiter involved. All along the frontiers, the older men, who could not be counted on as eligible for the draft, and the younger boys not as yet subject to conscription were gathered together in thousands to dig antitank ditches, erect barriers around endangered towns, and provide defensive positions against a threatening invasion. In some cases, they were joined by women workers, and in many places foreign labor was also employed. The work of these motley crews varied. Along the western front, many of them displayed little enthusiasm. The Security Service in Düsseldorf reported that the employment of the Hitler Youth in fortifications was considered useless. People believed that the regime was only trying to maintain itself a little longer.[30] A report from the Kreisleiter in Freiburg i. Br. noted that some of the workers on the fortifications were stopping work early and directed that all must work at least a full eight-hour day or lose their pay. A few days later, the Kreis organizational office reported that it had combed through all of the factory personnel to find those who could be used for fortification work and added that all factory personnel who were not working on Sundays were to be used for fortification purposes on that day.[31] Apparently, however, these efforts of the party leaders achieved little success. A report of the propaganda leader of the area indicated that the work on the fortifications there had begun with some enthusiasm, but that bad weather, enemy air attacks, and poor transportation arrangements had dampened morale considerably.[32]

Evidently, Freiburg's experience was not unusual. A follow-up directive from Bormann noted that the work was going too slowly in some Gaus and reminded the Gauleiters that they were personnaly responsible for seeing that enough defensive positions were constructed, regardless of whether or not they were getting the kind of collaboration they wanted.[33] Josef Bürckel, the Gauleiter of the West Mark, voiced open opposition. He wrote to the party chancellery, stating that efforts to refurbish and strengthen the German West Wall (called the Siegfried line by the Allies) were useless since there were no battle-ready troops available to occupy this line. Senseless destruction, he felt, should be avoided. But the party chancellery simply sent him one of its own agents, Willi Stöhr, to direct the construction work.[34] Bürckel committed suicide late in September as a consequence of his desertion of the city of Metz against Hitler's wishes. Stöhr became his successor. Bürckel was reported to have died of pneumonia and given an honorary party burial.[35]

Everywhere in the west, the work was amateurish in character. Often installations could be well concealed from ground observation but were easily seen from the air and proper camouflage materials were no longer available.[36] Barbed wire, mines, and antitank weapons were lacking. The original bunkers had cement covers only one and one half to two meters thick, far too light for war at this stage, and the bunkers were made for thirty-seven-milimeter cannons, and could not be converted for the seventy-five-millimeter cannons, because the ammunition chests in them would not accommodate shells of that caliber. At best, they could be made useful for the protection of soldiers against the weather and the enemy artillery fire.[37]

On the eastern front, the fortification work was apparently more effective. This was due largely to the energy and determination of the Gauleiter of East Prussia, Erich Koch. Ambitious, self-centered, and brutal, Koch managed to organize hundreds of thousands of workers and achieve good results. A whole network of potential defense installations was created. They were set up contrary to Hitler's belief that defensive positions behind the front lines made the troops fight less aggressively. In this one area, Guderian, Hitler's commander in the East, had been able to proceed contrary to Hitler's wishes. And Guderian praised the determination and hard work of those who had accomplished these defenses. They did, indeed, reflect the fervent efforts of thousands of women as well as the older men, some of them clawing at the dirt that needed to be cleared away with their hands as well as their spades.[38]

But the defenses lacked the possibility of a withdrawal since Koch shared Hitler's belief that the Russians would never be able to penetrate German territory. Successive lines of defense were not constructed. Nor were those that were constructed occupied by seasoned troops or provided with sufficient artillery support. Guderian was prevented from effective action in this respect by Hitler's draining of troops, armor, and cannons for the unsuccessful drive in the West. The lines stood vacant. When they were later occupied by troops that had already been broken on the front, the defenses were far less effective.[39]

The whole process of fortification work changed the domestic scene materially. Most of the Hitler Youth were taken over into the Reich Labor Service. Thousands of them were seen in the railroad stations, waiting, spades in hand, for their transportation to frontier areas.[40] Often they were accepted into the new work in a dramatic party festival with their spades polished to a gleam and presented in a salute to their leaders. Their new work gave them access to cigarette rations not available to them as Hitler Youth and to movie presentations previously counted too "adult" for their viewing.[41] Older men also joined the work. A sixty-two-year-old court president from Wuppertal led a troop of fortification workers for two months, earning the respect of his regional superior for his courage and dedication, in contrast to the declining morale of some of his colleagues.[42]

The young and the aged were also joined in the ranks of the

Volkssturm, which began its existence in this same period. Although Hitler had earlier vetoed the plans of several Gauleiters to raise their own specific home guards, he entrusted Martin Bormann, in a decree of September 24, 1944, with the task of forming a general "people's storm troop" against the enemy.[43] In this action, he was seeking to restore the romantic mood of the late Napoleonic period when the people rose up in a mighty storm against the invader. Bormann added the injunction that this new militia was to be strictly a "party matter" with those involved "true to the Führer unto death."[44] If any leader, he charged, found himself regarding the situation he confronted as hopeless, he was to turn over the command to someone else who would keep on fighting, even if the new leader might be the youngest on the scene.[45]

Heinrich Himmler, the head of the SS, was given, in consultation with Bormann, the management of the details of the military organization and equipment of the Volkssturm. He, in turn, entrusted the direction of this task to SS General Gottlob Berger. Berger worked in cooperation with a small staff of the regular army under the leadership of staff officer Colonel (later Major General) Hans Kissel. But actual execution of the enlistment of the Volkssturm rested largely in the hands of the Gauleiter.[46]

The call for the Volkssturm sought to recruit the thousands of men from sixteen to sixty who had been left out of the fighting previously. These were to be divided into four levies; the first included those between the ages of twenty and sixty who were capable of military service and could be used either for unlimited or temporary service in the Volkssturm without endangering vital functions in the homeland. The average age of these men was fifty-two, many of them having served in World War I. Although designed for use in their home Gaus, they could in an emergency be used elsewhere. Only this levy could be used for securing defensive positions on the frontiers. The second levy involved those of the same ages who were employed in vital work at home so that they could not be employed militarily unless the enemy were in a position that immediately threatened their homes. Until the enemy stood before their doors, they remained basically weekend warriors, since most of them were employed in the munitions industries and the long hours of work left only Sunday free for their training. Although physically better off than the first levy, fewer of them had had any real military experience. And their training often resulted in serious disruptions of normal business—thus Bormann had to note that the failure to unload railroad cars on Sunday because of

Volkssturm duties could delay this process for as many as 7,000 cars a day, a stiuation which could not be permitted.[47] The third levy consisted of youths from sixteen to nineteen who had not been called to military service. These were to get their military training as a part of their service with the Hitler Youth or Reich Labor Service rather than by joining the ranks of the older Volkssturm men. Those of ages sixteen or less were not supposed to be used for direct military service even if they volunteered for it themselves unless special tasks were assigned to them by the Führer himself.[48] But both in the west and especially in the east, these boys were involved in some military actions and the general public reaction was that the party was now preparing to sacrifice even the children in seeking to evade defeat.[49] The fourth levy, finally, consisted of those who were unfit for any armed service but who might still be used as watch or security personnel. The determination of their unfitness was to be rechecked by a new physical conducted by doctors named by the Kreisleiters. After the original enrollment of the Volkssturm men (and the big festivals for this) the different levies were to be separated into different battalions.[50]

With the urging and often compulsion of party agencies, thousands of men turned out for Volkssturm service. In the West, those who took part often regarded their role as somewhat humorous and at best useless.[51] In the East, things were taken more seriously. In Königsberg, thousands of Volkssturm men listened on October 18 to a speech by Himmler that inaugurated their services—some were already fighting two days later.[52] In the castle park of Breslau, 80,000 people watched "with enthusiasm" the swearing in of 20,000 Volkssturm men.[53] Similar scenes were played out in Berlin and other cities.[54]

But enrollment did not mean successful employment. Efforts to provide some sort of uniform were only partially successful. Party uniforms were made over for Volkssturm service—many of the recipients were unhappy since they realized, especially in the east, that if the enemy identified the source of their garments, they were likely to receive harsh treatment.[55] All uniforms were supposed to be dyed—some *einsatzbraun*, some field gray.[56] Many still wore civilian clothes with only an arm band to identify their service.

Training for all levies was sporadic and poorly organized. Some of those in the east went off to battle without ever having fired a rifle or a carbine.[57] Those who did receive some training, only on Sundays for the second levy, learned to fire a rifle and to use a bazooka without killing themselves. But the demands occasioned by these new levies far outstripped the potential supplies of small arms. The first levy would have required for full equipment 1,700,000 hand weapons; the second 2,800,000 for a total of over 4,000,000. Although the most threatened Gaus were reasonably well supplied, rifles for those in the second levy were critically short.[58] A program for the production of "Volk rifles" and "Volk machine pistols" was begun, but it did not achieve reasonable production until the end of January 1945, with an estimate of 15,000 to be produced in February.[59] By the end of 1944, therefore, any propaganda advantage of this enrollment of the last available manpower of Germany into a great popular effort to resist the enemy had been lost. The major consequence of this effort was to add, to the already heavy state bureaucracy, new agencies seeking to supply these civilian soldiers (they did have legal military status) with pay books and social security arrangements for themselves and their dependents.[60]

The party's ever more dominant role in German life during this period, which was reflected in its management of the fortification work and of the raising of the Volkssturm, was also extended to the implementation of measures for air-raid protection and the repair of damages. The air-raid protection office, which had previously been an independent government agency, was transferred by a Führer decree of July 25, 1944, to party control and placed under the Gauleiters and Kreisleiters with the appropriate regional and local offices.[61]

But the shortage of funds to meet the problems created by the increasing weight of air raids became quickly apparent. The temporary auxiliary housing (*Behilfsheime*) that had been begun with such intensive propaganda support was virtually abolished. An internal memorandum of the propaganda office reported that these primitive buildings with primitive fittings had not been popular. People wanted their own "home" even if it were only a couple of rooms. Moreover, the memorandum said, repair of buildings gained more space more easily than the construction of new buildings did.[62] The post-air-raid help was also reduced. If only a few persons were rendered homeless after a raid, the welfare agency of the party was not to set up special arrangements for aid.[63] It was also instructed to hold to the minimum necessary the distribution of stamp-free food. This led to popular complaints about the miniscule payments for damages.[64]

All the while, the fear of air raids continued to be the largest single factor affecting public morale. But food shortages also caused concern. The wheat harvest declined and the meat ration suddenly rose since fodder for the existing cattle became scarce.[65] Potato supplies declined and people began again to "hamster" in the countryside to obtain them.[66] In Berlin, Ursula von Kardorff dispatched a request to a friend to send a box of them from the country.[67] Another housewife, Elsie Wendel, tried to make use of partly frozen ones in her cellar. According to Nazi instructions, she boiled them in vinegar water, but they smelled horrible and tasted even worse. She could only follow others in trading clothing for food.[68] Transportation problems affected the delivery of potatoes, other vegetables, and milk.[69]

The beginning of serious fodder shortages, referred to above, led the government to restrict the holdings of small animals to three geese, three ducks, two turkeys, two guinea fowls, and two rabbits.[70] Although food supplies were not yet at a critical stage, the propaganda ministry rejected a proposal that complaints about food shortages be counteracted by comparing the food supplies available in this war with those available in the first world war. To Goebbels and probably to more Germans than the party anticipated, the signs of coming difficulties were too apparent.[71]

The "swap" business continued to expand.[72] Prices for desirable goods tended to reach sky-high levels. Soap for washing clothes was almost unavailable. The party suggested that ivy leaves could be boiled to make a brew that would render dark-colored clothing clean without a gram of soap.[73] The only new consumer product on the scene was a baby buggy proudly labeled as six centimeters longer than the old ones. The notice of its coming availability was issued on November 14 and it was promised for three months from that time.[74] How many, if any, actually appeared cannot be determined. Clothing conditions for women worsened—the task of darning the stacks of disintegrating stockings and sewing together dilapidated underwear darkened the life of the German Hausfrau.[75]

In the cities, streetcar transportation became more difficult. Some stops were eliminated, occasioning inconvenience.[76] In the countryside, the major problem was the continuing addition of new evacuees. Some came from newly bombed cities, some from eastern and western areas being evacuated from the enemy. To these were added Black Sea Germans[77] and Esthonians[78] brought into the country and "friendly" and "allied" groups evacuated from France, Holland, and Belgium. These new additions to the existing numbers of prisoners of war, foreign workers, and concentration-camp inmates created the impression in many areas of unbearable overcrowding and added to the existing tension the signs of nerves rubbed raw.

There were also increasing health problems. The two main categories of difficulty were tuberculosis and sex-related diseases. These were reported from many areas of Germany and reflected problems of heating, the shortage of medical attention, and purported bad habits of hygiene on the part of some of the Hitler Youth groups and foreign visitors.[79] All of these reports also stressed the serious shortage of medical assistance in the countryside that was due to gasoline shortages.[80] The party made some effort to remedy this situation by getting army medical officers to care for civilians, at a fee, when located in an area where this was possible.[81]

The old fears of the multitude of foreigners in the midst of the German homeland continued. Willy Beer, going home in Berlin on the last streetcar of the night, found himself the only German on the car. It was, he felt, a remarkable world in which the capital city resounded with many languages and the night belonged not to the Germans but to the French, the Dutch, the Rumanians, all attended by merry maidens whose faces reflected the love of color of their homelands.[82] Ursula von Kardorff reported similar impressions of scenes in the Friedrichstrasse railroad station. Slavs with high cheekbones, fair-haired Danes and Norwegians, well-dressed Frenchwomen, Poles showing their hatred of Germans, and cool Italians mingled there to laugh, sing, and swap goods after working in the armaments factories. Even this fairly level-headed observer retailed the rumors of foreign workers sending information to the enemy that was returned to the Germans in the broadcasts of the foreign radio stations and referred to them as the potential Trojan horse of this war.[83]

These fears were shared by the authorities. On November 24, 1944, the minister of the interior ordered that the camps of foreigners should be closely watched to foil at the outset any opposition and, if difficulties did appear, to make an example of those involved.[84] Supervision of the camps was also to be tightened in order to prevent excessive fraternization, to look for illegal pamphlets or radio material, and to seek out weapons or plans for flight.[85] The office of the state police in Augsburg found weapons held by newly arriving foreign workers.[86] In Hamburg, party members and political leaders formed an emergency guard available in case of a rising of the foreign workers.[87]

In addition, there were reports that foreign agents were providing foreign workers with instructions on how to fake illnesses.

Gasoline laced with garlic could be used to cause stomach troubles. Milk injections in the buttocks produced high fever. Abnormal heart signs were the effect of pills of an unknown character. Boils or skin damage could be produced by gasoline, caustic, or sulfur. Pulverized roots produced a bloody stool. The appearance of a kidney infection could be faked by adding an egg-white solution to urine, tuberculosis by sniffing up fine graphite powder, and fevers by adding one quarter or one half tablet of quinine to a pipe full of tobacco.[88]

With some trepidation and concern 150,000 women were enrolled as auxiliaries in the army. Most of them were used to manage the searchlights for the antiaircraft batteries.[89] Special instructions were given that they were to be protected from capture if at all possible. Yet they were not to be armed even to protect themselves from capture.[90] And women were not to be enrolled in the Volkssturm.[91] Even in these late, desperate days the party continued to regard women as persons whose sex ought to have separated them from the hardships of war. Party leaders found great difficulty in dealing with their role. Although they wanted to picture them as "hard" for "hard times," they also wanted to retain the view of them as primarily the mothers of the future race, to protect them from being *entfraulicht*, from losing their womanly character.[92] Among the themes of those who sought to educate the new air force auxiliaries were the following: "The wooden barracks must become a home. Where women live, there is no dark, dusty corner." "The woman in a soldier's post but still a woman." "Love is the noblest feeling. (It moves mountains. The love for a man, mother love, love of country, homeland, and mother . . .)." "The attitude of air force helpers. The [male] soldier should not value us too lightly. If he does, however, we will convince him of our sense of duty."[93] Here, late in the war, the woman was pictured as the companion of man in life, in work, and in fighting. And it was suggested that when in the future the proper relationship between the work of men and of women was found, it would be in a truly National Socialist Germany. In country areas, the party also sought to get more work from the women. The girls sent to work on the farms lost all festival days and evenings, all opportunity for amateur theatricals and dances and other recreation. They were also to be trained in using tools or small machines so that they could work at least fifty hours a week (possibly up to sixty) on war-related home work when their agricultural work was not needed.[94]

The role of German youth in this period is not easily judged. Arthur Axmann, the head of the Hitler Youth, reported with pride to

Hitler that 70 percent of the youth of age sixteen had volunteered for military service. Hitler received the message "with pride and joy" as "a shining example of the will to struggle and a readiness for fanatical service and sacrifice."[95] And there are, indeed, signs that for many of these lads, whose schooling had begun under the National Socialist state, there was a genuine attachment to the regime and its ideals. They had been exposed from their childhood on to propaganda for sacrifice. In this period, a youth publication quoted from Karl von Clausewitz's confession of 1812: "I declare and inform the world now and the world to come . . . that I am willing to find a glorious death in defense of the freedom and worth of the homeland." Those who took this oath encouraged others to follow them in giving "testimony on the holy altar of history."[96] There was, as Milita Maschmann, herself a leader of the League of German Girls, related, a certain appeal in this new service to these youths who were no longer dismissed because they were still too young. And she recounted seeing a young wounded antiaircraft helper who was asked by an officer whether he was in pain. "Yes," he replied, "but it doesn't matter. Germany must triumph."[97] Many of these youths were, indeed, to make the ultimate sacrifice in useless military efforts in the east and in Berlin. But the diary of Klaus Granzow probably reflects more accurately the mood of many recruits whose enthusiasm for military service declined sharply with the realization of its futility during the last stages of the war.[98] And for many other youths, as has already been seen in earlier parts of this volume, the regime had lost its lure with the growing hardships attending the air raids.

But in this period, the regime moved with increasing vigor and severity against any kind of dissent. The youth received new attention from both the Reich Minister of Justice Thierack and the SS Chief of Police Himmler. The records of the regional court president of Cologne reflect the strong action of the police against youth bands in this period with action against one large band numbering 128 members and other actions against twenty smaller bands. In all, some 500 were arrested, only 220 of them Germans. Although these bands were supposed to have been responsible for twenty-nine murders, only three members were sentenced to death and the executions were not well attended by party officials, who "were too busy elsewhere." One must assume that many band members arrested were allowed to enter the military instead of being sent to prison. This would tend to explain the relatively large numbers of young soldiers who were executed in the closing phases of the war for desertion of their duty.[99]

The "satanism"[100] of the regime reached new heights—or should it be depths? Roland Freisler's courtroom performances, in which he berated, scolded, and denounced those being tried for their part in the July 20 assassination attempt on the life of Hitler, were broadly known.[101] Similar performances against lesser criminals took place. Willy Beer went to observe the work of the "People's Court" in hopes of a last view of a friend. He found the friend had already been condemned to death two days previously. But Freisler sat in judgment over Social Democratic prisoners. In blood-red robes, standing out from the lesser judges, Freisler asked planned questions for which no answers were needed and denounced witnesses who displeased him. "And he knows how to construct contradictions where there are none, knows how to proclaim guilt where no proof has been presented, knows how to proclaim crime where only one heart has spoken to another." Never before had the name of justice been so misused, concluded Beer.[102]

As was to be expected, the degree of enforcement of the laws against treason varied from place to place. The joke ran the rounds in Berlin that a person could be arrested because he or she had laughed (about the regime) in the air-raid shelters.[103] In Düsseldorf, party leaders complained that morale-threatening statements in the bunkers and elsewhere were not being dealt with severely enough.[104] But a housemaid in a hotel in a small town where pro-German Cossacks under a German officer were quartered got away with the threat that "if that rascal Hitler came around here, I'd put him down the lavatory and close the lid on him."[105] In southern Germany, the police had difficulties dealing with the jokes about the antics of the imaginary character Weiss Ferdl: Weiss Ferdl was seen carrying his radio around Munich and his friend asked him why. Weiss Ferdl answered that he was taking it to confession since it told only lies and no longer knew the truth. In another anecdote, Weiss Ferdl was seen carrying a sack of rags around the city. His friends asked him what was in it. "The government," said Weiss Ferdl. His friends looked in and said, "There's nothing here but a bunch of old rags" (in German a pun for "a bunch of plain bums"). "I didn't say it, you did," replied Weiss Ferdl. But severe punishment for telling Weiss Ferdl jokes was regarded as unnecessary. The tellers were released with a warning.[106]

Reports indicated that conditions in prisons and concentration camps worsened. Food supplies in the growing group of satellite concentration camps around the Natzweiler concentration camp in Alsace (most of these were in the Wüttemberg area) grew short and starvation and hard work began to take a heavy toll of prisoners.[107] In the prisons in Berlin, no protection against air raids was provided. Prisoners could only huddle against a wall and hope the bombs would not make the prison their target.[108] But bombs did reduce the number of prisons available in many areas and did slow down the actions of the courts. The number of court personnel also declined with the air war as well as with the drain of lawyers into the military.[109]

Hitler's appeal for the Volkssturm read by Himmler at the circus building in Munich and broadcast by radio to the entire country carried notes of uncertainty not previously present in the Führer's addresses. There was the warning that if Germany were defeated, the delivery to the enemy of the so-called "war criminals" (the worthwhile men, he interjected) would be followed by innumerable columns of others marching into the Siberian tundras. He warned against the existing hatred of Germany by all its enemies. All of Germany's difficulties, he alleged, were due to "betrayal after betrayal." Anyone who sought to "place other men in a conflict of conscience" was, he said, preparing his own way to death. And he promised that "the times of defeats" would not bring surrender. All in all, the speech lacked the crispness and vigor of Hitler's earlier speeches and, delivered by someone else, failed to make a dent in the general feelings of gloom.[110]

More and more, each person turned inward for survival during this period. Ursula von Kardorff went to mass both morning and evening and wrote that "it is the only thing that keeps me going."[111] In spite of Nazi antichurch activity, the churches continued to survive and draw good attendance.[112] Perhaps Lili Hahn best summarized the situation after the end of a tormenting incident. She had been forced into a sexual relationship with an SS man by threats to send her Jewish mother to a concentration camp. An unwanted child from this hateful union was aborted. Now, still looking for survival herself, she wrote: "Everyone is so overcome by his own personal worries that he no longer cares about the fate of Germany. It is far more important that one gets something to eat, that shoes will last a little longer, and above all whether there will be an air raid. Will we have a roof over our heads tomorrow, or even be alive?"[113]

The Christmas celebrations of 1944 found most Germans seeking the traditional religious expressions in spite of the party's efforts to undermine them. For most people, this was difficult. New candles were unavailable unless one belonged to the SS. All married SS leaders, subordinate leaders, and ordinary SS men who did not already have the proper Christmas lights and all widows of SS men were to be furnished new ones.[114] These reflected a nonreligious view associated with "the birth of the light." Several versions were suggested. One dealt with a newborn child lying in a golden cradle in the hall of one's ancestors, reflecting their sunny, godlike life. Another pictured a tree remaining green through the year's dark nights and passing on its light by the flames on its branches. A third, the most popular, was of a virgin with golden hair shut up in a dark tower, but after her release from captivity appearing shining with new life. This was given a visual portrayal with a small light in the lower part of the tower, which symbolized light in the darkness, to be followed in the beginning of the new year with the kindling of a great light at the top of the tower. There was, noted an SS memorandum, no foreign spirit involved in this Christmas memento.[115] Himmler's Christmas card, sent together with the lights, wished the SS members "all good luck and fortune," warned that 1945 would be the decisive year of the war, and set forth the slogan "Through mothers and heroes our victory will come! In unshatterable loyalty and deepest thankfulness we greet the leader sent to us by the Lord God: Adolf Hitler."[116]

Party Christmas celebrations even altered the words sung to the most famous Christmas carol. "Silent night, holy night" became "Lofty night" (*Hohe Nacht*).

Lofty night of the clear stars
which stand like broad bridges
Over the deep distance
to where our hearts lie.

Lofty night of the great fires
which are lit on all the mountains
today the earth must renew itself
Like a newborn child.

Mothers, you are all the fires,
All the fires placed on high.
Mothers, deep in your hearts
Beats the heart of the wide world.[117]

Little wonder that these new songs left those who attended the party- or army-sponsored celebrations dissatisfied. Hugo Hartung went from the areligious celebrations of the army into the cathedral, where he found more candles than ever and more people saying their normal prayers.[118] Klaus Granzow found the "odious" celebration of the miltary ridiculous, although he and his comrades who took part were rewarded with plenteous servings of punch. In a strange church, the pastor sang off key and the organ was shrill, but when he returned to the barracks, he and his comrades sang the old Christmas songs and "now it is really Christmas."[119] And Joachim Günther, traveling back and forth across Germany in a military hospital train, found in an old schoolbook picked up in Halberstadt a poem that made Christmas for him, as it spoke of the holy night coming in on the wings of the angels, the bells, and the joy of sweet songs, and the thousand candles which should finally celebrate the coming of peace.[120]

Bormann, with ironic double face, approved of people having Christmas trees if they could get them, and three days of vacation were permitted.[121] And, strangely enough, it appears that many did manage to find trees or at least branches, to decorate them sometimes with the silver streamers dropped by the bombers to throw off the radar, and to dig out motley shapes of candles to provide a little Christmas spirit. And, somehow, many of them managed to find some last remnants of special food and drink to provide some semblance of holiday enjoyment.[122]

The enemy did not help the Christmas celebrations. Two thousand bombers attacked Cologne, and the Christmas carols had to be sung in the church crypts as Christians had once sung in the catacombs.[123] Hamburg was bombed but the Christmas trees and candles still burned in the church that Mathilde Wolff-Mönckeberg attended and the old carols gave comfort.[124] Berlin was bombed and the inhabitants began to say that the Allies would have to bring their own targets if they wanted new ones.

By this time, of course, the only entertainment available was the movies, with the film ministry still producing movies. Goebbels's favorite, "Opfergang," (the rite of sacrifice) premiered in Berlin on December 29, 1944.[125] Home talent productions could be produced locally.[126] And there were, as one German newspaper pointed out, "a thousand friends" in the public library to help pass the time.[127] But this year had been, as the same newspaper observed, "the year of the hardest burdens."[128] And the year's end brought little hope for a happy New Year. Brave speeches by party leaders could not hide the increasing fury of the air warfare.[129] Those in the country area now faced attacks, unsheltered by air-raid bunkers, and some contemplated moving back into the cities.[130] And some news of Russian actions in the east crept into wider German consciousness—the most shocking of them the story that in taking the town of Nemmersdorf, the Russians had not only repeatedly raped all women and girls but had nailed several alive to the barn doors.[131]

The Germans now began to face their ultimate trials—an end of their hopes, accompanied by sheer terror of the consequences. Some, in these late days, realized that Nazi pictures showing enemy atrocities were hypocritical. "Have we not killed the Jews by the thousands. Do not our soldiers relate that in Poland the Jews had to shovel their own graves?"[132] But even those who made these late-day confessions of guilt were seldom aware of the depth and extent of the evil of which they spoke. Few of those at home could have known or even believed that in these days when the party was screaming about the shortage of railroad transportation in the west,[133] trains were still rushing from Hungary to the death camps in Poland, seeking to exterminate the last remnants of Jews in that country before it would be occupied by the Russians.[134] Both the German people and the invaders from both sides learned more of the extermination camps, the harshness of internal concentration camps, and the brutality of the SS guards in the days that followed. Priceless art treasures stolen from abroad escaped only by accident the destruction planned by the professed devotees of *Kultur* in case they should lose the war.[135] Beneath the prevailing apathy in the days that followed lay also the profound emotions associated with the realization of failure, defeat, the dangers of enemy terrorism, and, above all, the deep disillusionment with the system that had once gained such profound devotion.

9. The End Comes— With Death and Terror

Germany had suffered grievously in the years before 1945. The hail of bombs had taken a heavy toll on its cities. Buildings, homes, and people had shared the consequences of an unparalleled destruction. Hundreds of thousands of soldiers had lost their lives in Hitler's ill-managed campaigns. Millions of people at home had suffered from privation, homesickness, and unhappiness in unfamiliar places of refuge as well as from the tangible fears of the raids and the vague dread of an uncertain future.

But these trials and privations faded into insignificance before the horrors of the closing months of World War II. The bombs continued to fall—every bomb might save the lives of some of the Allied soldiers moving into German territory. The pressure of the Nazi regime upon its civilian population and its soldiers increased as defeat became ever more inevitable. Soldiers, weary of the battle front, and civilians who had lost their confidence in failed leadership became victims of the numerous "special courts" that dispensed death sentences without trial and without mercy. Orders from above directed the destruction of bridges, transportation facilities, and industry in areas about to be occupied by the enemy— orders that would have crippled Germany's capacity for existence for years to come. And, above all, the great flight of Germans in from the east brought the death of thousands in the "treks" through snow and bitter cold, the death of women, children, and old men seeking to escape the merciless vengeance of the oncoming Soviet troops.

The "home front," in this last period of the war, frequently became the battle front as well. As the enemy troops approached from the east and the west, the regime sought to enroll old men, young boys, and even some women into the military, to hold armament makers at their work benches until evacuation was no longer possible, and to dictate the sacrifice of thousands in senseless and futile last-ditch stands against overwhelming enemy forces.

More and more in these last days of the war, personal factors dictated the course of events in each of the different parts of Germany. Some party bureaucrats continued to carry on their assigned tasks as though the tide of events had not turned against them. Others were desperately aware of the coming denouement. In some areas, foolish resistance efforts were made. In others, government agents helped to mitigate the problems of a peaceful transition to enemy authority. There was no longer one home front; there were many. And the relationship between the fading authority of the central government and the local authority of Gauleiters, Kreisleiters, and Ortsgruppenleiters became ever more tenuous. As a consequence, an ordered and systematic accounting of these days is impossible. But some impression of the confusion and uncertainty and of the variations of popular reactions may be attempted.

The month of January saw the beginning of major catastrophes on the eastern front. German-occupied territory began to shrink precipitately. Soviet armed forces, with an enormous advantage of men and materiel (infantry 7.7 to 1; artillery 6.9 to 1; mortars 10.2 to 1; tanks 4.7 to 1), drove ruthlessly deep into southern Poland, pierced Hungary all the way to Budapest, and began to place extreme pressure on German armies along the Baltic Sea and in East Prussia. Field Marshal Heinz Guderian sought vainly to warn Hitler of the desperate danger confronting German forces in the east and to obtain Hitler's consent for redisposition of forces to strengthen the defense of German territory. But Hitler maintained his stubborn insistence that every square meter of territory held by Germany had to be defended to the death.[1] His attitude was shared by the Gauleiters in the east, such as Arthur Greiser, the Gauleiter in the Warthegau, the extended version of the East Prussian area that had gathered in Polish territory occupied by Germany after the defeat of Poland. Greiser's childlike faith in the Führer's promises that the troops would hold fast against the Russians led him to deny evacuation to the Germans in his Gau. By January 18, the Germans settled in former Polish territories began to reap the harvest of Soviet revenge as Soviet troops pushed into the eastern boundaries of the Warthegau, burning the villages they overran, killing the male inhabitants, and engaging in the orgies of mass rape that were to mark their progress westward. Before them fled the Germans who had made themselves masters in these new territories, pushing their few possessions on little sleds or, if they were lucky, loading themselves and their small remnants of household goods on horse-drawn wagons or sleds.[2] Their numbers mounted rapidly. By the end of the war, two million of these refugees had fled the scourge of Soviet forces.[3]

Before the end of January, Soviet troops had reached Elbing in the former East Prussian state, had virtually cut off the city of Königsberg from land connections to the west, and had reached the Oder River and the Upper Silesian industrial area. On the last day of the month, a Soviet submarine sank a ship of the Nazi Kraft durch Freude organization, the *Wilhelm Gustloff*, loaded with five thousand refugees.[4] But other thousands were perishing in the snows and bitter cold of the icy winter as they sought to escape the Soviet fury. Gauleiter Greiser, shaken by his view of the refugees and the lack of weapons on the part of the Volkssturm, lost all energy for a stern resistance. Moving to a delayed order for evacuation and announcing that he would use the Volkssturm only to protect the refugees, Greiser decided to give up Posen without a last-ditch defense. Hitler recalled Greiser from his post. The former Gauleiter escaped punishment only because Himmler persuaded Hitler that Posen was not a German city.[5] But shortly afterward, Posen became one of Hitler's "fortresses" to be defended to the end. With several changes of command, it suffered and bled until February 23 when the weary and wounded surrendered to the Soviet armies. As at Stalingrad, plans of the commanders to break out to the west were rejected by Hitler and Himmler. And with surrender, many Germans who had not left the city when Greiser did or who had been caught there on their treks westward became the victims of Polish vengeance against their former masters and of the Soviet mass rapes and executions. Stories of the time alleged the use of flame throwers to dispose of "excess baggage" behind their lines.[6]

Posen was only one of a series of "fortress" cities to be sacrificed by Hitler in these closing months of the war. By the end of January, Königsberg had been placed under General Otto Lasch, who held his "fortress" until April 8. Yet his efforts were not strong enough to satisfy Hitler, who condemned the general and his family to death for his surrender. Breslau became the Nazis' shining example of how a fortress city should be defended. Gauleiter Karl Hanke earned accolades for his "heroism." Surrounded on all sides by Russian forces by February 15, the city's defenders, with an armament of two hundred cannons and seven tanks, held out against bitter Soviet attacks until May 6. But its defense was only made possible by a brutal expulsion on January 20 of all its nonessential men, women, and children. In bitter cold and snow, without means of transportation, reliable guides, or any planned assistance along the way, these unfortunate victims had been ordered out of the city in the late hours of the afternoon. Dragging themselves through the icy winds of winter, the women sought to shelter their babies by pressing them close to their bodies. Those infants who were suckling refused the milk from the cold breasts of their mothers, who often froze their breasts in this vain effort to feed the young. Babes and young children who died from exposure could not be buried—their half-mad mothers grubbed a shallow grave in the snow of the streets and left the bodies behind.[7]

From all the threatened areas of the East the civilians streamed westward like a gigantic swarm of ants, without plan or tangible objective. In deserted railroad stations they often waited endlessly for trains that never came or, if fortunate, mounted in massive numbers on one of the last trains moving westward, coming into old Germany with only the clothes on their backs and perhaps a few meager remnants of their earlier possessions. Many escaped by boat across the Baltic with fabulous numbers leaving through the last few ports open to the north. Before Kolberg was taken on March 18, 68,000 of its inhabitants had been evacuated by sea. The Hela peninsula north of Königsberg saw 96,000 wounded, 81,000 refugees, and 66,000 soldiers evacuated in the first half of April. In these evacuations, there was suffering and death as well as the relief at escaping the dangers of Soviet occupation. One story told of a mother who saw her children safely aboard an evacuation ship but was unable to join them. Pitifully, she followed their route to eastern Germany and hunted desperately for her lost children. Finally, she adopted a doll left unguarded in a doll's baby buggy as her lost child. The soul of her infant, "Jutta," she maintained, spoke to her from behind the painted lips and rouged cheeks of the doll.[8]

Perhaps nowhere else was the blatant evil of the Nazi regime more strikingly underscored than in these grim events on Germany's east. Evacuations began too late, were initiated without preparation and planning, and sent thousands of helpless people on foot through snow and sub-zero cold without aid by the party on their journeys or places prepared for their reception. Too frequently, evacuees were overtaken by the Soviet forces and had to redeem with their suffering the earlier evils of the Nazi regime—its brutality against Soviet prisoners of war and against much of the civilian population during their victorious drive into Soviet territory. Some of the refugees were overrun by Soviet tanks. Some were herded together into houses that were then set afire. Many of the men were shot as they made futile efforts to protect wives or daughters from mass rapes. Young girls and old women were repeatedly violated by Soviet soldiers. One witness told of a woman of sixty who had died from the mistreatment of repeated rape but whose body still awaited a line of Soviet soldiers. Another told of a youth of fourteen who became mentally deranged after being forced to hold the flashlight for the continued raping of his mother by Soviet soldiers.[9]

As early as January 21, Soviet forces had established themselves on the Oder River north and south of Breslau. From that point on, the threat to all of eastern Germany, to the industrial sections of Upper Silesia, the farmlands of Silesia and Pomerania, and the capital itself, Berlin, was clear. Only major changes of strategy could have moderated the suffering of the closing months of the war. The military leaders sought these with all the persuasiveness they could summon. Their proposals included the transfer southward into East Prussia of German armies in the Courland area along the Baltic, the reduction of defensive strength in the west by the withdrawal of as much as possible of the tank forces wasted in the Ardennes offensive, and the permission for armed forces trapped in untenable positions in the east to break through to defensive positions in the Reich, a move that would probably have allowed an accompanying withdrawal of civilian refugees seeking to flee the Soviet forces. All of these were negated by Hitler and the coterie of Nazi leaders, Bormann, Goebbels, and Himmler, still talking of a final victory.

In justice, it must be admitted that these actions might well have led to an earlier end of the war. Before the middle of January, even the official army reports made it clear that the Ardennes offensive (the Battle of the Bulge) had reached an unsuccessful end.[10] At the same time, the terrible struggle in the Hürtgen forest near Aachen was finally reaching its end. But not until February 23 did the Western Allies launch a major offensive out of a hard-won bridgehead over the Rur River. In March, the American forces under Patton began to clear the western bank of the Rhine of German forces.

Cologne fell on March 7 and on that same day, the Allied forces captured the Ludendorff bridge at Remagen and began to invest the eastern side of the Rhine. Through the remainder of March, more German cities fell to Allied forces—Koblenz, Worms, Wesel, Germersheim, Ludwigshafen, Darmstadt, Hanau, Aschaffenburg, Mannheim, and Frankfurt. But the industrial Ruhr, defended by German forces surrounded in a "kettle," held out until the middle of April. The real industrial centers of Germany were in the west and some imagined hope of victory could be preserved as long as they remained German.

The air raids continued, taking added toll of the refineries and synthetic oil production and visiting additional death and destruction on German cities. Strafing attacks were directed not only against military targets but also against civilians on city streets and the farmers in their fields along with their trucks, their tractors, and their cattle. Goebbels was incensed at the indiscriminate use of the "Jabos," the dive bombers, and condoned moves for the lynching of their pilots if they were shot down.[11]

Berlin received its proper attention, but Hitler was safe beneath twenty-five feet of reinforced concrete. The raid of February 3, however, removed from the scene Roland Freisler, the virulent and detestable head of the Nazis' People's Court. This punishment from heaven saved lives and earned the deep satisfaction of those who had condemned his methods and feared his vengeance.[12]

In an incompletely explained and, from a postwar standpoint, badly conceived aberration of Western strategy, Dresden, deep in eastern Germany, received a Hamburg-like attack on the night of February 13/14, 1945. That Dresden became an Allied bombing target was not in itself surprising. As the range of bombing from England came to cover most of eastern Germany, a number of locations there were designated prime bombing targets. Brüx, to the south of Dresden in the area of the Sudetenland, Böhlen, Ruhland, and Pölitz to the north and west, were high on the list of cities chosen for attention because of refining or synthetic oil plants. For all of these, Dresden was a potential secondary target.[13] Contrary to later East German and Soviet claims, Stalin welcomed bombing activities in eastern Germany, especially against Berlin. On a number of occasions, he called for an intensification of bombing there.[14] Dresden was the scene of intensive railroad movements and these were everywhere acceptable targets for Allied attacks. And as Soviet forces attacked German cities, their air forces wreaked destruction upon them in support of the ground forces.

But the plans for the Dresden raids clearly indicate the intention to cause the maximum overall damage possible. Carried out by experienced British air crews against a city poorly prepared for air raids and taking place while considerable numbers of refugees from the eastern areas were passing through its streets and railroad stations, the Allied attacks were to create, for the second time during the European war, a vision of the apocalypse. Dresden and Hamburg were paired as the European equivalents of the later bombings of Hiroshima and Nagasaki.

Two attacks were carried out during the night of February 13/14. The first came at 22:03 (10:03) and lasted somewhat over half an hour. Seven hundred seventy-two British Lancasters, the planes that carried the heaviest bombing loads of the European war, dumped their deadly cargoes on the most closely built-up portions of Dresden. Three hours later, at 1:28, a second fleet of 550 Lancasters found so much destruction and fire that they dispersed their efforts over less-damaged portions of the city.[15] On Ash Wednesday, February 14, a large fleet of American Flying Fortresses and Liberators found much of the city already turning to ashes but added 1,800 explosive bombs and 136,800 fire sticks to spread the existing damage. A day later, a second flight of American bombers, partially hampered by serious cloud cover over the city, dropped another 3,700 explosive bombs onto the ravaged city.[16]

It is obvious that these raids, like most of those carried out in western Germany, were designed to create the maximum general destruction and to kill as many civilians as possible. Even the American raids, professedly aimed at the railroad marshalling yards, employed far too many incendiaries and not enough explosive bombs to comport with the primacy of railroad targets.[17] Just as the second British raid came at a propitious time to prevent effective fire-fighting efforts in the city, so the noon raid of the American planes added another dimension to the terror aspect of Allied planning. The "overkill" character of the Allied bombing in the later days of the war is underscored in the tragedy of Dresden.

But the raids also underscored the shortcomings of Nazi administration. Martin Mutschmann, the Gauleiter of Saxony, bore a heavy burden of guilt for the loss of life involved. Although his own villa was provided with an elaborate steel and concrete bunker, he had left his capital city woefully short of air-raid shelters for its inhabitants. In a controversy with the local SS agent concerning the adequacy of air-raid shelters, Mutschmann had been able to silence his critic. As a consequence, much of the population of Dresden was without any reasonable refuge at the time of the city's greatest travail.[18] Moreover, the withdrawal of antiaircraft defenses to protect oil-refining areas had left the city with almost no antiaircraft defenses. The Allied planes confronted no dangerous fire at all during the raids.[19] And in the aftermath, although German reports kept raising the estimate of the number of people killed during the raids, the major emphasis, as it had earlier been in the west, was on the loss of cultural treasures. These, Mutschmann later told a Soviet interrogator, could never be replaced. It was obvious that he felt the loss of people was less significant.[20]

The consequences of the raids, like those of the Hamburg catastrophe of July 1943, were embroidered with false exaggerations. The streets of Dresden, these accounts claimed, had been so full of the fleeing lines of refugees that fire and air-raid relief efforts had been imperiled by the bodies crowded together on the streets. Estimates that the city had doubled its population because of refugees and that hundreds of thousands had perished as a consequence were broadly accepted during the war and long thereafter. Only relatively recently has a German account returned some measure of reasonableness to the estimate of results. Götz Bergander's book on the Dresden raids provides a sober accounting of the subject. The estimates of one half million or more refugees in Dresden cannot be substantiated. In this city, virtually untouched by the war until the time of the bombings, it was impossible that one half million refugees could have been accommodated; there was no stoppage of traffic on its roads and no enormous camps of refugees on the green areas of the city. At the most, several hundred thousand refugees may have been in Dresden.

Moreover, the constant increase in estimates of the number killed in the raids does not comport with the facts. Official reports justify an estimate of between 25,000 and 35,000 killed. Figures that rose to 100,000 to 200,000 killed lost touch with reality. If accurate, whole divisions of men would have been required to pull the bodies from the cellars and stack them up in open places. The streets were never blocked by bodies and stories of burning dead bodies in cellars are contravened by the simple fact that lack of oxygen in these enclosed areas would have made it impossible to carry out such supposed operations. A lack of trucks and fuel to supply them made impossible efforts to carry hundreds of thousands of bodies out of the city.[21] Legends of fighter planes strafing refugees, firefighters, and civilians during and after the raids are contradicted by specific records showing that these planes were employed elsewhere, not in Dresden.[22]

Although Bergander's study somewhat moderates the degree of tragedy associated with the Dresden raids, it does not wipe away the vision of endless blocks of gutted houses, in which only a few days previously there had been teeming life, of new thousands of refugees added to the flood of human misery moving across eastern Germany, and of Allied planners who could now add another mark to the list of German cities "virtually destroyed" and new figures to the estimates of those killed or made homeless by the raids.[23] The personalized brutality of Soviet forces against German civilians had its counterpart in the impersonal brutality of American and British forces raining death and suffering on an unseen foe far beneath them.

In these days of dissolution, of the progressive march of enemy forces into the interior of the Reich, of intensive bombing from the air and bombardment from hostile cannons, of the ever-increasing harshness of a dying regime, the primal urge for survival, for *Überleben*, dominated the minds of most Germans. There was in this quest for survival a kind of drive for personal victory—whatever might happen, one had surmounted the difficulties of war and emerged as one of a lucky elite.

For most civilians, this was, of course, an unthinking, unplanned, unreasoned reaction. For the literate minority, these were days of self-questioning, of broad and resolute reading of old favorites and of new, sometimes enemy, authors. As Joachim Günther shuttled back and forth across Germany, Hungary, and even the Balkans on a German hospital train, he read novels and classics and pondered on their relationship to the existing current of events.[24] Gottfried Benn debated literature and life in his letters to F.W. Oelze. Although painfully aware of the coming tragedy, Benn thought he had made the proper choice of remaining in Germany. One could not deal with the downfall of a people by producing "literary arabesques" in Miami.[25] Horst Lange continued his constant reading, including American and French literature, while giving strong expression to his deep disillusionment in his diary notes.[26] Fritz Hartung read Jack London stories, and Mathilde Wolff-Mönckeberg found her solace in Goethe's poetry.[27]

Music still offered relief for many Germans although the emergency decrees and air-raid conditions reduced this form of entertainment. Wilhelm Furtwängler still conducted the Berlin symphony orchestra in concerts in the Admirals' Palace in Berlin. When the lights went out because of a cut-off in the electric supply, both he and the audience waited an hour until service was restored to complete the concert.[28] Erna Berger sang and her accompanist continued to play when an electric outage interrupted her concert.[29] Even government officials recognized the need of calm and recommended that quieter, less complex music be played on the radio during the nighttime hours.[30] And the most popular movie of the period featured "Music in Salzburg."[31]

Religion also served as an opiate. For Catholics, the mass provided a relief from the strain of war.[32] Protestant church services also gained larger than usual audiences. Willy Beer attended services in the church of anti-Nazi Martin Niemöller in Dahlem and found there a sense of calm—the audience, which filled the church to overflowing, sang and listened and prayed with no sense of panic.[33]

But for most Germans, these were days filled with endless work— for those in the factories the long hours of the Jäger program, if the factory where they worked could still get raw materials and power supplies. And with all of the growing problems of food, transportation, and fuel, daily life tended to become a dull routine, overshadowed by the horror stories attached to the increasingly oppressive nature of the regime. During these last months of the war, there was, indeed, a kind of undeclared civil war in Germany, a one-sided war conducted by the Nazi party and its agents in the government, in the army, and in the police not only against open opposition but also against the weary, the irresolute, the weak-minded, and the incautious, who might in some way, by action or word, reveal their apprehension that the war was already lost and that what remained was charade and illusion.

The party's distrust of the military leadership had grown ever stronger since the failed assassination effort of July 20, 1944. Efforts to effectuate the establishment of National Socialist leadership officers throughout the army had been only partially successful. An officer named Ruder, who headed a "special staff" of the party chancellery devoted to this matter, reported in November 1944 that 50 percent of the professional officers lacked the "spiritual capacity" that would fit them for effective leadership.[34] A new directive of March 13, 1945, added emphasis to their role. The task of these "warlike, fanatical National Socialists" was "the political activation and fanaticization" of their troops.[35] That it was possible to find such persons is reflected in the diary of Wilhelm Prüller, who was enrolled in training sessions for the post of National Socialist leadership officer in Bamberg in February and March of 1945. In his mind, even in these closing months of the war, there was no doubt of the party leadership and he maintained his true devotion to the cause of resistance.[36]

On the eastern front, Bormann reported in another one of his directives, some officers had shown themselves incapable of fanaticizing their soldiers. They were, he declared, more interested in eating well and consorting with foreign whores.[37] The only military figure who received a favorable comment in Bormann's reports was Admiral Karl Dönitz, whose messages to his followers were as fanatical in tone as those of Bormann himself. "We must," wrote Dönitz, "slap the face of every German who wavers in his loyalty. His motives are fear, cowardice, and weakness. We are the strong and the true." And Dönitz cited as an example to follow the American report that indicated that at Iwo Jima 14,000 Japanese had been found dead and only 180 became captives.[38]

The party chancellery dispatched ever more numerous advisements to party leaders, reminding them of their role as the exemplification of steadfastness and loyalty. "Now it is up to us to show that we are worthy of a Führer [such as] Adolf Hitler."[39] Party leaders, Bormann directed, were to hold their offices to the last minute and then join the soldiers in their final defense actions.[40] Party leaders were not to send their wives out of threatened frontier areas until general evacuation was ordered and were not to seek safety for themselves or their families in the Salzburg or Berchtesgaden areas.[41] (His own wife had long been there in relative security.) It was better, Bormann declared, "to die among the ruins" than to retreat.[42]

All possible efforts were to be made to counteract sabotage or a collapse of the will to resistance. The most significant measure for preserving authority was the use of Standgerichte, standing courts with emergency powers to hand out rapid judgments, including the death penalty. "The Führer," Bormann wrote, "expects every Gauleiter to see that these courts combat divisiveness, cowardice, and defeatism with death judgments: Whoever is not ready to fight for his people, but rather fails them in their most serious hour, is not worthy of living further and must be turned over to the hangman."[43] Political crimes were defined in a later memorandum as high treason, treason by malicious lies, misuse of the pulpit, defamation of the state, criticism of the federal or state governments, attacks on the uniforms of the party or state, misuse of the radio, and others.[44]

Obviously, the role of the Standgerichte was a broad one. A judge in Bamberg reported that the prisons there were filled and there were no local means of executing the death penalty— those condemned had to be sent to Frankfurt am Main for execution.[45] In Berlin, the arrests began to mount although the worst days were yet to come. The growing unrest of the Nazi *Bonzen*, said one observer, was beginning to show. Unjust arrests gained the comment that "that sort of thing only makes it worse. Hate and anger are increased."[46] But hate and anger normally remained unspoken and hidden. As one Berlin observer remarked, "There are no signs of unrest to be remarked on the part of the people, no shouting or crying, no tears. Complete apathy. No one has the strength to stir up an uproar against Hitler and the total state, let alone against the war and fate."[47]

But under the surface there were signs of deep opposition. A report of the chief of the security police listed critical statements from "thoroughly quiet and proper countrymen who are by no means to be counted in opposition circles."[48] Perhaps the most eloquent outward sign of opposition was silence. The dedication of a war memorial in Markt-Schellenberg was attended by units of the regular army and the Volkssturm as well as the civilian population. When the army leader at the close of his speech raised a "Sieg Heil" to the Führer, the only response was silence.[49] The stage was set for the conflict between those who knew the end was near and those who would not admit this even to themselves. Already in the west inhabitants of little damaged cities were seeking to prevent fanatical Nazis from using them as bastions for a last-ditch stand against the enemy.

Meantime, the party still sought resolutely to carry out its daily administrative responsibilities. The establishment of the Volkssturm had created a desperate need for uniforms for them. Once again a great *Volksopfer* (popular sacrifice) drive was initiated to fill this need and also to provide some source of clothing for those thousands of evacuees who had fled from the east with nothing but the clothing on their backs. Once again, this was initiated as if, even after five and one half years of minimum clothing rations, every person's closet was still filled with excess items of apparel. The call anticipated that the party would use its "often demonstrated strength" to thrust aside all opposition in order to achieve the seemingly impossible goal of collecting 100,000 tons of textile materials. Old clothing, uniforms for eating and drinking clubs, streetcar personnel uniforms, and so forth were suggested. Carnival outfits could be contributed—there would be no need after the war to dress as tame Englishmen, American gangsters, or red Bolsheviks. Dress outfits and old party uniforms were suggested—some of the party faithful were not unhappy at this last stage of the war to rid themselves of at least part of their party accoutrements. Unused camping materials—tents, blankets, cooking wear, shovels, steel helmets were collected.[50] There was a sort of textile tax, one observer said, in the party's method of collecting these sacrifices.[51]

Yet there was a recognition on the part of the party leaders that they had garnered serious criticism throughout Germany because of their failure to plan the evacuation of the eastern territories and their failure to provide sufficient aid to those refugees on their treks back into the Reich.[52] New directives ordered punishment for soldiers who plundered deserted homes in the east, ordered every effort to provide help for refugees in reaching safe destinations, required party agents to store the family goods of these refugees, and directed party leaders to offer rides when possible to these refugees and to show concern for their fate.[53]

The plight of these refugees added to the existing strain within Germany on food supplies and other materials. Von Rheden, the staff leader of the Reich Office for the Country People, had begun to signal the coming of a food emergency late in 1944. In the midst of the paper shortage of the late war period, he still found it necessary to spend thirty pages detailing the internal regulations of his office and a seventy-six-page memorandum on the working lines of his office for 1945.[54] In this last document, Rheden proclaimed: "We stand today in the most difficult battle for the Reich with which fate has ever confronted the German farmer." With ideology held high, the document stressed Hitler's designation of Germany as a *Bauernreich* (farmer's state), a state undergirded by its "countryfolk character." The full realization of the living principles of this ideology required farmers to get together to join their souls in this great struggle. The writer suggested a *Dorfstube*, a simply furnished room in each village where farmers could get together to sing, spin, recite poetry, work together to produce simple things needed for daily life, and, above all, to realize their place within "the wellsprings of the nation." They also were expected to join in a great battle to increase production. In all this, the farmer was to realize that he was now the inheritor of the role of the independent farmers of the Peasant War and of the struggles against Napoleon.

Ridiculous as this document was, and not because of it but because of their own hardy and determined spirit, the German farmers did hold out until the end. But this was a time of many difficulties. The government forbade special food distributions within the different Gaus even though transport was often unavailable to carry food from one Gau to another.[55] Wood for the farmers' gas generator tractors was often stolen for firewood, and repair of the tractors was extremely difficult.[56] Although government controls on fodder looked to the reduction of the raising of cattle and other animals, farmers hesitated to slaughter them because of their increasing distrust of the value of money.[57] In March, the government required drastic cuts in the raising of poultry. Geese, ducks, turkeys, and guinea fowls were completely forbidden and the number of chickens was regulated. Rabbit holdings were also to be reduced and goats' milk and goat meat were to be counted into the rationing system.[58]

By this time, with the Western Allies beginning to move into German territory, the ration periods were being extended, sugar removed from the rations, the bread ration cut in half, and special instructions issued for the use of rye when grinding and transport were not available.[59] And once again came the desperate suggestion that Germany's forest areas still offered the needed salad, vegetables, fruits, and mushrooms.[60] There were also references to land still unused and an encouragement to establish vegetable gardens near the large cities—victory gardens on the eve of defeat.[61] The rationing agencies did, however, seek to meet the population's food needs in their areas until those territories were occupied by the enemy. Sometimes bean soup had to be substituted for the already unpopular ersatz coffee in the morning and a dry marmalade of rye meal, sugar, and dried fruit replaced the real thing. Mathilde Wolff-Mönckeberg described how she and her husband picked out five small potatoes apiece per day and found bread so scarce that she couldn't even provide a sandwich for her husband to help him survive a long night's watch for air raids.[62] And Willy Beer reported that in Berlin ordinary people could no longer buy restaurant meals and even the black market had frozen up.[63] Even Goebbels complained in his diary on March 1: "We shall very soon be forced to reduce by 35-50% the ration of the most important items, fat and bread. As a result they will fall below the tolerable minimum subsistence level. . . . To all of our people's miseries that of hunger will now be added."[64] But in spite of the widespread complaints of the wartime period, Germans looking back to those last few days of the war found things at least adequate in comparison with the really fundamental shortages that came during the occupation period.[65]

The German farmer had, indeed, made valiant efforts to feed his fellow countrymen. Everywhere across Germany, as enemy troops moved in, they found the German famers busily cultivating the fields and preparing to try to feed the millions of refugees from the east now within the shrunken homeland. Undoubtedly the enemy troops themselves often plundered food stores kept by individuals or by government agencies. But so did the civilian population, and last-minute special food distributions prior to enemy occupation had reduced available rations. The shortage of fertilizer, of seeds, of seedling potatoes, the final destruction of transportation facilities, the return to their homes of hundreds of thousands of foreign farm workers, the exhaustion of the last reserves of farm horses, and the degeneration of farm tractors all contributed to the food shortages that came in 1946 and 1947. Germany was to reap a harvest of hunger because of the Nazi system itself and its last stubborn struggle against catastrophe.[66]

The sense of malaise occasioned by growing food shortages was accentuated by serious shortages of coal for heating and electricity for lighting and cooking. Homes began to be cold and dank without available heat and a wintry chill descended upon trains carrying refugees and evacuees. Even an army hospital train, as it moved about Germany, provided heat only for the cars occupied by the medical officers and train personnel.[67] In Berlin and many other large cities, electricity was often available only a few hours a day. Sometimes one had to do family cooking late at night or during air raids in order to use this rationed power resource.[68] Electric hot-water heaters and washing machines could no longer be used. Even the radio became subject to rationed employment. And streetcar stops were reduced to save current.[69] Transportation resources shrank due to coal shortages and the strafing of trains and railroad yards. The authorities sought to concert means for repair of damaged tracks, and other facilities, to distribute railroad cars for safer storage until they could be used again, and to hold train usage to vital purposes.[70]

Because of paper shortages, most newspapers shrank to a two-page miniscule size, and in some places they ceased publication.[71] Party directives required that all reports now be typed single-spaced.[72] Communications became increasingly difficult. Normal mail communications between some Gaus and the central office in Berlin were interrupted by air raids or enemy action.[73] The postal ministry sought to limit the long- distance calls of the Gauleiters to ten minutes and those of the Kreisleiters to three, but the party headquarters obtained the restoration of unlimited usage for the Gauleiters and of six minutes for the Kreisleiters.[74] Yet the exigencies of war sometimes generated strange needs. In January, a request came from Lippstadt for 24,720 sanitary napkins for the Luftwaffe female helpers stationed there.[75] In Württemberg, orders were issued for the seizure of all wicker suplies available.[76]

In the west, the war during this period centered largely on German territory. Very early, the party became aware that it would not be able to kindle in the West the spirit of resistance that it regarded as appropriate. Reports that the population of Mühlhausen had received entering French troops with flowers aroused the ire of party leaders.[77] Stories of the chocolate bars given out to children by American soldiers circulated widely. In most cases, it was not that people were really glad to see an enemy occupation. It was just that they were so dispirited, so weary of war, that an end seemed a relief. "Alles vorüber, alles vorbei"—everything over, everything done with"—was the motto, the end of a failed regime, a lost war; not a joyful occasion but an end of the past, the beginning of coping with the future.

In this end phase of the war, Hitler issued his most criminal order, an order that would have condemned hundreds of thousands of his fellow Germans to additional, unnecessary, and futile suffering and death. This was his so-called "Nero decree," which sought to require the Germans to follow the scorched-earth example that the Russians had set when the Germans invaded in 1941. But the Russians had had hundreds of miles to withdraw from the front lines, to pull back and preserve their industry. In a Germany threatened on both sides and overfilled with refugees, this was not possible. Hitler's decree, issued on March 19, directed that all military, transportation, communications, industrial, and supply locations in territories threatened by the enemy were to be destroyed before they could become useful to the enemy.[78] The population was to be evacuated from areas in the west threatened by the enemy "in a general southeasterly direction." Although Bormann's repetition of this order on March 23 spoke of recognizing the difficulty of carrying it out and suggested that it must be solved with the necessary understanding and improvization, a second order speaking of cutting off the enemy from the rear and destroying him was less sympathetic. "The enemy," Bormann wrote, "must be brought in the next few days to realize that he has intruded into a hinterland filled with a fanatical will to resist." And Bormann added a phrase that had been part of Hitler's original decision: "Any concern for the [civilian] population can play no role under present circumstances."[79] Bormann added on Easter day, April 1, 1945, another directive emphasizing a fight to the end against enslavement and ordering all Gauleiters, Kreisleiters, and other political leaders to fight or fall within their areas of responsibility. They must, he said, lift high their hearts and overcome all weakness.[80] On April 13, he was still demanding that operative bridges be destroyed to prevent their use by the enemy although he suggested that other facilities (not specified—factories, and so on) should not be destroyed since lost areas might be recovered.[81]

As a consequence of these orders, the end of the war in western Germany carried with it notes of unnecessary tragedy. Everywhere the Allied troops moved, the German population was confronted with this last challenge of the Nazi regime. Should they remain true to the Führer, true to their sense of patriotism, true to soldierly oaths, and defend to the end their farms, their little villages, and their great cities, whereby peaceful rural areas would suffer the kind of destruction previously reserved for the cities, and cities would lose the last remaining places of residence as well as gas, electricity, and water connections, or should they give in without resistance? Railroad bridges provided the only remaining means of provisioning many cities. Starvation, cold, and exposure would be the price paid by hundreds of thousands for following the Führer's orders. Common sense and compassion for the people dictated disobedience. A fanatical sense of obedience and honor voted for faithfulness until death.

As a result of this dilemma the fate of each village, town, and city on the western front varied according to the character and beliefs of a few men. The pages of Goebbel's "last entries" in his diary highlight his bitter disappointment with the course of events on the western front. Through the early days of March 1945, he voiced his surprise at the relatively good reception accorded the Anglo-American forces. He was shocked at the ineptitude of the Volkssturm in the west. He bewailed the lack of resistance in Cologne, which was, he felt, well qualified to defend itself. He believed that the people were still Nazi at heart but too easily submissive to the enemy in the areas that were overrun. When he heard that people in the west were helping deserters, he asked himself, "What else is to be expected of them when they receive the enemy with white flags?"[82] And as events revealed the rapid movement of Allied troops into western Germany, Goebbels continued to complain of the lack of morale of both the people and the troops. He blamed the long air war, its continued destruction, and the late use of fighter bombers for the loss of morale. On March 21, he noted that 353,000 had been killed and 457,000 wounded by the air raids up to December, 1944 and commented that "this is a war within a war, sometimes more frightful than the war at the front." Soon, however, he was also talking of the failure of the western Gauleiters to provide adequate leadership. Some, he felt, were too old to act forcefully, others just too weak. And he found no examples of either Gauleiters or Kreisleiters leading their people in battle and losing their lives for the cause. As for the people themselves, those in the west, he felt, had lived too close to the French and, like them, had been weakened by excessive civilization. The Germans in the east were tougher since they were closer to the more primitive Poles and Russians.[83] Goebbels was particularly angered by the reception extended to the Americans by the Germans. The heavily fortified area of Trier fell into enemy hands without a fight. People in the Hanau-Frankfurt area met the Americans with white flags, and some of the women even demeaned themselves to welcome and embrace American soldiers. In Limburg, the Americans were received with demonstrations of joy and flowers. Kassel and Mannheim surrendered by telephone. Everywhere, Goebbels felt, the Germans were exchanging the swastika for the white flag and German women were even kissing American soldiers.[84]

But not everything went as smoothly and simply as Goebbels's diary suggests. The Gauleiter in Cologne demanded resistance and the city did not surrender until heavily battered by American artillery fire, that added new victims to those already killed in the air raids. Thirty-two thousand hard-core survivors emerged from the bunkers and cellars to greet the occupying forces. The remainder of the population had taken shelter outside the city. The Volkssturm here as elsewhere was poorly armed with old-style and hunting rifles and a few pieces of ammunition each. Both the Volkssturm and the police groups who sought to defend the city were older men—in their forties, fifties, and sixties—or children—of fourteen, fifteen, or sixteen years. No heavy weapons protected the city. To expect real resistance with such forces was nonsensical. The first American tanks were met with a gift of wine and a bouquet of tulips, and the givers of these gifts received cigars, cigarettes, and oranges in return. But some of the Americans also paid for their entry into the city with their lives. And all of the city's bridges were destroyed before it was taken.[85]

The surrender of Stuttgart without resistance was managed by its chief burgomaster, Dr. Karl Strölin, who brought together a group of the city's leaders determined to save it from a senseless and useless destruction. All of them worked in the face of deadly peril, since the local Gauleiter, Wilhelm Murr, sought to carry out the orders for last-ditch resistance. A line of fortifications about the city had been built. Calls for the establishment of "Werewolf" resistance had been issued, looking to implement Goebbels's concept of defense to the end and revenge against defeatists. The food storage areas had been opened to provide extra supplies for the inhabitants in case of siege. And Murr had labeled Stuttgart a communications center that had to be defended, refusing efforts to declare it an open city or a hospital city in order to receive special consideration. Strölin's letter to the commander of the enemy forces nearing the city, offering its surrender without resistance, was in Nazi eyes treason, and orders for his arrest were issued but by accident never delivered. Similar efforts to surrender the neighboring city of Heilbronn had brought the execution of the acting burgomaster there, his wife, his brother-in-law, a pastor of the city, and eleven other persons. The newspapers of Stuttgart still called for resistance, although the party leaders fled. Efforts to prevent the destruction of the thirteen bridges around the city were only partially successful. Only the one carrying the city's water lines remained.

In the end, it was the general commanding the troops of the area who was most responsible for the city's salvation. As he withdrew his forces without resistance, Strölin remained and carried out the surrender of the city without heavy bombardment by the entering French forces. Not without some personal danger as well as some mishandling by the French, Strölin's cohorts were able to carry out peacefully the establishment of a German administration to carry out the directives of the French occupying forces.[86]

Surrender efforts in Bavaria combined disorganized local protests against the contemplated defense of towns and cities with the most significant organized opposition to Nazism existing in this last stage of the war. Many of the efforts to prevent a dead-end defense of the towns were shattered by the actions of SS and police agencies. In Neuhoff a.d. Zenn, the Volkssturm was ordered to build tank barriers of logs. Many of them refused to obey the order and the barriers made by those who followed orders were sawed up by the women of the town on the night of April 6 and hauled away for firewood. The police searched out culprits and erected gallows to frighten the people. Eight Volkssturm men were arrested along with the burgomaster. Even the Ortsgruppenleiter (the party leader of the town) was arrested but released soon after. Three days later, not only those already arrested but all of the Volkssturm men, twenty-eight in all, were taken to prison in Nuremberg. The leader was condemned to death but the entry of the Americans into Nuremberg prevented his execution. The others were marched towards Dachau but also freed by the Americans on April 25.[87]

In Bad Windesheim, the women of the town engaged in open mutiny against the move to make it part of a defensive area for the retreat of a German division. They joined together in a crowd of two hundred to three hundred, with many children present, to try to get the major commanding the troops there to withdraw his forces. In an effort to calm the people, the major had a sergeant from the town who had won the knight's cross speak to them—but to no avail. The next day, the major chose one of the women to designate as the leader of the demonstration and held her on display before the city hall for one and one half hours. But the Gestapo in Nuremberg learned of the incident and sent two SS men, one of whom shot the woman before the eyes of her husband—once in the neck, once in the left eye, and once in the mouth.[88]

A similar mass demonstration took place in Regensburg on April 23. About eight hundred to one thousand men gathered before the office of the Kreisleiter. Random arrests were made. The cathedral pastor of Regensburg, Dr. Johann Maier, tried to act as moderator for both sides but was arrested and executed along with one of the leaders of the demonstration.[89] Erlangen came under fire on April 15. Houses and a hospital were damaged. Recognizing the weakness of his defense forces, the lieutenant colonel charged with its defense gave in to the chief burgomaster's plea for surrender. But the colonel's efforts to obtain a cease-fire from his own troops ran into difficulty in one area where the defenders wanted to continue resistance. During his attempt to silence this small group of fanatics, the colonel was killed by "friendly" fire, but the city was not heavily damaged.[90]

The hoisting of a white flag could still bring death. A miller near Seenheim was caught in the middle between Americans and fanatical Nazis. On April 11, two American soldiers came to the mill. Expecting American occupation, the miller put a white flag on his mill. The following day, a German major came by and saw the white flag. The miller was shot and his mill and surrounding buildings burned to the ground [91] In Ansbach, an anti-Nazi student was hung before the city hall for his efforts to get the people to fight the "Nazi executioners" and raise the white flag. The military commander who ordered and personally carried out the execution instructed that the body be left for display until it "stank." A few hours later, American troops occupied the city.[92]

Most of the efforts to secure surrender without resistance were motivated by the desire to avoid further destruction rather than by political considerations. But in Bavaria, a significant anti-Nazi movement existed, which displayed itself in this period under the name of "the Bavarian Freedom Movement" (Freiheitsaktion Bayern—FAB).[93] This movement had roots going back into the prewar period. By 1942, it had gained as its leader a Captain Dr. Rupprecht Gerngross, the chief of an interpreters' company in the Munich area. Gerngross recruited for his unit a number of opponents of the Nazi regime and began to plan for a *Putsch*. But the presence of strong SS units nearby meant that any chance for a successful coup would have to wait until enemy forces were at hand. Armored troops in Freising joined the plans and, on April 24, were able to reach American forces with the promise of the surrender of Freising without resistance—thus opening the road to Munich.

Meanwhile, action in Munich moved, on April 27 and 28, to open revolt. Plotters obtained control of the radio stations, of the two major newspaper buildings, and of the town hall. They also reached the state governor of Bavaria, General Ritter von Epp, and sought to persuade him to join the movement. A radio appeal to the people announced that "the yoke of the Nazis in Munich" had been broken and called for the eradication of both Nazism and militarism, "which has driven Germany into many senseless wars and especially in its Prussian form has brought unspeakable suffering to all Germans."[94] But Munich's Gauleiter, Paul Giesler, had determined on stubborn defense of "the capital city of the [Nazi] movement." And his determination was backed by the new military commander of the city, Major General Rudolf Hübner, who had formerly headed one of the standing courts dealing with deserters. Opposition groups were expelled from the radio stations and a general search for those involved in the uprising set into motion. Some of those involved were captured and executed. Family relatives of Gerngross were arrested, but the Volkssturm men who guarded them could not be brought to shoot them and they were released. A group of men who had worn white arm bands or hoisted white flags were allowed to volunteer for special duty, but once armed and released, they took off for safety in the Gauleiter's own automobile. The Gauleiter himself, having restored order, soon also fled the city, and in spite of all the mock heroics of the Nazi defenders, the city was occupied by American forces with minimum difficulties.[95]

In Augsburg, a similar "freedom action" was more successful. Although the local commander here, too, refused until the last minute to take official responsibility for surrender, the opposition movement took control of most of the city, removed tank barriers, hoisted white flags, and made contact with incoming American forces. The military commander was taken prisoner, and the city suffered no last-minute artillery barrages.[96] But in Penzberg, Altötting, Götting, Burghausen, and Landshut persons involved with the Bavarian Freedom Movement were executed in the last days before these towns were occupied by American troops.[97] And in Nuremberg, Gauleiter Karl Holz sought with "fanaticism" to defend the city that had been the scene of the great party rallies and the seat of power of the archpriest of anti-Semitism, Julius Streicher. With overtired and undertrained troops, harassed by the enemy dive bombers, which strafed everything that moved on the streets, and overwhelmed by the great numbers of American tanks and the constant shelling of American artillery, Holz found that fanaticism could not prevent defeat.[98]

In the Ruhr "kettle," resistance also proceeded to the bitter end. In spite of air raids, the old men and women still clung to their "home" city of Duisburg, surviving the last of 299 air raids on March 29, 1945. Some found the dangers of artillery bombardment more frightening. One Duisburger riding his bicycle across town on March 30 suddenly found himself in an area where forty artillery shells fell in rapid order and counted himself lucky to have survived. There were still children in the city. Perhaps the parents knew that they would be safer than in evacuated schools. The SS took nine school boys from one of the evacuated schools to serve in the Volkssturm and they all perished in the fighting. Even as Essen was taken by the enemy, the town's police president ordered eight more of the prisoners in the city jail executed on April 9, 1945. Two days later, he left the city, and three days later the city surrendered. In the woods nearby, General Model, the commander of the troops in the "kettle," considered his own fate. "In ancient times," he said, "a defeated commander took poison." On April 21, 1945, he shot himself in a wooded area outside the city.[99]

Hamburg had the unique distinction of being the only city in which a Nazi Gauleiter was the key to an arranged surrender. The Gauleiter, Karl Kaufmann, had one of the better reputations attributed to Nazi leaders. In the aftermath of the July catastrophe of 1943, he had appealed for Hitler to visit the city to see the effects of the bombings. He had warned Albert Speer about the growing antagonism against him on the part of other Gauleiters. He also had the reputation of caring for his people. Now, in the late spring of 1945, as British forces moved closer to his old Hansa city, he was desperately anxious to spare it the destruction that would cramp its livelihood far into the future. Although his decision in this respect had been taken earlier, it was strengthened by the serious destruction visited upon the neighboring city of Bremen late in April when *its* Gauleiter sought to follow the orders for last-ditch defense. Kaufmann was fortunate in having in the area a sympathetic military commander, Major General Alwin Wolz, who was able to prevent the destruction of the city's port facilities and aided in contacting the commander of the approaching English forces. But, as was usual in these cases, affairs had to be handled with care in view of the danger of outside intrusion on the part of higher authorities. Admiral Dönitz was anxious that Hamburg's port facilities be kept available as long as possible, since it was one of the last places to which refugees from the east could be brought. It was not, therefore, until the death of Hitler and the transfer of authority to the succession government of Dönitz that Kaufmann could proclaim that the city would not be defended. Kaufmann said that he took this action to protect women and children from "senseless and irresponsible destruction" and declared that "this war is a national catastrophe for us and a misfortune for Europe. May all those who bear the responsibility for it recognize this fact."[100]

In Berlin, however, the Gauleiter was the truest Nazi of them all, Joseph Goebbels, and there was no one to speak against the destruction of the city and to show concern for the lives of its men, women, and children. The city had continued to suffer grievously from air attacks. Ursula von Kardorff, who had already seen so many raids, wrote that the one that came on February 3 was the worst of all. This one brought her, at long last, to the decision to leave the city.[101] Ruth Andreas-Friedrich told of a friend who spent nine hours after this raid shut up in a cellar with three stories of rubble burying it and twenty-six women crying from fear.[102] And Willy Beer described the mammoth, panic-filled drive of great masses of people into the huge above-ground air-raid bunker at the zoo on March 1. With the shelter virtually full, another thousand or fifteen hundred were still struggling to enter. He and others passed the thousands of mothers with babies sitting below to join others clinging to the stairs of the bunker. The great structure had become, he said, a monument not to Germany's greatness as previous monuments had been, but a monument to fear.[103]

The city remained filled with refugees from the east. Westbound trains departed from the city only at night, but many people left on foot or in private cars. Somehow, black-market contacts could provide gasoline, and private cars still moved through the streets in considerable numbers.[104] Refugees tended to criticize the regime more openly—they had lost everything and were no longer so afraid.[105] Other opposition groups looked forward to the victory of the enemy and sang of Hitler's coming fate to the tune of "Lili Marlene":

> There on the lamp posts before the Party Chancellery
> Hang our party bosses.
> The Führer is among them.
> There we want to stand together,
> We want to see our Führer
> As once on the first of May.[106]

But no one sang such songs or made nasty comments too openly. As noted above, Leo Findahl was most impressed during these days with the sense of "complete apathy."[107]

The quiet was enforced by stern police measures. As the end came closer, police action became more and more severe. Police raids nabbed and executed deserters. By April 4, Ruth Andreas-Friedrich was writing that there were "forty fanatics in every district of the city" seeking to give Hitler a chance to live a week longer.[108] But from the middle of April on, things worsened. Hitler was determined to make everyone accept his optimistic orders for a dead-end defense of Berlin. On April 16, he issued the slogan "Berlin remains German. Vienna will again become German, and Europe will never become Russian."[109] This was followed by the order that every commander who failed to obey his orders would lose his life within five hours.[110] On April 23, Hitler placed the command of the city in the hands of Lieutenant Colonel Bärenfänger, a twenty-seven-year-old front-line infantry officer holding the highest order of the Iron Cross. By noon of that same day, commando squads of the SS, the SD, the SA, and political leaders occupied all of Berlin, arresting all who failed to show the proper defensive spirit and decorating the street lamps with new bodies of political opponents.[111]

This is not the place to repeat the oft-told stories of the confusion in Hitler's bunker, of the comings and goings of officers and political leaders still paying homage to the figure of a political leader who had lost touch with reality, who issued orders that were nonsensical but were carried out by men who knew they were nonsensical. No one can really judge how many Berliners, or how many Germans, for that matter, were still heartened by Goebbels's description of Hitler on

his birthday—"He is the heart of the resistance against the destruction of the world. He is Germany's bravest heart and the most
glowing will of our people."[112] But it is obvious that many still
believed in the Führer's leadership. Old men with potbellies and
young, beardless boys died on the barricades around the city. Faith
died hard. But Hitler's death brought no tears to the eyes of his
followers. With the demigod gone, each man sought his own
salvation.

Berlin suffered the pangs of hell during its last days. Flame
throwers destroyed houses in which there was resistance—women
and children paid the price along with the soldiers. The invaders
encountered harsh resistance. Civilians joined in the fighting—a
Silesian woman who had escaped Soviet atrocities in the east fought
fanatically with the antitank *Panzerfäuste* abandoned by others. The
toll of Russian lives lost in the city was heavy and Soviet vengeance
harsh. Again the women, old and young, were greeted with the call
of "Komm, Frau" and subjected to multiple rape. And harshness and
severity of treatment threatened all with death or forced labor. Those
who had escaped the city and the armies still fighting sought, in the
closing days of the war, to move westward to surrender into British
or American hands. Both military and civilians found the utmost
reluctance on the part of the British and American authorities to
allow either military forces or civilians to enter their assigned areas
of Germany. In the long run, the soldiers came off better than the
civilians. The armies of Generals Walter Wenck and Walter von
Tippelskirch got across the Elbe into American or British territories.
Some civilians managed to accompany the troops, hiding in their
mass movements, but many, faced by unsympathetic Western commanders, found the last escape routes from Soviet forces closed.[113]

In the last stages of the fighting, many party functionaries
donned army uniforms to fight or civilian clothes to flee. Pictures of
Hitler, swastikas, copies of *Mein Kampf*, and party uniforms were
dumped into ruined buildings or consigned to the fire.[114] The once
proud Hoheitsträger, the Nazi bearers of authority, the "golden
pheasants," as their fellow Germans called them, sought flight or
committed suicide. They and lesser Nazis were to be brought to
justice by the victors for their role in the institutions and activities of
the Nazi regime. Eight of the Gauleiters committed suicide. Six of
them were executed or killed. Seven were tried and given sentences
but survived.[115] Some party functionaries found their way into
Switzerland and from there to Italy and often to South America.[116]

The Nazi dream of conquest had perished. Any idealism attached to this dream had been stained with the blood of the Jews killed in the concentration camps and the death of millions of soldiers in the war it had waged—enemy soldiers, German soldiers, the soldiers of Germany's allies. Nazism had brought upon the German people the greatest travail a nation ever confronted. The survival of those who lived through all these trials was not the product of Nazi organization or Nazi propaganda. It was the product of the stubborn will to survive of a hardy people that now turned to the task of creating a new state and a new government.

Forty Years Later— In Retrospect

The travail of the Germans was not over with the end of the fighting. Those who had "survived" confronted new trials. Many who had trekked across snow and ice faced the permanent loss of homes in the territory beyond the eastern boundary at the Oder-Western Neisse line. Those who had once appropriated land belonging to the Poles found territory they had considered German in the possession of the Poles. Inside the Oder-Neisse boundary, a third of the remaining territory was governed by German Communists under the direction of the Soviet Union. In that area, one harsh dictatorship had been replaced by another. The administration of the rest of Germany, although less exploitative than that of the Soviet zone, was strict and severe. Industries considered potentially martial were stripped of their factories. Food supplies suffered from the extravagant distributions and plundering raids of the last portion of the war and from the diversion eastward of Soviet-zone food supplies by the occupying authority. Hunger in 1946 and 1947 was more extreme than it had been in the Nazi years. But human feelings in the western zones of Germany healed quickly. Nonfraternization rules passed quickly into oblivion. Allied military leaders sought to learn from the Germans the experiences they had in dealing with the Russians. Soon, perhaps too soon, the quest for de-Nazification lost its drive and the sense of partnership against communism took precedence over the memories of war.

What remains now of all this after forty years? The recent celebrations of "D-Day" have raised this question for many survivors. This book has set forth some of the answers. It has pictured a nation gripped by a regime that held a people captive, caught up in a propaganda that justified the murder of approximately six million of Europe's Jewish population. Could anything be sadder than the picture of those Jews, who considered themselves Germans, being expelled from the body politic of the nation to which they belonged and carried brutally to places of shameless execution? And did their German countrymen weep for the death of their compatriots? Forty years later—weep for the Jews!

But the Allied fighting involved death by fire and explosion from the skies, cities ravaged by firestorms that turned homes into charred ashes and living beings into cinders. This was a war from above in which nameless pilots and bombardiers visited death upon thousands of nameless victims below. He that provokes the dragon perishes in his fiery breath—but forty years later, weep for those who perished in agony in the air raids!

Hitler in his grandiose plans for domination sent his armies deep into Soviet territories. Millions of Russians perished in the fighting. Millions of others suffered in the ignominy and hardships of German captivity. Forty years later—weep for the Soviet soldiers and civilians who were victims of the Nazi armies!

Millions of other eastern peoples—Poles, Ukrainians, Rumanians, Hungarians—were forced from their homes to work in German factories and on German farms, treated as if they were on a level with the cattle in the fields. Some perished, some survived the hardships of this involuntary servitude. Forty years later—weep for those who suffered modern slavery!

Millions of German soldiers, led into adventures beyond the capability of their nation, perished on the battle fronts. Some died seeking victory at Stalingrad. Some died in an effort to slow the drive of the enemy towards their homeland. Some died in the senseless effort to hold fortresses that were not fortresses against enemies who outnumbered them and outmatched them in weapons and equipment. Were their last futile efforts to stem the tide of defeat glorious or insane? Should these German soldiers be honored for their loyalty and dedication to a regime that did not deserve either loyalty or dedication? Whatever the answer, after forty years—weep for the German soldiers whose lives were so recklessly lost!

And the hundreds of thousands of Germans in the east who lost their lives fleeing from the wrath of Soviet soldiers—what of them?

What of the thousands of German women subjected to gang rape by Soviet soldiers? What of the others seeking without success to shelter their children from the bitter winds of icy winter? Were they all guilty of Hitler's sins because they had lived in Hitler's Germany? After forty years—weep for those who perished or suffered escaping the brutality of another regime!

And Allied soldiers, too—those who lost their lives on the beaches of Normandy, in the battles towards and into Germany. Certainly, we still weep for them forty years later. If they were alive, they too would weep for those for whom we have asked tears to be shed.

Perhaps this was the last war in which, for Americans, the concepts of right and wrong, good and evil, were so clearly underscored. Forty years later, I still believe that I was distinctly on the side of the angels in World War II. But forty years later, I also feel that there were elements of self-satisfaction in my thinking that led me to ignore some aspects of the events in which I took part. Fustel de Coulanges once said that all men are the resume, the summary, and the epitome of all previous history. World War II left us all with a residue of suffering that we have not yet fully comprehended.

Notes

1. The End of Optimism

1. Story of the thousand-bomber attack largely based on Josef Fischer, *Köln* '39—'45. *Der Leidensweg einer Stadt. Miterlebt v . . .* , pp. 88-89.

2. Ibid., pp. 98-99; Erich Hampe, *Der zivile Luftschutz im Zweiten Weltkrieg, Dokumentation und Erfahrungsberichte,* pp. 121-22.

3. See my article, "The Allied Bombing of Germany, 1942-1945, and the German Response: Dilemmas of Judgment," *German Studies Review,* 5, no. 3 (Oct. 1982): 325-37.

4. Ibid., pp. 329-30, largely based on Sir Charles Webster and Noble Frankland, *The Strategic Air Offensive against Germany, 1939-1945,* 1, pp. 99, 322-24.

5. Hampe, *Der zivile Luftschutz,* p. 125.

6. U.S. Group CC, Infantry Division, Statistical Office of German Industries, Reichsgruppe Industrie, Bundesarchiv, Koblenz.

7. Hampe, *Der zivile Luftschutz,* p. 125.

8. Ibid., p. 122.

9. See Andreas Hillgruber and Gerhard Hümmelchen, *Chronik des Zweiten Weltkrieges. Kalendarium militärischer und politischer Ereignisse,* pp. 131-55.

10. Among the recent studies of significance in respect to the role of the bureaucracy are Peter Hüttenberger, *Die Gauleiter. Studie zum Wandel des Machtgefüges in der NSDAP;* Peter Diehl-Thiele, *Partei und Staat im Dritten Reich. Untersuchungen zum Verhältnis von NSDAP und allgemeiner innerer Staatsverwaltung, 1933-1945.*

11. On the role of Bormann see the recent study by Jochen von Lang and Claus Sibyll, *Der Sekretär: Martin Bormann, der Mann der Hitler beherrschte* (in English, *Bormann, the Man Who Manipulated Hitler*). I will be citing records of Bormann's office from two sets of microfilmed materials: T 81, records of the National Socialist German Labor Party, and T 580, records of the National Socialist German Labor Party

from the Berlin Documents Center. There are some materials in each file not available in the other. Bormann's "Confidential Information" reports to the Gauleiters Kreisleiters, and Ortsgruppenleiters, will be cited as "VI" for *Vertrauliche Informationen*, his circulars as "Rs" for *Rundschreiben*, his directives as "An" for *Anordnungen*, and his publicity releases as "Bg" for *Bekanntgaben*, with appropriate record file and reel number. A small "g" in the number indicates that the material was secret (*geheim*); the letters "gRs" stand for "top secret" (*geheime Reichssache*).

12. Printed selections of these are found in Heinz Boberach, ed., *Meldungen aus dem Reich. Aus den geheimen Lageberichten des Sicherheitsdienstes der SS, 1939-1944*. Many local reports cited in this book are not found in Boberach.

13. The best collection of newspaper holdings of the National Socialist period are to be found in the Institut füer Zeitungsforschung in Dortmund.

14. Leonard Mosley, *The Reich Marshal: A Biography of Hermann Goering*, p. 289; cf. Hans Brunswig, *Feuersturm über Hamburg*, p. 28, citing *Hamburger Tageblatt*, Aug. 10, 1939.

15. See Anthony Verrier, *The Bomber Offensive*, p. 77.

16. Best told in David Irving, *The Rise and Fall of the Luftwaffe: The Life of Field Marshal Erhard Milch*.

17. Hampe, *Der zivile Luftschutz*, pp. 17ff., 28, 46-48, 291ff.

18. Fischer, *Köln*, p. 68.

19. Ibid., pp. 102-4; cf. similar report in respect to Rostock, Rs 27g, June 4, 1942, T 81, reel 2.

20. From Hillgruber, *Chronik*, pp. 131-55.

21. Bernhard Zittel, "Die Volksstimmung im Dritten Reich im Spiegel der Geheimberichte des Regierungspräsidenten von Schwaben," *Zeitschrift des Historischen Vereins für Schwaben* 66 (1972): 35.

22. See report of Oberlandesgerichtspräsident (President of the Higher Regional Court) for Bamberg, Jan. 5, 1942, Bundesarchiv, Koblenz, R 22, 3355. These reports from various regions are hereafter cited OLGP with city and appropriate archival designation.

23. From Stuttgart, July 15, 1941, cited in Paul Sauer, *Württemberg in der Zeit des Nationalsozialismus*, pp. 363-64.

24. Report of Generalstaatsanwalt (Prosecuting Attorney), Stuttgart, Dec. 1, 1941, cited in Sauer, *Württemberg*.

25. VI 17, 28, Jan. 7, 29, 1942, T 81, reel 2; Kurt Preis, *München unterm Hakenkreuz. Die Hauptstadt der Bewegung: Zwischen Pracht und Trümmern*, p. 181.

26. Rs 4, Feb. 5, 1942, T 81, reel 2.

27. Rs 5g, Feb. 8, 1942, ibid.

28. Rs 20, Feb. 13, 1942; cf. 3, Jan. 22, 1942, ibid.

29. VI 225, 249, Mar. 4, 7, 1942, ibid.

30. VI 278, Mar. 14, 1942, ibid.

31. OLGP, R 22, 3355, Bamberg, Apr. 30, 1942.

32. Ibid., Apr. 1, 1942.

33. Louis Lochner, ed., *The Goebbels Diaries, 1942-1943*, p. 64.

34. Ibid., pp. 223-25. It was at this point that the decision to replace the original leader of the Nazi Agricultural Organization, Richard Darré, by the more practical (bureaucratic) Herbert Backe was made.

35. Sauer, *Württemberg*, p. 366.

36. E.g. OLGP, R 22, 3355, Bamberg, Aug. 3, 1942.

37. VI 728, Jul. 28, 1942, T 81, reel 3.

38. VI 779, Aug. 25, 1942, ibid. Underscoring in original.

39. VI 730, Jul. 28, 1942, ibid.

40. VI 924, Oct. 23, 1942, ibid.

41. VI 811, Sept. 4, 1942, ibid.

42. VI 582, Jun. 22, 1942, T 81, reel 2.

43. OLGP, R 22, 3355, Bamberg, Feb. 28, 1942.

44. An A47, Aug. 4, 1942, T 81, reel 8.

45. Tobacco came under rationing on Feb. 1, 1942. See Sauer, Württemberg, p. 366. On newspapers VI 722, Jul. 28, 1942, T 81, reel 3.

46. VI 18, Jan. 3, 1942, T 81, reel 2.

47. Rs 25, Mar. 6 18g. Mar. 30, 1942, T 81, reel 2. For Speer's role, see his well-known Inside the Third Reich: Memoirs, pp. 189ff.

48. Hüttenberger, Die Gauleiter, pp. 184-85.

49. See, e.g., report of Gauwirtschaftsberater in Wien, Mar. 6, 1942, T 81, reel 5.

50. The publicity attached to the pilfering of supplies by a Nazi official of the public welfare service is reflected in OLGP, R 22, 3375, Kiel, Sept. 11, Oct. 2, 1942. The mild penalty that the man received aroused angry comment.

51. Rs 10, Jan. 24; 16, Jan. 29, 1942, T 81, reel 2; VI 774, Aug. 18, 1942, T 81, reel 3. For criticism of party leaders, see also OLGP, R 22, 3355, Bamberg, Feb. 2, 1942.

52. On Sauckel's work, see Edward Homze, Foreign Labor in Nazi Germany. The figures that follow are derived from pp. 129-53.

53. Newspapers were published in Berlin in the languages of Italian, Spanish, Dutch, Danish, Walloon, French, Slovak, Bulgarian, Croat, White Russian, Russian, Ukrainian, and West Ukrainian workers. See VI 815, Sept. 11, 1942.

54. See, e.g., Wolfgang Domarus, Nationalsozialismus, Krieg und Bevölkerung. Untersuchungen zur Lage, Volksstimmung und Struktur in Augsburg während des Dritten Reiches (Miscellanea Bavaria Monacensia. Dissertationen zur Bayerischen Landes- und Münchner Stadtgeschichte, ed. Karl Rosl and Michael Schattenhofer, no. 71), p. 158. Hereafter cited NS-Krieg.

55. The "Landwacht." An 15, Apr. 10, 1942, T 81, reel 8.

56. See, e.g., SD report from Bayreuth, Aug. 31, 1942, in Martin Broszat, Elke Fröhlich, and Felix Wiesemann, eds., Bayern in der NS-Zeit, vol. 1, Soziale Lage und Politisches Verhalten der Bevölkerung im Spiegel vertraulicher Berichte, pt. 7, p. 628.

57. SD, Bayreuth, July 20, 1942, ibid., p. 627.

58. OLGP, R 22, 3355, Bamberg, Oct. 6, 1942. Before Thierack's appointment, the same judge was reporting that people were saying, "Yes, haven't there already been enough people in Germany beheaded or shot?" Ibid., June 29, 1942.

59. The best general sources for the Wannsee Conference and its outcomes are Lucy Dawidowicz, The War Against the Jews, 1933-1945, pp. 182-86; Yehuda Bauer, A History of the Holocaust, pp. 200-207. The most notable study of the German reaction to these measures is found in Sarah Gordon, Hitler, Germans and the "Jewish Question," pp. 172-245.

60. See, e.g., Frances Henry, Victims and Neighbors. A Small Town in Nazi Germany Remembered, pp. 98-100; cf. Leonard Gross, The Last Jews in Berlin, pp. 57, 72, 118, 156, 193-94, 206-7.

61. Henry, Victims and Neighbors, pp. 119-20; Gordon, Hitler, Germans and the "Jewish Question," pp. 196-97.

62. VI 285, Mar. 14, 1942, T 81, reel 2; VI 653, July 10, 1942, T 81, reel 3; An 97, July 3, 1942, T 81, reel 8; VI 786, Aug. 25, 1942, T 81, reel 3.

63. See Ian Kershaw, Popular Opinion and Political Dissent in the Third Reich: Bavaria, 1933-1945, pp. 362-71.

64. Lochner, Goebbels Diaries, Mar. 26, 1942, p. 146.

65. SD, Berchtesgaden, Jan. 2, 1942, in Broszat, Bayern in der NS-Zeit, I, 7, p. 626; OLGP, R 22, 3355, Bamberg, Feb. 28, 1942; VI 231, Mar. 4, 1942, T 81, reel 2; VI 800, Sept. 1, 1942, T 81, reel 3.

66. Sauer, *Württemberg*, p. 409. But he says some executions continued until the end of the war.
67. Rs 44g, Aug. 26, 1942, T 81, reel 2.
68. VI 466, May 15, 1942, ibid.
69. VI 338, Mar. 28, 1942; 667, July 14, 1942, T 81, reel 3; 282, Mar. 14; 360, Apr. 1, 1942, T 81, reel 2.
70. Domarus, *NS-Krieg*, p. 110, fn. 4; Zittel, "Volksstimmung," p. 39.
71. SD report from Berchtesgaden, Sept. 28, 1942, in Broszat, *Bayern in der NS-Zeit*, 1, pt. 7, p. 630.

2. The Last (Somewhat) Merry Christmas

1. I have found little detailed information on the use of the guillotine. The only photograph I have seen showed the one used at Plötzensee prison, which indicated that the victim was executed lying down. Friedrich Reck-Malleczewen spoke of eleven being used in the Reich and the one in Munich getting out of order so that one had to be borrowed from Stuttgart. *Diary of a Man in Despair*, p. 176.
2. For the church opposition to the Nazis, see J.S. Conway, *The Nazi Persecution of the Churches, 1933-1945*; Benedicta Maria Kempner, *Priester vor Hitlers Tribunen*; also Terence Prittie, *Germans against Hitler*; Hans Rothfels, *The German Opposition to Hitler: An Assessment*.
3. Nadler, *Eine Stadt im Schatten Streichers. Bisher unveröffentlichte Tagebuchblätter, Dokumente, und Bilder vom Kriegsjahr 1943*, p. 54.
4. From Würzburg, Dec. 14, 1942, in Broszat, *Bayern in der NS-Zeit*, 1, pt. 7, pp. 631-32.
5. Von Kardorff, *Diary of a Nightmare: Berlin, 1942-1945*, p. 20.
6. Fischer, *Köln*, p. 121.
7. VI 756, Aug. 15; 841, Sept. 22, 1942, T 81, reel 3.
8. VI 1029, Dec. 18, 1942, ibid.
9. VI 912, Oct. 20, 1942, ibid.; cf. OLGP, R 22, 3373, Kiel, Dec. 15, 1942; SD Report, Linz, Jan. 4, 1943, T 81, reel 7; von Kardorff, *Nightmare*, p. 22.
10. Nadler, *Stadt im Schatten*, p. 54.
11. Fischer, *Köln*, p. 121.
12. See program, T 81, reel 65.
13. SD, Linz, Dec. 22, 1942, T 81, reel 7.
14. Ibid.
15. *Westfälische Landeszeitung*, Jan. 4, 9/10, 1943.
16. *Münchener Neueste Nachrichten*, Jan. 9/10, 1943.
17. Lochner, *Goebbels Diaries*, p. 258.
18. Ibid., p. 243.
19. Ulrich von Hassell, *The Von Hassell Diaries, 1939-1944: The Story of the Forces against Hitler inside Germany*, pp. 271-72.
20. Bg 16, Dec. 24, 1942, T 81, reel 8.
21. SD, Linz, Nov. 29, Dec. 27, 1942, Jan. 11, 25, 1943, T 81, reels 6, 7; SD, Friedberg, Jan. 4, 1943, in Broszat, *Bayern in der NS-Zeit*, 1, pt. 7, p. 632.
22. Warlimont, *Inside Hitler's Headquarters, 1943-45*, pp. 267ff.
23. SD, Würzburg, Dec. 14, 1942, in Broszat, *Bayern in der NS-Zeit*, 1, pt. 7, pp. 631-32.
24. Ibid., Jan. 12, 1943, p. 633.
25. Max Domarus, ed., *Hitler. Reden und Proklamationen, 1932-1945. Kommentiert von einem deutschen Zeitgenossen*, 2, pt. 2, pp. 1967-68.

26. Gottfried Benn, *Briefe an F.W. Oelze, 1932-1945*, p. 325, letter dated Dec. 4, 1942.

27. Horst Lange, *Tagebücher aus dem Zweiten Weltkrieg*, ed. and with comments by Hans Dieter Schäfer, p. 113, dated Dec. 11, 1942.

28. Von Kardorff, *Nightmare*, pp. 21-22, Dec. 28, 1942; p. 20, Dec. 26, 1942.

29. Jan. 2, 1943, in Broszat, *Bayern in der NS-Zeit*, 1, pt. 7, p. 574.

30. Nov. 30, 1942, T 81, reel 6.

31. Rs 2, Jan. 7, 1943, T 580, reel 15; SD, Linz, Jan. 25, 1943, T 81, reel 6.

32. VI 1018, Dec. 11, 1942, T 81, reel 3.

33. SD, Linz, Jan. 18, 1943, T 81, reel 7.

34. VI 905, Oct. 20, 1942, T 81, reel 3.

35. SD, Linz, Dec. 7, 1942, T 81, reel 6.

36. VI 974, Nov. 20, 1942, T 81, reel 3.

37. SD, Linz, Jan. 18, 1943, T 81, reel 7.

38. Zittel, "Volksstimmung," p. 49.

39. SD, Linz, Jan. 25, 1943, T 81, reel 7.

40. Ibid.

41. OLGP, R 22, 3366, Hamburg, Dec. 3, 1942.

42. Sauer, *Württemberg*, p. 365.

43. Zittel, "Volksstimmung," p. 45.

44. Ibid., p. 49.

45. Ibid.; SD, Linz, Jan. 25, 1943, T 81, reel 6.

46. Mathilde Wolff-Mönckeberg, *On the Other Side: To My Children from Germany, 1940-1945*, p. 61.

47. *Münchener Neueste Nachrichten*, Jan. 7, 1943.

48. Ibid.; cf. *Westfälische Landeszeitung*, Jan. 4, 1943.

49. See bills listed in Propaganda Ministry Treasury Reports, Jan. 13, 21, 1943, T 580, reel 573.

50. See his account in *Ich glaubte an Hitler*, pp. 269ff.

51. VI 985, Nov. 27, 1942, T 81, reel 3.

52. VI 996, Nov. 27, 1942, ibid.

53. SD, Bayreuth, Nov. 6, 1942, in Broszat, *Bayern in der NS-Zeit*, 1, pt. 7, p. 630.

54. OLGP, R 22, 3360, Danzig, Dec. 7, 1942; cf. VI 20, Jan. 22, 1943, T 81, reel 3.

55. Zittel, "Volksstimmung," p. 54.

56. Ibid.; Sauer, *Württemberg*, p. 419.

57. Schutzpolizei, Dienstabteilung, Schw. i. Bayr., T 580, reel 119.

58. See Regierungspräsident von Oberbayern, Nov. 9, 1942, von Ober- und Mittelfranken, Nov. 5, 1942, Kriegstagebuch des Rüstungskommandos, Nürnberg, Nov., 1942, cited in Ludwig Eiber, "Frauen in der Kriegsindustrie, Arbeitsbedingungen, Lebensumstände und Protestverhalten," in Broszat, *Bayern in der NS-Zeit*, vol. 3, *Herrschaft und Gesellschaft im Konflikt*, ed. Martin Broszat, Elke Fröhlich, and Anton Grossman, pt. B, pp. 620-21.

59. Jill Stephenson, *The Nazi Organisation of Women*; cf. Leila Rupp, *Mobilizing Women for War: German and American Propaganda, 1939-1945*, pp. 115-36. She notes that government pay for soldiers' wives in Germany was more generous than in the United States and that there was less financial incentive for them to work in the factories (pp. 169ff).

60. VI 897, Oct. 6, 1942, T 81, reel 3; Rs 185, Nov. 27, 1942, T 81, reel 1.

61. Homze, *Foreign Labor in Nazi Germany*, pp. 272-75.

62. Ibid., pp. 122-28.

63. See SD report, Friedberg, Nov. 16, 1942, in Broszat, *Bayern in der NS-Zeit*, 1, pt. 7, p. 631.

64. Cited in Ulrich von Hassell, *Diaries*, p. 341.

65. Andreas-Friedrich, *Der Schattenmann. Tagebuchzeichnungen, 1939-1945*, Oct. 11, Nov. 22, 1942, pp. 99, 102.

66. Reck-Malleczewen, *Diary of a Man in Despair*, Oct. 30, 1942, p. 161.

67. The autobiographical story of Inge Scholl, *Students against Tyranny: The Resistance of the White Rose, Munich, 1942-43*; cf. Richard Hanser, *A Noble Treason: The Revolt of the Munich Students against Hitler*.

68. Scholl, *Students*, p. 73.

69. Ibid., pp. 77-80.

70. Ibid., p. 85.

71. Ibid., p. 89.

72. Ibid.

73. Hanser, *A Noble Treason*, pp. 219-20.

74. Ibid., p. 221.

75. Zittel, "Volksstimmung," p. 50.

76. Von Hassell, *Diaries*, Nov. 26, 1942, p. 272.

77. Prittie, *Germans against Hitler*, p. 232.

78. See Ger von Roon, *German Resistance to Hitler: Count von Moltke and the Kreisau Circle*.

79. Bundeszentrale für politische Bildung, Bonn, *Germans against Hitler, July 20, 1944*, pp. 60-64; Rothfels, *The German Opposition to Hitler*, pp. 134-37.

80. Von Roon, *German Resistance*, pp. 133-38; Conway, *Nazi Persecution of the Churches*, p. 103.

81. Rs 198, Dec. 18, 1942, T 81, reel 1.

82. Werner Johé, *Die gleichgeschaltete Justiz. Organisation des Rechtswesens und Politisierung der Rechtssprechung, 1933-1945, dargestellt am Beispiel des Oberlandesgerichtsbezirks Hamburg*, pp. 55, 92.

83. Ibid., p. 92, fn. 21.

84. See Hubert Schorn, *Der Richter im Dritten Reich. Geschichte und Dokumente*, p. 57ff.

85. Cited in Johe, *Gleichgeschaltete Justiz*, pp. 54-55.

86. SD, Würzburg, Nov. 23, 1942, in Broszat, *Bayern in der NS-Zeit*, 1, pt. 7, p. 631.

87. Schorn, *Der Richter*, pp. 187-503.

88. Jan. 11, 1943, T 81, reel 7.

89. SD, Linz, Jan. 25, 1943, T 81, reel 6; Franz Josef Heyen, *Nationalsozialismus im Alltag. Quellen zur Geschichte des Nationalsozialismus vornehmlich im Raum Mainz-Koblenz-Trier*, pp. 305-7.

90. NSV, Baden, Gaupropagandawalter, Jan. 5, 1943, T 81, reel 40.

91. VI 917, Oct. 20, 1942, T 81, reel 3.

92. OLGP, R 22, 3366, Hamburg, Oct. 10, 1942.

93. Fischer, *Köln*, pp. 117-18.

94. Ibid., p. 120.

95. VI 1012, Dec. 11, 1942, T 81, reel 2.

96. VI 886, Oct. 15, 1942, ibid.

3. Stalingrad and All-Out Warfare

1. Alexander Werth, *Russia at War, 1941-1945*, p. 930.

2. Heinz Schröter, *Stalingrad*, pp. 43-44.

3. Clark, *Barbarossa*, p. 181.
4. Schröter, *Stalingrad*, p. 147.
5. Ibid., pp. 184-86; cf. Jay W. Baird, *The Mythical World of Nazi War Propaganda*, p. 187.
6. From C. Bertelsmann, ed., *Letzte Briefe aus Stalingrad*, p. 20.
7. Ibid., p. 23.
8. Ibid., p. 37.
9. Baird, *Mythical World*, pp. 176-82.
10. Schröter, *Stalingrad*, pp. 218, 247.
11. Von Kardorff, *Nightmare*, p. 28.
12. Nadler, *Stadt im Schatten*, pp. 64-66.
13. Baird, *Mythical World*, p. 182.
14. Nadler, *Stadt im Schatten*, p. 67.
15. Domarus, *Hitler*, 2, pt. 2, pp. 1975-76.
16. Baird, *Mythical World*, p. 185; cf. *Westfälische Landeszeitung*, Feb. 4, 1943.
17. Nadler, *Stadt im Schatten*, p. 73.
18. Ibid., p. 76.
19. Christabel Bielenberg, *The Past Is Myself*, p. 110.
20. Baird, *Mythical World*, p. 186; Domarus, *Hitler*, 2, pt. 2, pp. 1984-85.
21. See, e.g., SD, Linz, Jan. 30, 1943, T 81, reel 6; SD, Würzburg, Feb. 1, 1943, in Broszat, *Bayern in der NS-Zeit*, 1, pt. 7, p. 633.
22. SD, Linz, Feb. 22, 1943, T 81, reel 6.
23. Von Kardorff, *Nightmare*, p. 30.
24. SD, Linz, Feb. 8, 1943, T 81, reel 6; Nadler, *Stadt im Schatten*, p. 65; Domarus, *NS-Krieg*, p. 136.
25. SD, Linz, Feb. 20, 22, 1943, T 81, reel 6.
26. Melita Maschmann, *Account Rendered: A Dossier on My Former Self*, p. 146.
27. E.g., SD, Friedberg, Feb. 8, 1943, in Broszat, *Bayern in der NS-Zeit*, 1, pt. 7, pp. 633-34; cf. OLGP, R22, 3355, Bamberg, Mar. 29, 1943.
28. Benn, *Briefe*, Jan. 2, 1943, p. 327.
29. See report of Kreisschulungsamt in Schwabach, Feb. 18, 1943, in Broszat, *Bayern in der NS-Zeit*, 1, pt. 7, p. 575.
30. Report of Kreisschulungsamt in Weissenburg, Feb. 20, 1943, ibid.
31. SD, Friedberg, Feb. 8, 1943, ibid., pp. 633-34.
32. Robert E. Herzstein, *The War that Hitler Won: The Most Infamous Propaganda Campaign in History*, p. 83.
33. Speech summary from *Völkischer Beobachter*, Süddeutsche Ausgabe, Feb. 20, 1943, p. 3.
34. Von Kardorff, *Nightmare*, pp. 31-32.
35. John Toland, *Adolf Hitler*, p. 1005.
36. Rs 6 gRs., Jan. 25, 1943, T 580, reel 16.
37. Domarus, *Hitler*, 2, pt. 2, p. 1975.
38. VI 69, Feb. 10, 1943, T 81, reel 3.
39. Ibid.
40. Bg 5, Feb. 15, 1943, T 81, reel 8.
41. SD, Linz, Jan. 30, 1943, T 81, reel 6; Regierungspräsident, Oberbayern, Feb. 8, 1943, in Broszat, *Bayern in der NS-Zeit*, 3, pt. B, p. 622.
42. SD, Würzburg, Feb. 22, 1943, ibid. 1, pt. 7, pp. 634-35; SD, Linz, Feb. 20, 1943, T 81, reel 6.
43. Ibid., Feb. 22, 1943.
44. VI 69, Feb. 10, 1943, T 81, reel 3.

45. An A6, 7, 8, 9, 10, Feb. 10-19, 1943, T 81, reel 8; newspaper article, Apr. 12, 1943, cited in Hans-Georg von Studnitz, *While Berlin Burns: The Diary of. . .1943-1945*, pp. 57-58.

46. Kriegstagebuch des Rüstungskommandos, Nürnberg, Mar. 1943, in Broszat, *Bayern in der NS-Zeit*, 3, pt. B, pp. 624-25.

47. SD, Würzburg, Mar. 1, 1943, ibid., p. 623; OLGP, R22, 3364, Frankfurt a. M., Mar. 1943.

48. Kriegstagebuch des Rüstungskommandos, Augsburg, Mar. 7-13, 1943, in Broszat, *Bayern in der NS-Zeit*, 3, pt. B, p. 624.

49. Monthly report, Regierungspräsident von Ober- und Mittelfranken, Mar. 8, 1943, ibid., p. 623; SD, Würzburg, Apr., 1943, ibid., p. 625.

50. Lochner, *Goebbels Diaries*, Mar. 20, 1943, p. 312.

51. Monthly report, Regierungspräsident von Oberbayern, Apr. 8, 1943, in Broszat, *Bayern in der NS-Zeit*, 3, pt. B, p. 624; Kreisschulungsamt, Nürnberg, Apr. 18, 1943, ibid., p. 625; SD, Linz, Feb. 20, 1943, T 81, reel 6.

52. An 27, Apr. 9, 1943, T 81, reel 8.

53. Homze, *Foreign Labor*, pp. 147ff.

54. VI 49, Jan. 29, 1943, T 81, reel 3.

55. VI 182, Apr. 9, 1943, ibid.

56. VI 214, Apr. 27, 1943, ibid.

57. VI 209, Apr. 17, 1943, ibid.

58. VI 216, Apr. 17, 1943, ibid.

59. Kreisobmann to Kreisleiter, Mar. 11, 1943, ibid., reel 68.

60. VI 171, Mar. 29, 1943, reel 3.

61. Rs 21g, Apr. 10, 1943, T 580, reel 16.

62. Lagebericht, Muggenhof, Nürnberg, Apr. 11, 1943, in Eiber, "Frauen in der Kriegsindustrie," in Broszat, *Bayern in der NS-Zeit*, 3, pt. B, p. 625; VI 140 Mar. 19, 1943, T 81, reel 3; Rs 3g, Mar. 5, 1943, T 580, reel 15.

63. Report of Kreis School Officer, Nürnberg, Apr. 18, 1943, in Broszat, *Bayern in der NS-Zeit*, 1, pt. 7, p. 577.

64. OLGP, R22, 3374, Köln, Apr. 1, 1943.

65. Sauer, *Württemberg*, pp. 471-72.

66. An 17, Mar. 11, 1943, T 81, reel 1.

67. DAF, KdF, Gauvolksbildungswart, Strassburg, Apr. 5, 1943, T 81, reel 72.

68. Nadler, *Stadt im Schatten*, p. 80.

69. Lochner, *Goebbels Diaries*, Mar. 12, 13, 1943, pp. 295-97.

70. Speer, *Inside the Third Reich*, pp. 215-17.

71. SD, Friedberg, Apr. 9, 1943, in Broszat, *Bayern in der NS-Zeit*, 1, pt. 7, pp. 636-37.

72. SD, Berchtesgaden, Apr. 27, 1943, ibid., pp. 638-39; Kreisobmann, Strassburg, monthly report, Feb. 26, 1943, T 81, reel 71.

73. Wolff-Mönckeberg, *On the Other Side*, p. 62; Preis, *München unterm Hakenkreuz*, p. 203; Studnitz, *While Berlin Burns*, pp. 9-10.

74. Betriebsführer, Messerschmitt Works, Regensburg, Apr. 13, 1943, T 81, reel 65; Sauer, *Württemberg*, p. 373.

75. SD, Bad Kissingen, Apr. 22, 1943, in Broszat, *Bayern in der NS-Zeit*, 1, pt. 7, p. 637.

76. VI, 202, Apr. 13, 1943, T 81, reel 3.

77. SD, Linz, Jan. 25, 1943, T 81, reel 6.

78. Nadler, *Stadt im Schatten*, pp. 77-78.

79. NSDAP, Hauptamt VW, Amt Gesundheit, 25, Feb. 9, 1942, T 81, reel 39; VI 81, Feb. 16, 1943, T 81, reel 3.

80. VI 105, Feb. 26, 1943, T 81, reel 3.

81. Lochner, *Goebbels Diaries*, p. 278.
82. See memo, Himmler's personal staff chief, Apr. 6, 1943, T 580, reel 122.
83. SD, Halle, Mar. 23, 1943, T 580, reel 875; SD, Linz, Apr. 7, 9, 1943, T 81, reel 6.
84. VI 230, Apr. 22, 1943, T 81, reel 6.
85. SD, Linz, Mar. 29, 1943, T 81, reel 6.
86. NSDAP, Hauptamt für VW, Baden, Apr. 15, 1943, T 81, reel 39.
87. SD, Friedberg, Apr. 9, 1943, in Broszat, *Bayern in der NS-Zeit*, 1, pt. 7, p. 636.
88. Sigmund Graff, *Von S.M. zu N.S. Erinnerungen eines Bühnenautors (1900 bis 1945)*, p. 342.
89. *Münchener Neueste Nachrichten*, Apr. 12, 27, 1943.
90. Bg 6, Mar. 3, 1943, T 81, reel 8; Sauer, *Württemberg*, p. 473.
91. *Westfälische Landeszeitung*, Apr. 27, 1943.
92. Von Hassell, *Diaries*, p. 288.
93. Wolff-Mönckeberg, *On the Other Side*, p. 62.
94. Fischer, *Köln*, p. 121; Nadler, *Stadt im Schatten*, pp. 89-91.
95. Kuby, *Mein Krieg*, p. 308.
96. Rs 27, Feb. 12, 1943, T 580, reel 14; see comments in Nadler, *Stadt im Schatten*, pp. 78-79.
97. SD, Linz, Jan. 31, 1943, T 81, reel 6.
98. Verrier, *Bomber Offensive*, pp. 169-70.
99. Compiled from Hillgruber, *Chronik*.
100. OLGP, R22, 3363, Düsseldorf, Jul. 30, 1943.
101. Zittel "Volksstimmung," p. 180.
102. Wolff-Mönckeberg, *On the Other Side*, Mar. 2, 1943, p. 63.
103. Von Kardorff, *Nightmare*, pp. 35-36.
104. Lochner, *Goebbels Diaries*, Mar. 3, 1943, pp. 269-71.
105. Ibid., Mar. 9, pp. 280-83.
106. Ibid., Mar. 11, p. 293.
107. Hampe, *Der zivile Luftschutz*, p. 125.
108. Lochner, *Goebbels Diaries*, pp. 282, 293.
109. Ibid., pp. 323-24.
110. Nadler, *Stadt im Schatten*, pp. 93-100.
111. Kuby, *Mein Krieg*, pp. 322-23.
112. Andreas-Friedrich, *Der Schattenmann*, pp. 108-9.
113. Nadler, *Stadt im Schatten*, pp. 100-105.
114. SD, Linz, Mar. 13, 15, 1943, T 81, reel 6.
115. *Westfälische Landeszeitung*, Mar. 16, 1943.
116. *Münchener Neueste Nachrichten*, Mar. 11, 1943.
117. Nadler, *Stadt im Schatten*, pp. 106-8.
118. VI 124, Mar. 15, 1943, T 81, reel 3.
119. Rs 44, Mar. 18, 1943, T 580, reel 15.
120. Memo, Ahnenerbe Office, Berlin, Mar. 22, 1943, T 580, reel 122.
121. Rs 20g, Apr. 5, 1943, T 580, reel 16.
122. VI 188, Apr. 9, 1943, T 81, reel 3.
123. VI 222, 231, Apr. 22, 1943, ibid.
124. Lochner, *Goebbels Diaries*, Mar. 2, 1943, pp. 261-62; note of Hitler's approval, Mar. 9, p. 290; Mar. 20, p. 314.
125. Ibid., Mar. 6, 1943, p. 276; Mar. 11, p. 294.
126. Von Kardorff, *Nightmare*, pp. 34-35.
127. Andreas-Friedrich, *Schattenmann*, pp. 104-6.
128. Graff, *Von S.M. zu N.S*, pp. 333, 342.

129. Zittel, "Volksstimmung," pp. 46-47.
130. Domarus, Nationalsozialismus . . . in Augsburg, pp. 152-53.
131. VI 232, Apr. 22, 1943, T 81, reel 3.
132. An 16, Mar. 8, 1943, ibid., reel 3.
133. VI 185, Apr. 8, 1943, ibid., reel 3.
134. VI 152, Mar. 22, 1943, ibid.
135. Reck-Malleczewen Diary of a Man in Despair, pp. 175-78.
136. Domarus, Hitler, 2, pt. 2, p. 1966, fn. 29.
137. Friedrich Grimm, Mit offenem Visier. Aus den Lebenserinnerungen eines deutschen Rechtsanwalts, p. 218.
138. Domarus, Hitler, 2, pt. 2, p. 1966, fn. 29.
139. Reck-Malleczewen Diary of a Man in Despair, p. 177.
140. Hanser, Noble Treason, pp. 289-308.
141. The most complete discussion of the activities of these groups is found in Arno Klönne, "Jugendprotest und Jugendopposition. Von der HJ-Erziehung zum Cliquenwesen der Kriegszeit," Bayern in der NS-Zeit. Herrschaft und Gesellschaft im Konflikt, ed. Broszat et al., 4, pt. C, pp. 596ff. I have added to this study my own research in the records of the regional court presidents.
142. Klönne, "Jugendprotest," pp. 601-4.
143. OLGP, R 11, 3364, Frankfurt/M., Jan. 28, 1943.
144. Ibid.
145. Klönne, "Jugendprotest," p. 607.
146. OLGP, R 22, 3359, Celle, Feb. 1, 1943.
147. Report of school leader of Ortsgruppe Maxfeld near Nürnberg, Apr. 9, 1943, in Broszat, Bayern in der NS-Zeit, 1, pt. 7, p. 635.
148. Kreis school officer, Weissenburg, Apr. 21, 1943, ibid., p. 578.
149. Reichsgeschäftsführer, Ahnenerbe Office to Chief of Sicherheitspolizei, Feb. 1, 1943, T 580, reel 124.
150. SD, Linz, Feb. 1, 1943, T 81, reel 6.
151. Lochner, Goebbels Diaries, Mar. 2, 1943, pp. 268-69; Mar. 9, 1943, p. 285.
152. Rs 22g, Apr. 26, 1943, T 580, reel 16.
153. Dienststelle Rosenberg, Hauptamt Weltanschauliche Informationen, Mar., 1943, T 81, reel 41.
154. See Sauer, Württemberg, pp. 410-11.
155. Ibid.; cf. Heinz Höhne, The Order of the Death's Head: The Story of Hitler's S.S., pp. 179, 355, 490.
156. SD, Linz, Mar. 1, 1943, T 81, reel 6.
157. Sauer, Württemberg, p. 456.
158. An 5, Feb. 17, 1943, T 81, reel 8.
159. Sauer, Württemberg, p. 466.
160. Ibid., pp. 396-87; VI 53, Feb. 5, 1943; 17, Feb. 2, 1943, T 81, reels 3, 2, resp.
161. SD, Linz, Nov. 29, 1942, T 81, reel 6; Jan. 18, 1943, ibid., reel 7.
162. VI 1019, Dec. 18, 1942, T 81, reel 3.
163. Files of Propaganda Ministry Treasury, T 580, reel 583.
164. Rs 61, April 7, 1943, T 580, reel 15.
165. Westfälische Landeszeitung, Feb. 13/14, 1943.
166. SD, Würzburg, March 22, 1943, in Broszat, Bayern in der NS-Zeit, 1, pt. 7, pp. 635-36; cf. Domarus, Hitler, 2, pt. 2, p. 2001.
167. Ian Kershaw, Der Hitler Mythos. Volksstimmung und Propaganda im Dritten Reiche (Schriftenreihe der Vierteljahrshefte für Zeitgeschichte, Nr. 44), pp. 49ff.
168. Domarus, Hitler, 2, pt. 2, p. 1986.
169. Prittie, Germans against Hitler, pp. 196, 200.

4. Bombing Achieves Holocaust

1. Wolfgang Paul, *Der Heimatkrieg, 1939 bis 1945*, p. 152.
2. SD, Linz, May 21, 1943, T 81, reel 6; cf. Domarus, *Hitler*, 2, pt. 2, p. 2014. He was recalled Mar. 11; the news was released May 11.
3. Von Kardorff, *Nightmare*, Apr. 25, 1943, pp. 39-40.
4. SD, Bad Brückenau, June 4, 1943, in Broszat, *Bayern in der NS-Zeit*, 1 pt. 7, p. 642.
5. Ibid.
6. Rs 83, May 29, 1943, T 580, reel 16.
7. SD, Schwerin, July 20, 1943, T 81, reel 6: Hq, SD to Party Chancellery, July 22, 30, 1943.
8. Clark, *Barbarossa*, pp. 329-45.
9. From Hillgruber and Hümmelchen, *Chronik des Zweiten Weltkrieges*, pp. 169-74.
10. Fischer, *Köln*, pp. 122-24.
11. Ibid., p. 124.
12. Lochner, *Goebbels Diaries*, pp. 393, 397.
13. Ibid.
14. SD, Linz, June 29, 1943, T 81, reel 6.
15. SD, Linz, June 23, 1943; SD, Schwerin, June 29, 1943, ibid.
16. Ibid.
17. See Goebbels's comments in Lochner, *Goebbels Diaries*, pp. 382-84.
18. Hampe, *Der zivile Luftschutz*, p. 166.
19. Fischer, *Köln*, pp. 125-31.
20. The story that follows is based on ibid., pp. 135-37.
21. Benn, *Briefe*, July 30, 1943, p. 338.
22. Lange, *Tagebücher*, Aug. 3, 1943, p. 117.
23. Martin Middlebrook, *The Battle of Hamburg: Allied Bomber Forces Against a German City in 1943*, p. 95.
24. Paul, *Heimatkrieg*, pp. 67-68.
25. Middlebrook, *Battle of Hamburg*, p. 97.
26. Webster and Frankland, *Strategic Air Offensive*, 2, p. 190.
27. Ibid., pp. 150-51.
28. Hans Brunswig, *Feuersturm über Hamburg*, p. 195.
29. Ibid., pp. 12-13.
30. Ibid., pp. 166-89.
31. Ibid., p. 30.
32. Ibid., p. 173.
33. Ibid., pp. 180-82.
34. Ibid., p. 48.
35. Ibid., p. 172.
36. See map, ibid., pp. 198-99.
37. Ibid., pp. 199-206.
38. Ibid., pp. 208-10. Compare Middlebrook, *Battle of Hamburg*, pp. 175-233.
39. Brunswig, *Feuersturm*, pp. 206-8.
40. Ibid., p. 216.
41. With the later reduction of the number of casualties involved in the raid on Dresden late in the war, it appears that Hamburg still retains this dubious honor.
42. Ibid., pp. 211-20; Middlebrook, *Battle of Hamburg*, pp. 234-51; Gordon Musgrove, *Operation Gomorrah: The Hamburg Firestorm Raids*, pp. 65-82.
43. The description of meteorological conditions is from Brunswig, *Feuersturm*, pp. 264-73, and Musgrove, *Operation Gomorrah*, pp. 102-16.

44. See police reports cited in Percy Ernst Schramm, *Neun Generationen. Dreihundert Jahre deutscher "Kulturgeschichte" im Lichte der Schicksale einer Hamburger Bürgerfamilie (1648-1948),* 2, p. 572.
45. Reck-Malleczewen, *Diary of a Man in Despair,* pp. 188-89.
46. SD, Kitzingen, Aug. 30, 1943, in Broszat, *Bayern in der NS-Zeit,* 1 pt. 7, p. 649.
47. SD, Summary Report, Aug. 6, 1943, T 580, reel 875.
48. Schramm, *Neun Generationen,* 2, p. 573.
49. Brunswig, *Feuersturm,* pp. 244-46; circulation of rumor seen in von Kardorff, *Nighmare,* p. 51.
50. Middlebrook, *Battle of Hamburg,* pp. 146-47.
51. There are in later Sicherheitsdienst reports comments on anti-Nazi shouts and actions in Hamburg, but these seem to be scattered and unverified.
52. See map, Brunswig, *Feuersturm,* pp. 254-55.
53. Ibid., p. 256.
54. Ibid., pp. 257-58.
55. Ibid., pp. 261-63.
56. Fischer, *Köln,* pp. 162-66.
57. Nadler, *Stadt im Schatten,* pp. 170-74.
58. OLGP, R22, 3363, Düsseldorf, July 30, 1943.
59. Thomas M. Caffey, *Decision over Schweinfurt: The U.S. 8th Air Force Battle for Daylight Bombing,* pp. 259-81.
60. SD, Bad Neustadt, Aug. 20, 1943; SD, Friedberg, Aug. 22, 1943; SD, Bad Brückenau, Aug. 23, 1943; SD, Lohr, Aug. 23, 1943, in Broszat, *Bayern in der NS-Zeit,* 1 pt. 7, pp. 645-46.
61. SD, Schwerin, Aug. 3, 1943, T 580, reel 875.
62. Zofia Kruk, *The Taste of Fear: A Polish Childhood in Germany, 1939-1946,* p. 108.
63. SD, Schwerin, Aug. 24, 1943, T 580, reel 875, reveals that the people of the area knew the nature of experimentation at Peenemünde.
64. Andreas-Friedrich, *Der Schattenmann,* p. 118.
65. VI 438, 443, July 28, 1943, T 81, reel 4.
66. Wolff-Mönckeberg, *On the Other Side,* pp. 67-68.
67. For views of these matters see SD, Schwerin, Aug. 24, 1943, T 580, reel 875; OLGP, R22, 3358, Breslau, July 31, 1943.
68. OLGP, R22, 3363, Düsseldorf, July 30, 1943; 3374, Köln, July 30, 1943.
69. OLGP, R22, 3379, München, Aug. 21, 1943; 3358, Breslau, July 31, 1943; SD, Berchtesgaden, Aug. 30, 1943, in Broszat, *Bayern in der NS-Zeit,* 1, pt. 7, p. 648; Regierungspräsident von Oberbayern, Aug. 9, 1943, ibid., 3, pt. B, p. 629.
70. Bielenberg, *The Past Is Myself,* pp. 120ff.
71. Kuby, *Mein Krieg,* pp. 342ff.
72. Nadler, *Stadt im Schatten,* pp. 158-59; Kreis School Office, Fürth, Aug. 31, 1943, in Broszat, *Bayern in der NS-Zeit,* 1, pt. 7, p. 582.
73. See reports, SD, Schwerin, Aug. 3, 1943, T 580, reel 875; SD, Halle, July 15, 1943, T 81, reel 6; OLGP, R22, 3385, Rostock, Jul. 31, 1943.
74. OLGP, R22, 3364, Frankfurt a. M., July 27, 1943.
75. SD, Kitzingen, Aug. 30, 1943, in Broszat, *Bayern in der NS-Zeit,* 1, pt. 7, p. 649; cf. SD, Linz, July 6, 1943; SD, Hq., July 9, 1943, T 81, reel 6.
76. SD, Hq, July 15, 1943, ibid.; SD, Bad Neustadt, Aug. 20, 1943, in Broszat, *Bayern in der NS-Zeit,* 1, pt. 7, 645-46.
77. Irving, *The Rise and Fall of the Luftwaffe,* pp. 231-37.
78. SD, Weimar, July 9, 1943, T 81, reel 6; see also SD, Schwerin, July 13, 1943, ibid.; SD, Friedberg, July 18, 1943, in Broszat, *Bayern in der NS-Zeit,* 1, pt. 7, p. 643.

79. SD, Schwerin, Aug. 3, 1943, T 580, reel 875.
80. SD, Schwerin, July 13, 1943, T 81, reel 6; cf. SD, Friedberg, Aug. 22, 1943, in Broszat, *Bayern in der NS-Zeit*, 1, pt. 7, p. 646.
81. Lochner, *Goebbels Diaries*, p. 404; SD, Weimar, July 9, 1943, T 81, reel 6; SD, Bad Brückenau, Aug. 16, 1943, in Broszat, *Bayern in der NS-Zeit*, 1, pt. 7, p. 645.
82. SD, Berlin, Aug. 12, 1943, T 580, reel 875.
83. Not a literal translation but reflecting the tone of the German verse. SD, Bad Brückenau, Aug. 16, 1943, in Broszat, *Bayern in der NS-Zeit*, 1, pt. 7, p. 645; cf. SD, Weimar, July 9, 1943, T 81, reel 6, which attributes it to Zeiss factory workers.
84. For example Nadler, *Stadt im Schatten*, pp. 174-84; see letters to Goebbels, July 15, Aug. 12, 27, 29, 1943, T 580, reel 589.
85. VI 468, Aug. 13, 1943, T 81 reel 4.
86. Rs 110, Aug. 3, 1943; 35g, July 14, 1943; 104, July 22, 1943, T 580, reel 16.
87. Rs 120, Aug. 23; 126, Aug. 27, 1943, ibid.
88. Rs 50g, Sept. 1; 112, Aug. 14, 1943, ibid.
89. See stories of Wolff-Mönckeberg, *On the Other Side*, pp. 75-76; Andreas-Friedrich, *Der Schattenmann*, pp. 121ff.
90. Fischer, *Köln*, pp. 162-63.
91. Schramm, *Neun Generationen*, pp. 572-73.
92. SD, Linz, July 6, 1943, T 81, reel 6.
93. See Wolff-Mönckeberg, *On the Other Side*, p. 76; in Essen, the air raids in March destroyed 210 food stores and that of July 25 another 545. See Hubert Schmitz, *Die Bewirtschaftung der Nahrungsmittel und Verbrauchsgüter, 1939-1950. Dargestellt an dem Beispiel der Stadt Essen*, pp. 458-59.
94. See *Münchener Neueste Nachrichten*, Aug. 7/8, 21/22, 1943.
95. Von Kardorff, *Nightmare*, pp. 49-50.
96. See Alexander Werth, *Russia at War, 1941-1945*, pp. 732-37; for Seydlitz's role, James Donald Carnes, *General zwischen Hitler und Stalin. Das Schicksal des Walther v. Seydlitz*, pp. 179ff.
97. Rs 102, July 7, 1943, T 580, reel 16.
98. Kreis School Office, Neustadt, June 17, 1943, in Broszat, *Bayern in der NS-Zeit*, 1, pt. 7, p. 579.
99. *Köln*, p. 131.
100. SD, Halle, July 15, 1943, T 81, reel 6.
101. Sauer, *Württemberg*, p. 365; Schmitz, *Die Bewirtschaftung*, denies that soap was ever short during the war but admits that its quality declined greatly.
102. *Münchener Neueste Nachrichten*. Aug. 6, 1943.
103. Gau Treasurer, Franken, Nürnberg, to treasurer at Neustadt, July 7, 1943, T 81, reel 59.
104. VI 463, Aug. 5, 1943, T 81, reel 4.
105. Chief office of NSVW to Gau Hq. Baden, July 5, 1943, T 81, reel 39.
106. Sauer, *Württemberg*, pp. 367-68.
107. SD, Linz, July 6, 1943, T 81, reel 6; SD, Weimar, July 9, 16, ibid., vegetables available, fruit short; later, Aug. 30, only white cabbage in parts of area, T 580, reel 875.
108. OLGP, R22, 3359, Celle, July 29, 1943.
109. SD, Weimar, Aug. 30, 1943, T 580, reel 875.
110. Rs 103, July 15, 1943, T 580, reel 16.
111. See correspondence between Reichsstelle Rosenberg and Wilhelm Hartlieb, Aug. 5, 19, 1943, T 81, reel 41.
112. Rs 114, Aug. 18, 1943, T 580, reel 16.
113. SD, Friedberg, July 18, 1943, in Broszat, *Bayern in der NS-Zeit*, 1, pt. 7, p. 643.
114. Kreis School Office, Neustadt, Aug. 19, 1943, ibid. p. 581.

115. Kruk, *The Taste of Fear*, pp. 108-11.
116. VI 475, Aug. 13, 1943, T 81, reel 4; Sauer, *Württemberg*, p. 422.
117. Kreisobmann, Freiburg i. Br., Aug. 25, 1943, T 81, reel 69.
118. Ibid.; VI 450, Aug. 5, 1943, T 81, reel 4.
119. Zittel, "Volksstimmung," p. 54.
120. SD, Linz, June 11, 1943, T 81, reel 6.
121. SD, Halle, July 15, 1943, T 81, reel 6.
122. VI 429, July 14, 1943, T 81, reel 4.
123. Hüttenberger, *Die Gauleiter*, pp. 162-64.
124. VI 356, Aug. 5, 1943, T 81, reel 4.
125. SD, Schwerin, July 20, 1943, T 81, reel 6.
126. SD, Schwerin, Aug. 31, 1943, T 580, reel 875.
127. SD, Linz, Aug. 20, 1943, ibid.
128. Von Hassell, *Diaries*, July 19, 1943, p. 310.
129. SD, Schwerin, July 6, 1943, T 81, reel 6.
130. SD, Prague, Aug. 21, 1943, T 580, reel 875.
131. In-house memo, July 6, 1943, T 81, reel 4.
132. Fischer, *Köln*, p. 163.
133. Benn, *Briefe*, p. 339.

5. A Joyless Victory

1. Webster and Frankland, *Strategic Air Offensive*, 2, pp. 47-48. The cities "virtually destroyed" were Hamburg, Cologne, Essen, Dortmund, Düsseldorf, Hannover, Mannheim, Bochum, Mülheim, Köln Deutz, Barmen, Elberfeld, Mönchengladbach, Rheydt, Krefeld, Aachen, Rostock, Remscheid, Kassel, and Emden. "Seriously damaged" were Frankfurt a. M., Stuttgart, Duisburg, Bremen, Hagen, Munich, Nuremberg, Stettin, Kiel, Karlsruhe, Mainz, Wilhelmshaven, Lübeck, Saarbrücken, Osnabrück, Münster, Rüsselsheim, Berlin, Oberhausen.
2. Ibid., pp. 45-46.
3. Irving, *Rise and Fall of the Luftwaffe*, pp. 247-49; Ronald H. Bailey, *The Air War in Europe*, p. 135; Caffey, *Decision over Schweinfurt*, pp. 282-348.
4. Tony Wood and Bill Gunston, *Hitler's Luftwaffe: A Pictorial History and Technical Encyclopedia of Hitler's Air Power in World War II*, pp. 102-5. *Schräge Musik* was not used until early 1944. Cf. Webster and Frankland, *Stategic Air Offensive*, pp. 194-98; Bailey, *Air War in Europe*, pp. 132-39; Irving, *Luftwaffe*, pp. 225-27; 236-37.
5. SD, Schweinfurt, Oct. 25, Nov. 1, 1943, in Broszat, *Bayern in der NS-Zeit*, 1, pt. 7, pp. 654, 656-57; SD, Bad Neustadt, Oct. 15, 1943, ibid., p. 653.
6. SD, Würzburg, Oct. 26, 1943, ibid., pp. 654-55.
7. SD, Kitzingen, Nov. 8, 1943, ibid., p. 658.
8. SD, Bad Kissingen, Oct. 30, 1943, ibid., p. 655.
9. SD, Bad Brückenau, Sept. 6, 1943, ibid., pp. 649-50.
10. Ibid.
11. SD, Schwerin, Oct. 5, 1943, T 580, reel 875.
12. Nadler, *Stadt im Schatten*, pp. 187-89.
13. Lochner, *Goebbels Diaries*, pp. 496-98, 528-29, 532-33.
14. Bielenberg, *The Past Is Myself*, p. 125.
15. Andreas-Friedrich, *Der Schattenmann*, pp. 129-30.
16. Lochner, *Goebbels Diaries*, p. 497. Weinrich lost his position in 1944. See Hüttenberger, *Die Gauleiter*, p. 209.
17. SD, Halle, Sept. 20, 1943, T 580, reel 875.

18. OLGP, R22, 3364, Frankfurt a. M., Nov. 27, 1943; Rs 132, Sept. 14, 1943, T 580, reel 16.

19. Rs 168, Dec. 6, 1943, ibid.

20. VI 546, 547, Oct. 8, 1943, T 81, reel 4.

21. VI 629, Dec. 9, 1943, ibid.; Rs 156, Nov. 6, 1943, T 580, reel 16.

22. Rs 138, Sept. 24; 144, Oct. 8, 1943, ibid.

23. Rs 49g, Sept. 2 1943, T 580, reel 16.

24. VI 365, Dec. 18, 1943, T 81, reel 4.

25. Rs 155, Nov. 2, 1943, T 580, reel 16; VI 545, Oct. 8, 1943, T 81, reel 4.

26. Rs 165, Nov. 26, 1943; 64g, 65g, Dec. 16, 1943, T 580, reel 16.

27. Paul, *Heimatkrieg*, pp. 202-8.

28. VI 582, Nov. 5, 1943, T 81, reel 4.

29. VI 637, Dec. 18, 1943, ibid.

30. Rs 151, Oct. 14, 1943, T 580, reel 16.

31. *Stuttgart NS-Kurier*, Oct. 10, 1943 in Heinz Bardua, *Stuttgart im Luftkrieg, 1939-1945* (*Veröffentlichungen des Archivs der Stadt Stuttgart*, Bd. 33, Stuttgart, 1967?), pp. 186-88.

32. Hampe, *Der zivile Luftschutz*, pp. 587-602. In Dortmund, similar exhibits of extinguishing phosphorus bombs emphasized the advantage of making a thin mud mixture for this purpose rather than using pure water. *Westfälische Landeszeitung*, Nov. 11, 1943.

33. Hampe, *Der zivile Luftschutz*, p. 604.

34. Lochner, *Goebbels Diaries*, pp. 521-30.

35. Dienststelle Rosenberg, Dec. 5, 1943, T 81, reel 41.

36. Report, Dec. 8, 1943, T 580, reel 562.

37. Report, Dec. 3, 1943, ibid.

38. Letter of Irmgard Gosebruch to Maria Kiesbye of the Auslandsamt in Rostock, Nov. 22, 1943, T 81, reel 74.

39. Von Kardorff, *Nightmare*, pp. 71-72.

40. Lange, *Tagebücher*, pp. 129-30.

41. Ibid., pp. 130-31.

42. Ibid., pp. 131-32.

43. Fischer, *Köln*, pp. 166-68.

44. Deakin, *Brutal Friendship*, pp. 528-69.

45. SD, Schwerin, Sept 10, 1943, T 580, reel 875; SD, Kitzingen, Sept. 13, Würzburg, Sept. 14, 1943, in Broszat, *Bayern in der NS-Zeit*, 1, pt. 7, pp. 651-52.

46. SD, Berlin, general reports, Sept. 10, 1943, T 580, reel 875.

47. Kreis School Office, Eichstatt, Oct. 1, 1943, in Broszat, *Bayern in der NS-Zeit*, 1, pt. 7, p. 582.

48. RS 52gRs, Sept. 11, 1943, T 580, reel 16.

49. SD, Schwerin, Oct. 5, 1943, T 580, reel 875; SD, Nürnberg, Würzburg, Oct. 5, 1943, in Broszat, *Bayern in der NS-Zeit*, 1, pt. 7, p. 653.

50. SD, Schwerin, Sept. 10, 20, 1943, T 580, reel 875; Rs 140, Sept. 29, 1943, T 580, reel 16.

51. Rs 152, Oct. 15, 1943, ibid.

52. Von Kardorff, *Nightmare*, p. 66.

53. Wolff-Mönckeberg, *On the Other Side*, pp. 80-91.

54. Boberach, *Meldungen aus dem Reich*, Sept. 30, 1943, pp. 352-54.

55. Ibid., p. 373.

56. Von Kardorff, *Nightmare*, p. 64.

57. Boberach, *Meldungen aus dem Reich*, p. 373.

58. Party Press, special service, Nr. 244, T 81, reel 32; Sauer, *Württemberg*, p. 395; Nadler, *Stadt im Schatten*, pp. 184-87.

59. Irving, *Hitler's War*, pp. 575-76.
60. See SD, Würzburg, Nov. 2, 1943, in Broszat, *Bayern in der NS-Zeit*, 1, pt. 7, p. 657.
61. *Hitler*, 2, pt. 2, p. 2049.
62. Following summary from ibid., pp. 2049-59.
63. Boberach, *Meldungen aus dem Reich*, pp. 357-60; SD, Würzburg, Nov. 9; SD, Bad Kissingen, Nov. 11; SD, Bad Neustadt, Nov. 14, 1943, in Broszat, *Bayern in der NS-Zeit*, 1, pt. 7, p. 658.
64. SD, Schwerin, Sept. 10, 1943, T 580, reel 875.
65. Von Kardorff, *Nightmare*, p. 62; remainder from Boberach, *Meldungen aus dem Reich*, pp. 375-86.
66. OLGP, R 22, 3387, Stuttgart, May 31, 1943; cf. 3374, Köln, Sept. 29, 1943; 3359, Celle, Jan. 29, 1944.
67. Rs 163, Nov. 25, 1943, T 81, reel 8 ("Not to be published").
68. N.S. Betriebsobmann, Aachen, proclamation, Nov. (?), 1943, T 81, reel 69.
69. Rs 56g, Oct. 5, 1943, ibid.
70. OLGP, R 22, 3360, Danzig, Oct. 7, Dec. 7, 1943.
71. SD, Schwerin, Oct. 5, 1943, T 580, reel 875.
72. SD, Prague, Nov. 4, 1943, T 81, reel 6.
73. Kreisleiter to Kreisobmann, Freiburg i. Br., Nov. 10, 1943, T 81, reel 65.
74. SD, Friedberg, Nov. 14, 1943, in Broszat, *Bayern in der NS-Zeit*, 1, pt. 7, p. 655.
75. Sauer, *Württemberg*, p. 423.
76. VI 539, Sept. 30, 1943, T 81, reel 4.
77. Karl Dietrich Bracher, *The German Dictatorship: The Origins, Structure, and Effects of National Socialism*, p. 422.
78. SD, Halle, Sept. 3, 10, 15, 1943, T 580, reel 875.
79. Irving, *Luftwaffe*, p. 258-59 (Nov. 1943).
80. Hans Kehrl, *Krisenmanager im Dritten Reich. 6 Jahre Frieden—6 Jahre Krieg. Erinnerungen*, p. 310.
81. Both Speer's *Inside the Third Reich* and Irving's biography of Erhard Milch, *The Rise and Fall of the Luftwaffe*, give dramatic pictures of the infighting with which Speer had to cope. In spite of Kehrl's supposed support for Speer, his book gives evidence of his own jealousy of Speer's position.
82. Domarus, *Hitler*, 2, pt. 2, p. 2065.
83. Speer, *Inside the Third Reich*, pp. 309-18.
84. Sauer, *Württemberg*, p. 365; cf. Schmitz, *Die Bewirtschaftung*, pp. 505-6.
85. Gau officer for maintenance and repairs, Strassburg, circular Nr. 74, Oct. 30, 1943, T 81, reel 65.
86. Schmitz, *Die Bewirtschaftung*, p. 529.
87. SD, Linz, Dec. 10, 1943, T 580, reel 877.
88. VI 519, Sept. 16, 1943, T 81, reel 4; Kreis office for old materials, Freiburg i. Br., Nov. 15, 1943, T 81, reel 65.
89. Nadler, *Stadt im Schatten*, p. 201; OLGP, R 22, 3387, Stuttgart, Dec. 4, 1943.
90. VI 614, Dec. 2, 1943, T 81, reel 4.
91. In-house memo, Nov. 11, 1943, T 580, reel 122.
92. Nadler, *Stadt im Schatten*, pp. 197-201; VI 622, Dec. 7, 1943, T 81, reel 4.
93. Ibid.
94. Sauer, *Württemberg*, p. 365, noted shortages; Schmitz, *Die Bewirtschaftung* denied that there were ever shortages there, pp. 534-35.
95. OLGP, R 22, 3374, Köln, Nov. 30, 1943.
96. Von Kardorff, *Nightmare*, pp. 64-65, 76.

97. The following is taken from the rations summaries detailed in Schmitz, *Die Bewirtschaftung*, pp. 466-67.

98. Ibid., p. 387.

99. Ibid., p. 420.

100. SD, Weimar, July 16, 1943, T 81, reel 6.

101. Kreisobmann, Freiburg i. Br., Sept. 25, 1943, T 81 reel 69.

102. SD, Schwerin, Sept. 28, 1943, T 580, reel 875.

103. SD, Linz, Nov. 12, 1943, T 580, reel 877; Kreisobmann, Freiburg i. Br., Nov., 1943, T 81, reel 69.

104. VI 568, Oct. 16, 1943, T 81, reel 4; Rs 160, Nov. 15, 1943, T 580, reel 16; SD, Weimar, Sept. 23, 1943, T 580, reel 875.

105. Kreisobmann, Freiburg i. Br., Nov. 1943, T 81, reel 69.

106. OLGP, R 22, 3355, Bamberg, Nov. 27, 1943.

107. SD, Schwerin, Sept. 10, 1943, T 81, reel 69.

108. SD, Bad Brückenau, Sept. 20, 1943, in Broszat, *Bayern in der NS-Zeit* 1, pt. 7, p. 652.

109. *Westfälische Landeszeitung*, Nov. 2, 1943.

110. Irving, *Hitler's War*, p. 553.

111. SD, Lohr-Marktheidenfeld, Oct. 11, 1943, in Broszat, *Bayern in der NS-Zeit*, 1, pt. 7, p. 653; Kreis School Office, Weissenberg, Oct. 23, 1943, ibid., p. 583.

112. *Deutsche Allgemeine Zeitung*, Sept. 26, 1943; *Völkischer Beobachter*, Süddeutsche Ausgabe, Oct. 5, 1943.

113. VI 573, Oct. 29, 1943, ibid.; DAF, Kassel, Parole No. 3, late 1943, T 81, reel 71.

114. Central Office of NSV, Nov., 1943, T 81, reel 40.

115. "Die Leistungen der NSV: Ein Rückblick in Zahlen," ibid.

116. An 5g, Oct. 30, 1943, T 580, reel 15; Rs 66gRs, Dec. 21, 1943, T 580, reel 16.

117. SD, Friedberg, Oct. 17, 1943, in Broszat, *Bayern in der NS-Zeit*, 1, pt. 7, p. 654.

118. VI 594, Nov. 13, 1943, T 81, reel 4; Kreisobmann, Monschau, to factory leaders of Kreis, T 81, reel 71.

119. Boberach, *Meldungen*, pp. 360-70.

120. An 57, Oct. 22, 1943, T 81, reel 8; NS Betriebszellenobmann, Aachen, Oct., 1943, ibid., reel 69; "Arbeitsrichtlinien für Werkscharen und Werksfrauengruppen," 4. Beilage 1943 der Schulungsschrift "Arbeit und Wirtschaft," ibid., reel 71.

121. Gaubeauftragter für Winterhilfswerk, Baden, Nov. 11-Dec. 10, 1943, T 81, reel 39; cf. Kreisobmann, Freiburg i. Br., Dec. 27, 1943, T 81, reel 8.

122. Rs 169, Dec. 14, 1943, T 81, reel 8.

123. An 60, Nov. 13, 1943, ibid.

124. Reich Propaganda Office, Westmark, Neustadt, Nov. 2, 1943, T 580, reel 590; internal memo, Ahnenerbe Office of SS, Nov. 22, 1943, T 580, reel 122; Hauptamt, NSV, Dec. 7, 1943, T 81, reel 40; office of Kreisleiter, Freiburg i. Br., directive Nr. 6, Dec. 11, 1943, T 81, reel 65.

125. Rs 161, Nov. 22, 1943, T 81, reel 8.

126. VI 652, Dec. 28, 1943, T 81, reel 4.

127. SD, Linz, Dec. 25, 1943, T 580, reel 877; Lili Hahn, *White Flags of Surrender*, p. 300; von Kardorff, *Nighmare*, pp. 77-78; Wolff-Mönckeberg, *On the Other Side*, pp. 77-79.

128. Nadler, *Stadt im Schatten*, pp. 202-4; Gauschulungsamt, Baden, Kreisleitung Waldshut, Dec. 23, 1943, T 81, reel 1.

129. Lange, *Tagebücher*, pp. 132-33.

6. Life Goes On

1. Domarus, *Hitler*, 2, pt 2, pp. 2071-74.
2. Ibid., pp. 2074-77.
3. Ibid., pp. 2082-86.
4. Description of affairs in this period from Fischer, *Köln*, pp. 170-78.
5. See diagram in Martin Middlebrook, *The Nuremberg Raid, 30-31 March 1944*, p. 81.
6. Von Kardorff, *Nightmare*, pp. 82-102.
7. March 3, 1944, T 580, reel 878.
8. OLGP, R 22, 3366, Hamburg, Jan. 31, Apr. 12, 1944; cf. Wolff-Mönckeberg, *On the Other Side*, pp. 87-96.
9. Sauer, *Württemberg*, pp. 357-58; Bardua, *Stuttgart im Luftkrieg*, pp. 68-81. See also bombing chart, Middlebrook, *Nuremberg Raid*, p. 81.
10. The story dramatically told in ibid.
11. Sauer, *Württemberg*, p. 357.
12. Zittel, "Volksstimmung," pp. 55-56; Domarus, *NS-Krieg*, p. 180.
13. Ph. Kessler, member of Reich Defense Council, Bergmann-Elektrische Werke AG, to Speer, secret, Apr. 6, 1944, T 81, reel 59.
14. SD, Schweinfurt, Apr. 12, 1944, in Broszat, *Bayern in der NS-Zeit*, 1, pt. 7, pp. 660-61.
15. Hahn, *White Flags of Surrender*, pp. 303-22; OLGP, R 22, 3364, Frankfurt, Mar. 30, 1944.
16. OLGP, R 22, 3373, Kiel, Jan. 31, 1944.
17. OLGP, R 22, 3381, Rostock, Apr. 3, 1944.
18. OLGP, R 22, 3362, Dresden, Feb. 22, 1944.
19. SD, Würzburg, Apr. 11, 1944, in Broszat, *Bayern in der NS-Zeit*, 1, pt. 7, p. 660.
20. Bg 20, Jan. 29, 1944, T 580, reel 17.
21. *Westfälische Landeszeitung*, Apr. 4, 1944.
22. Robert Kratzel, Dresden, to Reich Propaganda Minister, Mar. 31, 1944, T 580, reel 657.
23. Irving, *Hitler's War*, pp. 552-53.
24. See *Deutsches Wohnungs-Hilfswerk*, Mitteilungen, Jrg. 1944, Nr. 1, Feb. 15, 1944, T 81, reel 68; VI 85, Apr. 21, 1944, T 81, reel 4; DAF, Gausachwalter, Bayreuth, Feb. 14, 1944, Nr. 3, T 81, reel 68.
25. NSV, Finance Office, Nr. 2, Mar. 25, 1944, T 81, reel 37.
26. VI 65, Mar. 24, 1944, T 81, reel 4.
27. Reichsschatzmeister to Speer as Generalbevollmächtigter für die Regelung der Wirtschaft, Jan. 17, 1944, T 81, reel 59.
28. Bg 25g, Feb. 3, 1944, T 580, reel 17.
29. Chief of General Staff of OKL to Party Chancellery, secret, Apr. 10, 1944, ibid.; VI 57, Mar. 23, 1944, T 81, reel 4.
30. VI 38, Mar. 7, 1944, ibid.
31. Kreis Personnel Office, Freiburg i. Br., to Gau Personnel Office, Mar. 3, 1944, T 81, reel 65.
32. Conveyed in Gaupropagandaleitung to Reich Propaganda Ministry, Jan. 11, 1944, T 580, reel 660. My translation.
33. NSDAP, Reich Propaganda Ministry, Sonderlieferung, Nr. 18, Apr. 12, 1944, T 81, reel 68.
34. SD, Friedberg, Apr. 16, 1944, in Broszat, *Bayern in der NS-Zeit*, 1, pt. 7, p. 661.

35. Boberach, *Meldungen aus dem Reich*, pp. 399-401; Baird, *Mythical World*, p. 222.

36. OLGP, R 22, 3357, Braunschweig, Mar. 31, 1944.

37. Ibid.

38. SD, Friedberg, Apr. 16, 1944, in Broszat, *Bayern in der NS-Zeit*, 1, pt. 7, p. 661.

39. Bielenberg, *The Past Is Myself*, p. 133.

40. VI 5, Jan. 17; 40, Mar. 7, 1944, T 81, reel 4.

41. Declaration found in T 580, reel 26. For a defensive view of Seydlitz's actions during this period, see Carnes, *General zwischen Hitler und Stalin*, pp. 189ff.

42. See Sauer, *Württemberg*, p. 439.

43. See Harold C. Deutsch, *The Conspiracy against Hitler in the Twilight War*.

44. See background sketch in Paul, *Heimatkrieg*, pp. 277-85.

45. Graff, *Von S.M. zu N.S.*, p. 346.

46. Paul, *Heimatkrieg*, p. 284.

47. John W. Wheeler-Bennett, *The Nemesis of Power: The German Army in Politics, 1918-1945*, p. 678.

48. *Westfälische Landeszeitung*, Jan. 31, 1944.

49. Office of Kreisleiter, directive Nr. 3, Jan. 22, 1944, T 81, reel 65.

50. Bg 28, Feb. 9, 1944, T 81, reel 8.

51. An 8, June 8, 1944, T 580, reel 17; VI 49, Mar. 10, 1944, T 81, reel 4; Office of Kreisleiter, Freiburg, directives 5, 9, Feb. 11, Mar. 20, 1944, T 81, reel 65; von Kardorff, *Nightmare*, pp. 103-4; Herzstein, *The War Hitler Won*, p. 246.

52. An 15, Jan. 14, 1944, T 81, reel 8.

53. Bg 103g, n.d., 1944, T 81, reel 1.

54. Bg 88, Apr. 24, 1944, T 580, reel 17.

55. An 73, Mar. 30, 1944, T 81, reel 8.

56. VI 36, Feb. 17, 1944, T 81, reel 4.

57. Reich Propaganda Minister to Oberregierungspräsident, Apr. 24, 1944, T 580, reel 658.

58. Bg 55, Feb. 28, 1944, T 580, reel 17.

59. VI 89, Apr. 21, 1944, T 81, reel 4.

60. VI 33, Feb. 17; 71, Mar. 24, 1944, ibid.

61. Bg 18, Jan. 31, 1944, T 580, reel 17.

62. Kreis School Office, Fränkische Alb, Mar. 8, 1944, in Broszat, *Bayern in der NS-Zeit*, 1, pt. 7, p. 584.

63. SD, Wiesbaden, to RSHA, Berlin, Mar. 3, 1944, T 175, reel 276.

64. SD, Frankfurt, a. M., Mar. 6, 1944, ibid.

65. SD, Frankfurt a. M., June 19, 1944, ibid.

66. SD, Frankfurt a. M., Mar. 6, 1944, ibid.

67. Speech at Weimar, Jan, 22, 1944, "Die deutsche Arbeitsfront im 5. Kriegsjahre," T 81, reel 69.

68. Hupfauer, Rüstungs- und Kriegsproduktion, Mar. 25, 1944; Gauobmann, circulars 27, 30, 38, Apr. 5, 8, 28, 1944, T 81, reel 69.

69. *Der Geschäftsführer*, Informations-Dienst, Jan. 21, Mar. 23, 1944, T 81, reel 69; Kreisobmann, Zabern, Feb. 5, 15, 16, 1944, ibid.; Nachrichten der Reichsminister für Rüstungs- und Kriegsproduktion, Nr. 36, Apr. 3, 1944, T 81, reel 76.

70. Apelt, *Jurist im Wandel der Staatsformen. Lebenserinnerungen*, p. 255.

71. Schmitz, *Die Bewirtschaftung*, pp. 508, 529.

72. SD, Schwerin, Jan. 4, 1944, T 580, reel 877.

73. Boberach, *Meldungen*, Jan. 20, 1944, pp. 390-91.

74. Ibid.; cf. OLGP, R 22, 3359, Celle, Jan. 29, 1944.

75. See Thierack's judicial letter, VI 69, Mar. 24, 1944, T 81, reel 4.

76. Bg 24g, Jan. 31, 1944, T 580, reel 17.
77. Schmitz, *Die Bewirtschaftung*, p. 402.
78. OLGP, R 22, 3356, Berlin, Jan. 27, 1944; cf. Kreisobmann, Freiburg i. Br., Apr. 26, 1944, T 81, reel 69.
79. Schmitz, *Die Bewirtschaftung*, p. 420.
80. Kreisobmann, Freiburg i. Br., Apr. 26, 1944, T 81, reel 69.
81. VI 16, Feb. 7, 1944, T 81, reel 4.
82. *Westfälische Landeszeitung*, Mar. 10, 1944.
83. Ibid., Apr. 24, 1944.
84. VI 122, May 23, 1944, T 81, reel 4.
85. Arbeitsblatt für Werkfrauengruppen, Mar., Apr., 1944, Kurhessen, T 81, reel 71.
86. Bg 72, Feb. 18, 1944, T 580, reel 17; VI 72, Mar. 24, 1944, T 81, reel 4.
87. Rs 87, Apr. 24, 1944, T 580, reel 17.
88. VI 67, Mar. 24, 1944, T 81, reel 4.
89. NSV, Ernährungshilfswerk, directive Nr. 2, Apr. 11, 1944, T 81, reel 37.
90. *Völkischer Beobachter*, Brandenburg, Jan. 14, 1944, "Wandlungen im Landvolk," T 81, reel 42.
91. Forschungsstelle deutscher Bauernhof, Feb. 14, 1944, T 81, reel 41.
92. Sauer, *Württemberg*, pp. 420-22.
93. Kreisobmann, Freiburg i. Br. to Gauobmann, Strassburg, Feb. 28, Apr. 26, 1944, T 81, reel 69.
94. Domarus, *NS-Krieg*, p. 105.
95. OLGP, R 22, 3379, München, Mar. 28, 1944.
96. Wolff-Mönckeberg, *On the Other Side*, p. 87.
97. SD, Schwerin, Apr. 11, 1944, T 580, reel 877.
98. See damage reports, Feb. 14, 1944, T 580, reel 562, Apr. 6, 1944, T 580, reel 561.
99. *Westfälische Landeszeitung*, Jan. 25, Feb. 3, 9, 1944.
100. Wolff-Mönckeberg, *On the Other Side*, p. 86.
101. Bg 12, Jan. 14, 16, Jan. 24, 1944, T 580, reel 17.
102. SD, Frankfurt, Mar. 6, 1944, T 175, reel 276.
103. The overall story of the youth groups is told in Arno Klönne's article "Jugendprotest und Jugendopposition: Von der HJ-Einziehung zum Cliquenwesen der Kriegszeit," in *Bayern in der NS-Zeit, Herrschaft und Gesellschaft im Konflikt*, ed. Broszat et al., 4, pt. C, pp. 604-14 (for this period). The most detailed documentary assessment is found in the copy of the memorandum of the chief prosecutor in Cologne, dated Jan. 16, 1944 as an attachment to OLGP, R 22, 3374, Jan. 28, 1944. Reports of youth criminality are included in most of the *Oberlandesgerichtspräsidenten* reports for this period.
104. Ibid.; see also OLGP, R 22, 3373, Kiel, Apr. 6, 1944.
105. OLGP, R 22, 3359, Celle, June 1, 1944.
106. OLGP, R 22, 3373, Kiel, May 31, 1944.
107. Part of report of chief prosecutor in Cologne, Jan. 16, 1944, included in R 22, 3374, Cologne, Jan. 28, 1944.
108. Ibid.
109. Ibid.
110. Klönne, "Jugendprotest," in Broszat, *Bayern in der NS-Zeit*, 4, pt. C, pp. 611-12.
111. See fn. 107 plus reports from OLGP, R 22, 3357, Braunschweig, Jan. 18, 1944; 3383, Posen, June 12, 1944; 3364, Frankfurt, July 26, 1944; Klönne, "Jugendprotest," in Broszat, *Bayern in der NS-Zeit*, 4, pt. C, pp. 608-9. In a secret circular, Bormann indicated that youth crimes in 1942 had risen to 52,423 as compared to

24,562 in 1937 (more than double) and were still rising in reports obtained for 1943. Bg 204g, Aug. 29, 1944, T 580, reel 17.
112. VI 14, Jan. 28, 1944, T 81, reel 4.
113. Propaganda Office, Bayreuth, Sonderdruck aus der Wochenzeitschrift *Das Reich*, Apr. 23, 1944, T 81, reel 68; Boberach, *Meldungen*, Apr. 6, 20, 1944, pp. 411-19.

7. The Bombs Still Fall

1. See, for example, Boberach, *Meldungen aus dem Reich*, pp. 420ff. (May 4, 1944).
2. Ibid., pp. 424-25.
3. SD Reports to Party Chancellery, July 7, 1944, T 81, reel 6.
4. See Wheeler-Bennett, *Nemesis of Power*, pp. 596-98.
5. The following discussion is based on Hans Kehrl, *Krisenmanager im Dritten Reiche. 6 Jahre Frieden—6 Jahre Krieg. Erinnerungen*, pp. 367-85; Hampe, *Der zivile Luftschutz*, pp. 135ff.; Peter Becker, "The Role of Synthetic Fuel in World War II Germany: Implications for Today?" *Air University Review* 32, no. 5 (July-Aug., 1981): 45-53.
6. Fischer, *Köln*, pp. 178-79.
7. Joachim Günther, *Das letzte Jahr. Mein Tagebuch 1944/45*, p. 137.
8. Von Kardorff, *Nightmare*, pp. 105-6.
9. Ibid., p. 109.
10. Bielenberg, *The Past Is Myself*, p. 167.
11. Paul, *Heimatkrieg*, p. 263.
12. Ibid., p. 344.
13. OLGP, R 22, 3373, Kiel, Aug. 4, Sept. 30, 1944.
14. OLGP, R 22, 3366, Hamburg, Aug. 5, 1944.
15. Reck-Malleczewen, *Diary of a Man in Despair*, p. 144.
16. Broszat, *Bayern in der NS-Zeit*, 1, pt. 7, p. 671.
17. June 14, July 17, 1944.
18. Günther, *Das letzte Jahr*, pp. 231-32, 236.
19. Bardua, *Stuttgart im Luftkrieg*, pp. 82-122.
20. Ibid., p. 115.
21. See, e.g., von Kardorff, *Nightmare*, p. 111.
22. Bardua, *Stuttgart im Luftkrieg*, p. 122; a general order for the protection of shot-down pilots was issued by the Kreisstabsamt, Freiburg i. Br., May 4, 1944, T 81, reel 65.
23. SD, Schwerin, May 30, 1944, T 81, reel 6.
24. Bielenberg, *The Past Is Myself*, p. 154.
25. Rs 169, July 26, 1944, T 81, reel 37 or T 580, reel 17.
26. VI 93, May 8, 1944, T 81, reel 4.
27. VI 103, May 10; 127, May 26, 1944, ibid.
28. BSV, Finance Circular 14, May 5, 1944, ibid.
29. Paul, *Heimatkrieg*, pp. 290-93. See also description of gas drill in Klaus Granzow, *Tagebuch eines Hitlerjungen, 1943-1945*, p. 122.
30. Anlage, SD, Schwerin, Aug. 15, 1944, T 81, reel 6.
31. Reck-Malleczewen, *Diary of a Man in Despair*, p. 199.
32. Bielenberg, *The Past Is Myself*, pp. 132ff.
33. Granzow, *Tagebuch*, pp. 105, 111-12.
34. Studnitz, *While Berlin Burns*, p. 208 and passim.
35. Letter of Annemarie Roth to Central Office, July 15/16, 1944, T 81, reel 74.

36. Hillgruber and Hümmelchen, *Chronik des zweiten Weltkrieges*, pp. 217-18; cf. Jürgen Thorwald, *Die grosse Flucht. Es begann an der Weichsel, das Ende an der Elbe*, p. 15.

37. Boberach, *Meldungen*, July 13, 1944, p. 437.

38. Maertens, Königsberg, to Reich Propaganda Ministry and responses, July 10, 11, 13, 14, 15, 17, 18, 19, 20, 21, 1944, T 580, reel 658.

39. Domarus, *Hitler*, 2, pt. 2, p. 2121.

40. SD, Schwerin, July 4, 1944, T 81, reel 6.

41. Memo, Dr. Schäffer to State Secretary Dr. Neumann, June 12, 1944, T 580, reel 657.

42. See files of "Sonderstab Ruder" in materials of Party Chancellery, FA 91/1, Institut für Zeitgeschichte, Munich; Wilhelm Prüller, *Diary of a German Soldier*, pp. 179ff.

43. See Domarus, *Hitler*, 2, pt. 2, p. 2132; Bormann, Rs 153, July 26, 1944, T 580, reel 17.

44. VI 46, Mar. 10, 1944, T 81, reel 4; cf. Walter Warlimont, *Inside Hitler's Headquarters*, p. 439; An 170, July 4, 1944, T 81, reel 8.

45. Lemke, in-house memo to Sondermann, July 13, 1944, T 580, reel 658.

46. May 2, 1944, T 580, reel 877.

47. May 9, 1944, ibid.

48. See memoranda of Gerigk, head of Amtmusik, May 24, June 9, 1944, T 81, reel 22; Kuby, *Mein Krieg*, p. 406; von Kardorff, *Nightmare*, p. 112.

49. See undated memo, T 580, reel 122.

50. Correspondence of Viennese Cultural Union with Ministry of Propaganda, June 17, July 27, Aug. 1, 1944, T 580, reel 584.

51. Hildegard Brenner, *Die Kunstpolitik des Nationalsozialismus*, pp. 151-52.

52. Sauer, *Württemberg*, p. 472.

53. See Hugo Hartung, *Schlesien 1944/45, Aufzeichnungen und Tagebücher*.

54. See, e.g., Kreisleiter, Freiburg i. Br., Aug. 28, 1944, T 81, reel 65; Memo, Ahnenerbe Office of the SS, Aug. 30, 1944, T 580, reel 122.

55. VI 121, May 23, 1944, T 81, reel 4; original suggestion of army, secret, Apr. 25, 1944 and Party Chancellery replies, box 799b, Ordner Nr. 6, Party Chancellery, T 580, reel 875.

56. VI 202, Aug. 25, 1944, T 81, reel 4; Kreisleiter, Freiburg i. Br., May 25, 1944, T 81, reel 65.

57. An 159, July 28, 1944, T 580, reel 17.

58. VI 198, 201, Aug. 25, 1944, T 81, reel 4; cf. Kreis Propaganda Office, Freiburg i. Br., Aug. 10, 1944, T 81, reel 65.

59. Monthly report of Kreis Economic Office, Aschaffenburg, May, 1944, in Broszat, *Bayern in der NS-Zeit*, 3, pt. B, p. 630.

60. Aug. 9, 1944, T 81, reel 70; cf. Chairman of Armaments Commission VIb to Gau and Kreis Labor Offices, Aug. 12, 1944, ibid.

61. See, e.g., Amt für Soziale Selbstverantwortung, Office of Home Work, DAF, Aug., 1944, ibid.; *Der Geschäftsführer*, June 17, 1944, T 81, reel 69; Kreisobmann, Gelden, to DAF, Essen, Aug. 7, 1944, T 81, reel 70; similar Kreisobmann, Zabern, June 7, 12, 1944, T 81, reel 69.

62. Indication of continued solid work, Landräte in Bad Aibling and Rosenheim, July 31, 1944, in Broszat, *Bayern in der NS-Zeit*, 1, pt. 7, p. 669.

63. VI 200, Aug. 25, 1944, T 81, reel 4.

64. Ley's orders, July 25, 26, Aug. 4, 8, 1944, T 81, reel 69; Hupfauer, Amt für Soziale Selbstverantwortung, DAF, Berlin, ibid.; SD, Schwerin, June 6, 1944, T 81, reel 6.

65. Sauer, *Württemberg*, p. 423.

66. VI 101, May 8, 1944, T 81, reel 4.

67. SD, Warthegau, May 7, 1944, T 81, reel 6.

68. VI 206, Aug. 25, 1944, T 81, reel 4.

69. VI 158, June 30, 1944, ibid.

70. Ibid.

71. VI 159, June 30, 1944, ibid.

72. VI 173, July 10, 1944, ibid.

73. VI 172, July 10, 1944, ibid.

74. Kreisobmann, Freiburg i. Br., T 81, reel 69.

75. SD, Freiburg i. Br., May 29, 1944, in Broszat, *Bayern in der NS Zeit*, 1, pt. 7, pp. 662-63; SD, Warthegau, June 5-July 1, 1944, T 81, reel 6.

76. Schuppe, chief burgomaster of Kattowitz, July 10, 1944, ibid.; cf. OLGP, R 22, 3362, Danzig. Aug. 1, 1944.

77. SD, *Berichte zu Inlandsfragen*, Feb. 21, 1944, T 175, reel 266.

78. Domarus, *Hitler*, 2, pt. 2, pp. 2113-15.

79. Report of Gendarmerie, Anger, Kreis Berchtesgaden, Aug. 20, 1944, in Broszat, *Bayern in der NS-Zeit*, 1, pt. 7, pp. 672-73.

80. Rs 122, May 11, 1944, T 81, reel 8.

81. SD, Schwerin, July 11, 1944, T 81, reel 6.

82. See Boberach, ed., *Richterbriefe. Dokumente zur Beeinflussung der deutschen Rechtssprechung, 1942-1944*.

83. Thus, Leo Findahl, *Letzter Akt—Berlin, 1939-1945*, pp. 31ff.

84. Andreas-Friedrich, *Der Schattenmann*, pp. 143-45.

85. Report of Kreis School Office, Weissenburg, Aug. 26, 1944, in Broszat, *Bayern in der NS-Zeit*, 1, pt. 7, p. 590.

86. Anlage to report of OLGP, R 22, 3361, Darmstadt, Aug. 1, 1944.

87. Report of Kreis School Office, Rothenburg o.d. Tauber, June 20, 1944, in Broszat, *Bayern in der NS-Zeit*, 1, pt. 7, p. 588.

88. OLGP, R 22, 3356, Berlin, Aug. 3, 1944.

89. SD, Frankfurt a. M., June 12, 1944, T 175, reel 276.

90. Cf. Zittel, "Volksstimmung," p. 55.

91. Von Kardorff, *Nightmare*, June 10, 1944, pp. 112-13.

92. VI 135, May 30, 1944, T 81, reel 4.

93. VI 147, June 19, 1944, ibid.

94. Box #799b, Ordner Nr. 6 (2. Teil) from Party Chancellery, Friedrich, to Reichsleiter, secret, May 14, 1944, T 580, reel 875.

95. Ibid., June 19, 1944.

96. An 152g, July 24, 1944, T 580, reel 16.

97. SD, Schwerin, July 25, Aug. 8, 14, 1944, T 81, reel 6.

98. Ibid.

99. VI 203, Aug. 25, 1944, T 81, reel 4.

100. SD, Berlin, May 4, 1944, T 580, reel 878; SD, *Berichte zu Inlandsfragen*, May 4, 1944, T 175, reel 266.

101. From SD, *Berichte zu Inlandsfragen*, June 5, 1944, ibid.

102. Ibid., June 26, 1944; cf. Gendarmerie Station Kohlgrub, July 25, 1944, in Broszat, *Bayern in der NS-Zeit*, 1, pt. 7, p. 669.

103. Schmitz, *Die Bewirtschaftung*, pp. 402, 466.

104. Rs 212, Aug. 28, 1944, T 580, reel 17.

105. VI 94, May 8, 1944, T 81, reel 4; Rs 179, Aug. 14, 1944, T 580, reel 17.

106. Report of Gendarmerie Station, Kohlgrub, July 25, 1944, in Broszat, *Bayern in der NS-Zeit*, 1, pt. 7, p. 667; cf. VI 180, Aug. 1, 1944, T 81, reel 4.

107. Kreis School Office, Ansbach, Aug. 18, 1944, in Broszat, *Bayern in der NS-Zeit*, 1, pt. 7, 589.

108. SD, *Berichte zu Inlandsfragen*, May 18, 1944, T 175, reel 266.
109. Following from ibid., July 3, 27, 1944.
110. Lange, *Tagebücher*, Aug. 19, 1944, p. 192.
111. Beer, *Die Stadt ohne Tod, Berliner Tagebuch 1943/45*, Sept. 3, 1944, p. 74.

8. Germany's Darkest Winter

1. Fischer, *Köln*, pp. 184-91.
2. Report of the Oberbürgermeister, Dr. Strölin, Oct. 24, 1944, in Bardua, *Stuttgart im Luftkrieg*, pp. 251-53.
3. Preis, *München unterm Hakenkreuz*, p. 220.
4. Wolff-Mönckeberg, *On the Other Side*, pp. 94-101.
5. Sauer, *Württemberg*, p. 356.
6. Hans-Georg Kraume, *Duisburg im Krieg, 1939-1945*, pp. 70-76.
7. *Westfälische Landeszeitung*, Oct. 24, 1944.
8. Hillgruber and Hümmelchen, *Chronik des zweiten Weltkrieges*, pp. 232-56.
9. Ibid.
10. Hahn, *White Flags of Surrender*, p. 334.
11. OLGP, R 22, 3364, Frankfurt a. M., Nov. 29, 1944.
12. Hans Kramp, *Rurfront 1944/45. Zweite Schlacht am Hubertuskreuz zwischen Wurm, Rur und Inde*, pp. 80-88.
13. Ibid., pp. 155-56.
14. See Cornelius Ryan, *A Bridge Too Far*.
15. Kramp, *Rurfront*, pp. 123-27.
16. See details, ibid.
17. See, e.g., report of gendarmerie station Schwindegg, Nov. 27, 1944; monthly report of Landrat, Bad Aibling, Dec. 1, 1944, in Broszat, *Bayern in der NS-Zeit*, 1, pt. 7, pp. 675-76.
18. See Zittel, "Volkstimmung," p. 57.
19. Sauer, *Württemberg*, p. 479.
20. Rs 224g, Sept. 4, 1944, T 580, reel 17.
21. Report of the Regierungspräsident of Upper Bavaria, Sept. 6, 1944, in Broszat, *Bayern in der NS-Zeit*, 1, pt. 7, p. 674.
22. Kramp, *Rurfront*, pp. 105, 267; Hüttenberger, *Gauleiter*, pp. 190-91.
23. Kramp, *Rurfront*, pp. 165, 330, 396-97, 403, 418, 421.
24. Ibid., pp. 126, 340, 374, 404, 435, 479.
25. Ibid., pp. 428, 474.
26. Bormann's role is best covered in Jochen von Lang's book, *Der Sekretär. Martin Bormann: Der Mann, der Hitler beherrschte* (translated as *Bormann: The Man Who Manipulated Hitler*).
27. Ibid., pp. 277-81.
28. Wahl, ". . . es ist das deutsche Herz," p. 201.
29. Hüttenberger, *Die Gauleiter*, p. 191; cf. Rs 213, Sept. 2, 1944, T 580, reel 17; VI 260, Nov. 14, 1944, T 81, reel 4.
30. Hüttenberger, *Gauleiter*, p. 191.
31. Circulars Nos. 7, 12, 12a, Sept. 18, 25, 27, 1944, T 81, reel 65.
32. Circular, Oct. 5, 1944, ibid.
33. An 260g, Sept. 20, 1944, T 580, reel 17.
34. Hüttenberger, *Gauleiter*, p. 191.
35. Domarus, *Hitler*, 2, pt. 2, p. 2152.
36. Stellungsbaustelle, Gau Baden-Elsass, Oct. 12, 1944, T 81, reel 39.
37. Paul, *Heimatkrieg*, p. 64.

38. See reports of OLGP, R 22, 3360, Danzig, Dec. 5, 1944; 3386, Stettin, Dec. 1, 1944; Paul, *Heimatkrieg*, pp. 368-69.

39. Thorwald, *Die grosse Flucht*, pp. 25-29.

40. Studnitz, *While Berlin Burns*, p. 192.

41. Granzow, *Tagebuch*, pp. 114-16.

42. OLGP, R 22, 3363, Düsseldorf, Nov. 29, 1944.

43. Domarus, *Hitler*, 2, pt. 2, pp. 2150-51.

44. Rs 324, Oct. 14, 1944; An 336, Oct. 19, 1944, T 81, reel 1.

45. Rs 386, Nov. 8, 1941, T 81, reel 1; confirmed for all army units by Hitler's orders of Nov. 25, 1944, Domarus, *Hitler*, 2, pt. 2, p. 2168.

46. Kissel's book *Der deutsche Volkssturm 1944/45. Eine territoriale Miliz im Rahmen der Landesverteidigung* (Beiheft 16/17 of *Wehrwissenschaftlichen Rundschau*) is the standard source. A dissertation on the subject under my direction sought to set forth a military appraisement of the training and effectiveness of the *Volkssturm*. See Burton K. Wright, "Army of Despair: The German *Volkssturm*, 1944-1945" (Ph.D., Florida State University, 1982).

47. Rs 473, Dec. 9, 1944, T 580, reel 18.

48. Kissel, *Volkssturm*, pp. 35-36.

49. E.g., von Kardorff, *Nightmare*, p. 145.

50. Kissel, *Volkssturm*, pp. 35-36.

51. E.g., Sauer, *Württemberg*, p. 475; Gendarmerie Station, Feldkirchen, Nov. 24, 1944, in Broszat, *Bayern in der NS-Zeit*, 1, pt. 7, 675.

52. Kissel, *Volkssturm*, p. 23.

53. Breslau office of Reich Propaganda Ministry to Propaganda Ministry, Oct. 20, 1944, T 580, reel 657.

54. Herzstein, *War that Hitler Won*, p. 250.

55. Kissel, *Volkssturm*, p. 42.

56. Ibid.; cf. Studnitz, *While Berlin Burns*, p. 227.

57. Kissel, *Volkssturm*, pp. 44, 61-63. See also the story of dramatic critic Hugo Hartung, who became an air force soldier without any kind of weapons training even when his area was directly threatened by the Russians: *Schlesien, 1944/45. Aufzeichnungen und Tagebücher.*

58. See Kissel, *Volkssturm*, Anlage 10.

59. Ibid., Anlagen 11, 38.

60. Ibid., pp. 48-49.

61. An 201, Aug. 29, 1944, T 81, reel 8.

62. Sondermann, Office of Reich Minister of Propaganda and Schmidt of the Party Chancellery, memos of Sept. 13 and Oct. 19, 1944, T 580, reel 660.

63. NSV, Organization Office, circular 126, Oct. 3, 1944, T 81, reel 37.

64. Hermann Jatzke, director of *Nürnberger Zeitung* to Goebbels, Oct. 14, 1944, T 580, reel 657.

65. Rs 310g, Oct. 1, 1944, T 580, reel 17.

66. OLGP, R 22, 3379, Munich, Nov. 20, 1944.

67. Von Kardorff, *Nightmare*, pp. 151-52.

68. Wendel, *Hausfrau at War*, p. 203.

69. Gendarmerie station Ettal, Oct. 25, 1944, in Broszat, *Bayern in der NS-Zeit* 1, pt. 7, pp. 674-75.

70. Rs 466, Dec. 18, 1944, T 580, reel 18.

71. Reich Propaganda Ministry, Dr. Schäffer, to Gau Propaganda Leader, Thüringen, Dec. 2, 1944, T 580, reel 657.

72. OLGP, R 22, 3381, Nuremberg, Sept. 20, 1944.

73. Preis, *Munchen unterm Hakenkreuz*, p. 221.

74. VI 262, Nov. 14, 1944, T 81, reel 4.

75. Findahl, *Letzter Akt—Berlin*, pp. 103-4; Wolff-Mönckeberg, *On the Other Side*, p. 98.
76. Kreisobmann der DAF., Freiburg i. Br., Sept. 13, 1944, T 81, reel 65.
77. OLGP, R 22, 3383, Posen, Sept. 30, 1944.
78. Sauer, *Württemberg*, p. 372.
79. Amt für Volksgesundheit, Villingen, Oct. 6, 1944; Lörrach, Oct. 11, 1944; Konstanz, Oct. 11, 1944; Mannheim, Oct. 11, 1944; Waldshut, Oct. 11, 1944; Heidelberg, Oct. 12, 1944; Walfach, Oct. 13, 1944; Pforzheim, Oct. 13, 1944; Stockach, Nov. 18, 1944, T 81, reel 72.
80. See also Amt für Volksgesundheit, Bühl/Baden, Oct. 17, 1944; Karlsruhe, Oct. 24, 1944; Lahr/Schwarzwald, Nov. 6, 1944, ibid.
81. VI 259, Nov. 14, 1944, T 81, reel 4.
82. Beer, *Stadt ohne Tod*, p. 96.
83. Von Kardorff, *Nightmare*, pp. 152-53.
84. Sauer, *Württemberg*, p. 478.
85. Bg 256g, Sept. 19, 1944, T 580, reel 17.
86. Domarus, *NS-Krieg*, p. 160.
87. OLGP, R 22, 3366, Hamburg, Oct. 2, 1944.
88. Abwehrbeauftragte der N.S.D.A.P., Party Chancellery, to Abw. in Munich, Nov. 20, 1944, T 580, reel 26.
89. Rs 421, Nov. 30, 1944, T 580, reel 18; Sauer, *Württemberg*, p. 340; DAF, Bereichsfrauenwalterin, Kassel, Sept. 7, 1944, T 81, reel 7.
90. Rs 267g, Oct. 3, 1944, T 580, reel 17.
91. An 422, Nov. 30, 1944, T 580, reel 18.
92. See Sauer, *Württemberg*, pp. 339-40.
93. See DAF, Amt Luftwaffe, Gaudienststelle, Münster, Sept. 15, Oct. 17, 1944, T 81, reel 71; memo, "Der politische Auftrag der Amtswalterin," ibid.
94. VI 214, Sept. 13; 237, Oct. 5, 1944, T 81, reel 4.
95. Domarus, *Hitler*, 2, pt. 2, pp. 2153-54.
96. *Schaffende Jugend* (news publication of Jugendamt of DAF), Nov. 1944, T 81, reel 69.
97. Maschmann, *Account Rendered*, p. 157.
98. Granzow, *Tagebuch*.
99. OLGP, R 22, 3374, Köln, Jan. 30, 1945; Klönne, "Jugendprotest," in Broszat, *Bayern in der NS-Zeit*, 4, pt. C, p. 313.
100. Reck-Malleczewen, *Diary of a Man in Despair*, p. 210.
101. See descriptions by von Kardorff, *Nightmare*, pp. 133-34; Graff, *Von S.M. zu N.S.*, p. 355.
102. Beer, *Stadt ohne Tod*, pp. 84-90.
103. Ibid., p. 71.
104. OLGP, R 22, 3363, Düsseldorf, Nov. 29, 1944.
105. Bielenberg, *The Past Is Myself*, pp. 180-82.
106. Gestapo, Nürnberg-Fürth, Dec. 1944-Feb. 4, 1945, T 580, reel 119.
107. Sauer, *Württemberg*, pp. 442-43.
108. Von Kardorff, *Nightmare*, pp. 148-49.
109. OLGP, R 22, 3356, Berlin, Dec. 2, 1944; 3363, Düsseldorf, Nov. 29, 1944; 3361, Darmstadt, Dec. 1, 1944.
110. Domarus, *Hitler*, 2, pt. 2, pp. 2159-67.
111. Von Kardorff, *Nightmare*, p. 135.
112. Sauer, *Württemberg*, p. 457.
113. Hahn, *White Flags*, p. 338.
114. Reichsführer SS, personal staff, Berlin, Dec. 4, 1944, T 580, reel 122.
115. "Julleuchter," files of Ahnenerbe Office, undated, ibid.

116. Dated "Feld Kommandostelle," Dec. 21, 1944, ibid.
117. Gaupropamt, Düsseldorf to Abt. Propaganda of Reich Propaganda Ministry, program for Christmas 1944, sent on Feb. 22, 1945, T 580, reel 657. Bormann's order for suitable celebrations, An 416, Nov. 30, 1944, T 81, reel 8.
118. Hartung, Schlesien, pp. 37-39.
119. Granzow, Tagebuch, pp. 142-45.
120. Günther, Das letzte Jahr, p. 387.
121. Rs 438, Dec. 9; 448, Dec. 13, 1944, T 580, reel 18.
122. For example, Bielenberg, The Past Is Myself, pp. 189, 196; von Kardorff, Nightmare, p. 157; Hartung, Schlesien, p. 37; Wolff-Mönckeberg, On the Other Side, pp. 62-64.
123. Robert Grosche, Kölner Tagebuch, 1944-46. Aus dem Nachlass, pp. 80-81; Fischer, Köln, pp. 193-94.
124. Wolff-Mönckeberg, On the Other Side, pp. 102-04.
125. Herzstein, The War that Hitler Won, p. 318.
126. DAF, KdF, Gaudienststelle, Bayreuth, Oct. 4, 1944, T 81, reel 72.
127. Westfälische Landeszeitung, Nov. 17, 1944.
128. Ibid., Dec. 30/31, 1944.
129. Hitler's talk in Domarus, Hitler, 2, pt. 2, pp. 2121-24; Gauleiter Murr's in Sauer, Württemberg, p. 474.
130. Report of the Landrat, Bad Aibling, Dec. 30, 1944, in Broszat, Bayern in der NS-Zeit, 1, pt. 7, p. 678.
131. Thorwald, Die grosse Flucht, pp. 18-19.
132. SD Report, Nov. 6, 1944, in Sauer, Württemberg, p. 476.
133. Rs 473gRs, Dec. 30, 1944, T 580, reel 18.
134. Dawidowicz, War against the Jews, pp. 188-89.
135. Brenner, Kunstpolitik, pp. 160-61.

9.The End Comes

1. Thorwald, Die grosse Flucht, pp. 32-34.
2. Ibid., pp. 35ff.
3. Hillgruber and Hümmelchen, Chronik des Zweiten Weltkrieges. Jan. 23, 1945, p. 262.
4. Thorwald, Die grosse Flucht, pp. 181-84.
5. Ibid., pp. 70-72.
6. Ibid., pp. 74-81.
7. Ibid., pp. 87ff.; cf. Maria Maurer, Sturm über Deutschland. Erlebnisbericht einer Transportschwester, p. 9.
8. Fritz Nendel, ed., Spreu im Wind. Tagebuch einer Verschollenen.
9. Thorwald, Die grosse Flucht, pp. 97, 114ff., 208; similar acocounts are found in Herbert Hupka, ed., Letzte Tage in Schlesien. Tagebücher, Erinnerungen und Dokumente der Vertreibung, and Klaus Granzow, Letzte Tage in Pommern. Tagebücher, Erinnerungen und Dokumente der Vertreibung.
10. See Günther, Das letzte Jahr, Jan. 13, 1945, pp. 427-28.
11. See his Final Entries, 1945: The Diaries of Joseph Goebbels, ed. Hugh Trevor Roper, p. 152.
12. Von Kardorff, Nightmare, pp. 169-70; cf. Studnitz, While Berlin Burns, p. 243; Lange, Tagebücher, p. 199.
13. Götz Bergander, Dresden im Luftkrieg. Vorgeschichte—Zerstörung—Folgen, pp. 23-25.
14. Ibid., pp. 342-46.

15. Ibid., pp. 134-63.
16. Ibid., pp. 164-84.
17. See "Pentagon verteidigt Angriff auf Dresden," *Süddeutsche Zeitung*, Feb. 16, 1970, p. 7.
18. Bergander, *Dresden*, pp. 121-31.
19. Ibid., pp. 65-74.
20. Ibid., p. 132.
21. Ibid., pp. 248-61.
22. Ibid., pp. 228-41.
23. Domarus, *Hitler*, 2, pt. 2, p. 2201, notes that the R.A.F. had warned it would bomb all cities over 100,000 population and that it was foolish to allow Dresden and Würzburg to be filled with evacuees from both east and west.
24. Günther, *Das letzte Jahr*, passim.
25. Benn, *Briefe an F.W. Oelze*, p. 388.
26. Lange, *Tagebücher*, pp. 190ff.
27. Hartung, *Schlesien*, p. 70; Wolff-Moenckeberg, *On the other Side*, pp. 109-11.
28. Karla Höcker, *Die letzten and und die ersten Tage. Berliner Aufzeichnungen 1945*, pp. 6-7.
29. Ibid., p. 9.
30. Schaefer, Hauptreferant Volkstum to Schäffer, Reich Propaganda Minister, in-house, Feb. 24, 1945, T 580, reel 657.
31. Granzow, *Tagebuch*, p. 155.
32. Von Kardorff, *Nightmare*, pp. 135, 176; cf. Guenther, *Das letzte Jahr*, p. 431.
33. Beer, *Stadt ohne Tod*, p. 147.
34. NSDAP, Partei Kanzlei, FA 91/1, Anlage 2 to Bormann's circular 397/44 dated Nov. 10, 11, 1944 (Institut für Zeitgeschichte, Munich).
35. Rs 148, Mar. 14, 1945, T 81, reel 5.
36. Prüller, *Diary of a German Soldier*, pp. 179-86.
37. Rs 149g, Mar. 19, 1945, T 81, reel 5.
38. Bg 162g, Mar. 27, 1945, ibid.
39. Rs 43, Jan. 30, 1945, ibid.
40. Bg. 61, Feb. 8, 1945, T 580, reel 18.
41. Rs 86, Feb. 17; An 91, Feb. 19, 1945, ibid.
42. Rs 113, Feb. 24, 1945, ibid.
43. An 79g, Feb. 19, 1945, T 580, reel 18.
44. Rs 183g, Mar. 23, 1945, T 81, reel 5.
45. OLGP, R 22, 3355, Bamberg, Feb. 23, 1945.
46. Andreas-Friedrich, *Der Schattenmann*, pp. 204, 211.
47. Findahl, *Letzter Akt—Berlin*, pp. 87-91.
48. Mengler, Chief of Sicherheitspolizei and SD to SS Obersturmbannführer von Borcke, Berlin, Mar. 28, 1945, T 580, reel 660.
49. Report of gendarmerie post Schellenberg, Kreis Berchtesgaden, Mar. 24, 1945, in Broszat, *Bayern in der NS-Zeit*, 1, pt. 7, p. 684.
50. An 162, Dec. 27, 1944, T 81, reel 8; Rs 27, Jan. 26, 1945, T 580, reel 18; Sauer, *Württemberg*, pp. 482-83; Karl Pleyer, Kapellmeister in Munich to Goebbels, Jan. 8, 1945, T 580, reel 663.
51. Günther, *Das letzte Jahr*, p. 429.
52. See, eg. Rs 65, Feb. 12, 1945, T 580, reel 18; OLGP, R 22, 3366, Hamburg, Jan. 30, 1945; 3360, Danzig, Jan. 31, 1945; 3381, Nuremberg, Feb. 6, 1945. Maria Maurer, a transport sister, found little help available even within the Reich itself. *Sturm über Deutschland*, pp. 9-13.

53. Rs 156g, Mar. 24, 1945, T 81, reel 5; An 12gRs, Jan. 17, 1945, T 580, reel 18; Bg 20, Jan. 26, 1945, T 81, reel 8; Rs 54gRs, Feb. 6, 1945, T 580, reel 18.

54. Reichsamt für das Landvolk, internal directives, Nr. 4; Nr. 8, Oct. 30, 1944; Nr. 14, Nr. 20, Nov. 7, 1944, Nr. 22, Nov. 7, 1944; Stabsleiter to Reichshauptstableitungsleiter III, Nov. 10, 1944; VI, Nov. 14, 1944; "Arbeitsgrundlagen für die landvolkpolitische-, ernährungs-, und landwirtschaftliche Aufklärungsarbeit," Jan. 1945, T 81, reel 37.

55. Rs 30, Jan. 27, 1945; 72, Feb. 10, 1945, T 580, reel 18.

56. An 33, Jan. 28, 1945; 34, Jan. 29, 1945, ibid.

57. Gendarmerie station Feilenbach, Feb. 22, 1945, in Broszat, *Bayern in der NS-Zeit*, 1, pt. 7, p. 681.

58. Sauer, *Württemberg*, pp. 483-84.

59. Bg 43, Feb. 2; 68, Feb. 11; 99, Feb. 23; 109, Mar. 4, 1945, T 580, reel 18.

60. An 184, Mar. 26, 1945, T 81, reel 5.

61. Rs 143, Mar. 19, 1945, T 580, reel 18.

62. Wolff-Mönckeberg, *On the Other Side*, p. 103.

63. Beer, *Stadt ohne Tod*, p. 123.

64. Goebbels, *Final Entries*, p. 18.

65. See Hermann Vietzen, *Chronik der Stadt Stuttgart, 1945-1948; Veröffentlichungen des Archivs der Stadt Stuttgart*, 25, pp. 12-13; cf. Schmitz, *Die Bewirtschaftung*, p. 358; Sauer, *Württemberg*, p. 367.

66. Werner Abelshauser, *Wirtschaft in Westdeutschland, 1945-1948; Rekonstruktion und Wirtschaftsbedingungen in der amerikanischen und britischen Zone (Schriftenreihe der Vierteljahrshefte für Zeitgeschichte*, No. 30), pp. 132-35, shows the extreme shortage of fertilizer existing in 1945-1946. Importations of food might have moderated shortages, but food production was short everywhere during that period.

67. Günther, *Das letzte Jahr*, pp. 420-21.

68. Beer, *Stadt ohne Tod*, p. 153.

69. Sauer, *Württemberg*, pp. 480-81.

70. Decree of Hitler establishing special transportation staff under Speer, Feb. 22, 1945, T 81, reel 37; repair orders An 42g, Jan. 31, 1945, T 580, reel 18.

71. Sauer, *Württemberg*, p. 484; Reich Propaganda Minister to Reich Propaganda Officers in Essen and Düsseldorf, Jan. 12, 1945, T 580, reel 657.

72. E.g., Gauschwalter, Bayreuth, circular 3, Feb. 20, 1945, T 81, reel 68.

73. See letters of propaganda offices to Propaganda Ministry, Bayreuth, Jan. 15; Hannover, Feb. 25; Moselland, Feb. 14; Mainfranken, Mar. 16; Thüringen, Feb. 11; Reich Propaganda Minister to office in Württemberg, Feb. 28, 1945, T 580, reel 657.

74. VI 18, Feb. 15, 1945, T 81, reel 4.

75. Bereichsobmann, DAF Fritzlar, Jan. 9, 20, 1945, T 81, reel 71.

76. Sauer, *Württemberg*, pp. 484-85.

77. Günther, *Das letzte Jahr*, Feb. 5, 1945, pp. 460-61.

78. See Speer, *Inside the Third Reich*, pp. 436-43; Domarus, *Hitler*, 2, pt. 2, pp. 2213-15.

79. Rs 166gRs, Mar. 23; 180gRs, Mar. 30, 1945, T 81, reel 5.

80. Apr. 1, 1945, ibid.; cf. Domarus, *Hitler*, 2, pt. 2, p. 1224, fn. 149.

81. An 209gRs, Apr. 13, 1945, T 580, reel 18.

82. Goebbels, *Final Entries*, p. 39, Mar. 4; p. 71, Mar. 7; p. 79, Mar. 8, 1945.

83. Ibid., p. 93, Mar. 9; pp. 93, 104, 108-9, Mar. 11; p. 116, Mar. 12; pp 155, 159, Mar. 16; p. 178, Mar. 19; pp. 199, 202-4, Mar. 21; p. 243, Mar. 26; p. 317, Apr. 3, 1945.

84. Ibid., p. 202, Mar. 21; p. 246, Mar. 26; p. 268, Mar. 28; p. 313, Apr. 2; p. 318, Apr. 3, 1945.

85. Fischer, *Köln*, pp. 195-208; cf. John Toland, *The Last 100 Days*, p. 194.

86. Vietzen, *Chronik der Stadt Stuttgart*, pp. 14-32; cf. Sauer, *Württemberg*, pp. 488-98.

87. Hildebrand Troll, "Aktionen zur Kriegsbeendigung im Frühjahr 1945," in Broszat, *Bayern in der NS-Zeit*, 4, pt. C, p. 648.

88. Ibid.; cf. *Bayern in der NS-Zeit*, 7, pt. 7, pp. 685-86.

89. Troll, "Aktionen," in Broszat, *Bayern in der NS-Zeit*, 4, pt. C, pp. 654-55.

90. Ibid., pp. 656-57.

91. Ibid., pp. 657-58.

92. Ibid., p. 659.

93. Ibid., pp. 660ff.

94. Ibid., p. 664.

95. Preis, *München unterm Hakenkreuz*, pp. 232-48.

96. Domarus, *NS-Krieg*, pp. 180-96; Troll, "Aktionen," in Broszat, *Bayern in der NS-Zeit*, 4, pt. C, p. 670.

97. Ibid., pp. 671-77.

98. Ibid., pp. 686-88; Domarus, *Hitler*, 2, pt. 2, p. 2224. The saga of one of the SS army corps that had fought in the Saar, helped to defend Nuremberg, and continued to fight "true to its duty" until the final end in the Alps is found in Erich Spiwoks and Hans Stöber, *Endkampf zwischen Mosel und Inn. XIII. SS-Armeekorps*. The story fails to indicate that their fighting brought additional destruction to some of the places where they fought.

99. Kraume, *Duisburg im Krieg*, pp. 100-114; cf. Hans G. Kösters, *Essen Stunde Null. Die letzten Tage, März/April 1945*, pp. 104-5. Details of the end of the fighting in Southwest Westphalia, highlighting the actions of the Volkssturm represented in its territorial militia, are found in Willi Timm, *Freikorps "Sauerland," 1944-1945. Zur Geschichte des Zweiten Weltkrieges in Südwestfalen (Veröffentlichungen aus dem Stadtarchiv Hagen, no. 3)*.

100. Story told in Kurt Detlev Möller, *Das letzte Kapitel. Geschichte der Kapitulation Hamburgs*.

101. Von Kardorff, *Nightmare*, pp. 168-69.

102. Andreas-Friedrich, *Der Schattenmann*, pp. 205-7.

103. Beer, *Stadt ohne Tod*, pp. 128-31.

104. Studnitz, *While Berlin Burns*, pp. 232-49; cf. Andreas-Friedrich, *Der Schattenmann*, p. 201.

105. Ibid., pp. 204, 234.

106. Ibid., p. 251. The German words were: "An der Laterne vor der Reichskanzlei / hängen unsere Bonzen / der Führer ist dabei. / Da wollen wir beieinander stehn, / Wir wollen unsern Führer sehn, / wie einst am ersten Mai." For other comments on opposition groups, see Jochen Köhler, *Klettern in der Grossstadt, Volkstümliche Geschichten vom Überleben in Berlin 1933-1945*, p. 228.

107. Findahl, *Letzter Akt—Berlin*, p. 91.

108. Andreas-Friedrich, *Der Schattenmann*, p. 242.

109. Thorwald, *Die grosse Flucht*, pp. 325-26.

110. Ibid., p. 343.

111. Ibid., pp. 368-70.

112. Ibid., pp. 338-39.

113. Ibid., pp. 451-74.

114. Höcker, *Die letzten und die ersten Tage*, p. 18.

115. Hüttenberger, *Die Gauleiter*, pp. 213-20.

116. See Werner Brockdorff, *Flucht vor Nürnberg: Pläne und Organisation der Fluchtwege der NS-Prominenz im "Römischen Weg"*.

Bibliography

1. Unpublished Materials

Microfilmed Records in National Archives, Washington, D.C.:
> T 81, records of the National Socialist German Labor Party
> T 175, records of the Reich Leader of the SS and Chief of the German Police
> T 580, Nationalsozialistische Deutsche Arbeiterpartei (Non-Biographic Records from Berlin Documents Center, "Schumacher Material")
> Printed guides are available for T 81 and T 175. There is no printed guide for T 580 but various reels contain indices of contents derived from the various party agencies. As indicated in the notes, Bormann's orders, directives, and information circulars were taken partially from T 81 and partially from T 580. A significant amount of material was derived from the records of the propaganda ministry in T 580. Portions of the scattered reports from various party agencies for the war years, which are included in T 81, were useful.]

Records of *Oberlandesgerichtspräsidenten*, Reichsjustizministerium, R 22. Bundesarchiv, Koblenz.

Partial files, Wirtschaftsministerium, Kriegsschäden, R 12I/84-164. Bundesarchiv, Koblenz.

File of Sonderstab Ruder, Reichskanzlei, FA 91. Institut für Zeitgeschichte, Munich.

2. Memoristic and Special Accounts Dealing with the Home Front

Andreas-Friedrich, Ruth. *Der Schattenmann. Tagebuchzeichnungen, 1939-1945.* Berlin: Suhrkamp, 1947.

Apelt, Willibalt. *Jurist im Wandel der Staatsformen. Lebenserinnerungen.* Tübingen: Mohr, 1965.

Bardua, Heinz. *Stuttgart im Luftkrieg, 1939-1945.* In *Veröffentlichungen des Archivs der Stadt Stuttgart,* vol. 23. Stuttgart: Ernst Klett, 1967.

Beer, Willy [pseud., Matthias Menzel]. *Die Stadt ohne Tod. Berliner Tagebuch 1943/45.* Berlin: Carl Habel, 1946.

Benn, Gottfried. *Briefe an F.W. Oelze, 1932-1945.* Foreword by F.W. Oelze. Frankfurt a.M.: Fischer Taschenbuch, 1975.

Bergander, Götz. *Dresden im Luftkrieg. Vorgeschichte—Zerstörung—Folgen* (Heyne Geschichte, 27). Munich: Wilhelm Heyne, 1979.

Bertelsmann, C. *Letzte Briefe aus Stalingrad.* Detmold: S. Kortemeier, Drück Tölle, 1958.

Bielenberg, Christabel. *The Past Is Myself.* London: Chatto & Windus, 1970.

Boberach, Heinz, ed. *Meldungen aus dem Reich. Auswahl aus den geheimen Lageberichten des Sicherheitsdienstes der SS 1939-1944.* Munich: Deutscher Taschenbuchverlag, 1968.

_____, ed. *Richterbriefe. Dokumente zur Beeinflussung der deutschen Rechtsprechung, 1942-1944.* Boppard am Rhein: Harald Boldt, 1975.

Boelcke, Willi A., ed. *The Secret Conferences of Dr. Goebbels.* New York: Dutton, 1970.

Broszat, Martin, Elke Frölich, and Falk Wiesemann, eds. *Bayern in der NS-Zeit,* Vol. 1, *Soziale Lage und politisches Verhalten der Bevölkerung im Spiegel vertraulicher Berichte.* Munich, Vienna: R. Oldenbourg, 1977.

Broszat, Martin, Elke Fröhlich, and Anton Grossmann, eds. *Bayern in der NS-Zeit,* Vol. 3, *Herrschaft und Gesellschaft im Konflikt,* Part B. Munich, Vienna: R. Oldenbourg, 1981.

_____. *Bayern in der NS-Zeit.* Vol. 4, *Herrschaft und Gesellschaft im Konflikt,* Part C. Munich, Vienna: R. Oldenbourg, 1981.

Brunswig, Hans. *Feuersturm über Hamburg.* Stuttgart: Motorbuch Verlag, 1979.

Cesany, Maximilian. "Apokalypse an der Elbe. Vor fünfundzwanzig Jahren ging Dresden unter." *Christ und Welt* (Feb. 13, 1970), p. 32.

Domarus, Max, ed. *Hitler. Reden und Proklamationen, 1932-1945. Kommentiert von einem deutschen Zeitgenossen.* 2 vols. Munich: Süddeutscher Verlag, 1965.

Domarus, Wolfgang. *Nationalsozialismus, Krieg und Bevölkerung. Untersuchungen zur Lage, Volksstimmung und Struktur in Augsburg während des Dritten Reiches. Miscellanea Bavaria Monacensia. Dissertationen zur Bayerischen Landes- und Münchner Stadtgeschichte.* Ed. Karl Bosl and Michael Schattenhofer, no. 71. Munich: Neue Schriftenreihe des Stadtarchivs, 1977.

Dreckmann, Hans. *Hamburg nach der Kapitulation; Erinnerungen an 1945-1946, Geschichte der "ernannten Bürgerschaft."* Hamburg: Dammtor, 1970.

Findahl, Theo. *Letzter Akt—Berlin, 1939-1945.* Hamburg: Hummerich, 1946.

Fischer, Josef. *Köln '39-'45. Der Leidensweg einer Stadt. Miterlebt von.* . . . Cologne: J.P. Bachem, 1970.

Goebbels, Joseph. *Final Entries 1945: The Diaries of* . . . . Ed. Hugh Trevor Roper. New York: G.P. Putnam's Sons, 1978.

_____. *The Goebbels Diaries.* Trans. and ed. Louis Lochner. New York: Doubleday, 1948.

Görgen, Hans Peter. *Düsseldorf und der Nationalsozialismus.* Cologne: Spezialdruckerei für Dissertationen: Gouder & Hansen, 1968.

Gosztony, Peter, ed. *Der Kampf um Berlin 1945 in Augenzeugenberichten.* Düsseldorf: Rauch, 1970.

Graff, Sigmund. *Von S.M. zu N.S. Erinnerungen eines Bühnenautors (1900 bis 1945).* Munich, Wels: Verlag Wesermühl, 1963.

Granzow, Klaus. *Tagebuch eines Hitlerjungen. 1943-1945.* Bremen: Carl Schünemann, 1965.

_____, ed. *Letzte Tage in Pommern. Tagebücher, Erinnerungen und Dokumente der Vertreibung.* Munich: Langen Müller, 1984.

Grimm, Friedrich. *Mit offenem Visier. Aus den Lebenserinnerungen eines deutschen Rechstanwalts. Als Biographie bearbeitet von Hermann Schild.* Leoni am Starnberger See: Drussel, 1961.

Grosche, Robert. *Kölner Tagebuch, 1944-46. Aus dem Nachlass.* Ed. Maria Steinhoff with the help of Christian Pesch, Hubert Luthe, and Ludger Honnefelder. Cologne: J. Hegner, 1969.

Günther, Joachim. *Das letzte Jahr. Mein Tagebuch, 1944-45.* Hamburg: Classen & Goverts, 1948.

Hahn, Lili. *White Flags of Surrender.* Washington and New York: Robert B. Luce, 1974.

Hampe, Erich. *Der zivile Luftschutz im Zweiten Weltkrieg. Dokumentation und Erfahrungsberichte über Aufbau und Einsatz.* Frankfurt a. M.: Bernard & Graefe Verlag für Wehrwesen, 1963.

Hartung, Hugo. *Schlesien 1944/45. Aufzeichnungen und Tagebücher.* Munich: Bergstadtverlag W. H. Korn, 1956.

Hassell, Ulrich von. *The Von Hassell Diaries, 1939-1944: The Story of the Forces against Hitler inside Germany.* Garden City, N.Y.: Doubleday, 1947.

Heiber, Helmut, ed. *Hitlers Lagebesprechungen. Die Protokollfragmente seiner militärischen Konferenzen 1942-5.* Stuttgart: Deutsche Verlagsanstalt, 1962.

Henry, Frances. *Victims and Neighbors: A Small Town in Nazi Germany Remembered.* South Hadley, Mass.: Bergin & Garvey, 1984.

Heyen, Franz Josef. *Nationalsozialismus im Alltag. Quellen zur Geschichte des Nationalsozialismus vornehmlich im Raum Mainz-Koblenz-Trier.* Boppard am Rhein: Boldt, 1967.

Hitler, Adolf. *Hitler's Secret Conversations: His Private Thoughts and Plans in His Own Words, 1941-1944.* Intr. essay on "The Mind of Adolf Hitler" by H.R. Trevor-Roper. New York: Farrar, Straus and Young, 1953.

Höcker, Karla. *Die letzten und die ersten Tage: Berliner Aufzeichnungen 1945 mit Berichten von Boleslaw Barlog et al.* Berlin: B. Hessling, 1966.

Hupka, Herbert. *Letzte Tage in Schlesien. Tagebücher, Erinnerungen und Dokumente der Vertreibung.* Munich: Langen Müller, 1981.

Kardorff, Ursula von. *Diary of a Nightmare: Berlin, 1942-1945.* Trans. Ewan Butler. London: Rupert Hart-Davis, 1965.

Kehrl, Hans. *Krisenmanager im Dritten Reich. 6 Jahre Frieden—6 Jahre Krieg. Erinnerungen.* With critical annotations and afterword by Erwin Viefhaus. Düsseldorf: Droste, 1973.

Kempner, Maria. *Priester vor Hitlers Tribunen.* Gütersloh: Reinhard Mohn, 1966.

Kissel, Hans. *Der deutsche Volkssturm 1944/45. Eine territoriale Miliz im Rahmen der Landesverteidigung.* Beiheft 16/17 der Wehrwissenschaftlichen Rundschau. Arbeitskreis für Wehrforschung: Frankfurt a. M.: E.S. Mittler, 1962.

Köhler, Jochen. *Klettern in der Grossstadt. Volkstümliche Geschichten vom Überleben in Berlin, 1933-1945.* With a preface by Wolf Biermann. 2nd ed. Berlin: Das Arsenal, 1981.

Kösters, Hans G. *Essen Stunde Null. Die letzten Tage, März/April 1945.* Düsseldorf: Droste, 1982.

Kramp, Hans. *Rurfront 1944/45. Zweite Schlacht am Hubertuskreuz zwischen Wurm, Rur, und Inde.* Geilenkirchen: Fred Gatzen, 1981.

Kraume, Hans-Georg. *Duisburg im Krieg, 1939-1945.* Düsseldorf: Droste, 1982.

Kruk, Zofia. *The Taste of Fear: A Polish Childhood in Germany, 1939-1946.* London: Hutchinson, 1973.

Kuby, Erich. *Mein Krieg. Aufzeichnungen aus 2129 Tagen.* Munich: Nymphenburger Verlag, 1975.

Lange, Horst. *Tagebücher aus dem Zweiten Weltkrieg.* Ed. Dieter Schäfer. Mainz: Von Hase and Koehler, 1979.

Lochner, Louis P., ed. and trans. *The Goebbels Diaries, 1942-1943.* Garden City, N.Y.: Doubleday, 1948.

Maschmann, Melita. *Account Rendered: A Dossier on My Former Self.* Trans. Geoffrey Strachan. London: Abelard-Schuman, 1964.

Maurer, Maria. *Sturm über Deutschland. Erlebnisbericht einer Transportschwester.* Lippstadt: C. Jos. Laumanns, 1971.

Menzel, Matthias. *See* Beer, Willy.

Möller, Kurt Detlev. *Das letzte Kapitel. Geschichte der Kapitulation Hamburgs. Von der Hamburger Katastrophe des Jahres 1943 bis zur*

Übergabe der Stadt am 3. Mai 1945. Hamburg: Hoffmann & Campe, 1947.

Nadler, Fritz. *Eine Stadt im Schatten Streichers. Bisher unveröffentlichte Tagebuchblätter, Dokumente und Bilder vom Kriegsjahr 1943.* Nuremberg: Fränkische Verlagsanstalt, 1969.

Nendel, Fritz, ed. *Spreu im Wind. Tagebuch einer Verschollenen.* Bonn: Verlag der Europäischer Bücherei, H.M. Hieronimi, 1949.

Pingel, Falk. *Häftlinge unter SS-Herrschaft. Widerstand, Selbstbehauptung und Vernichtung im Konzentrationslager.* In Historische Perspektive, 12. Hamburg: Hoffmann & Campe, 1978.

Preis, Kurt. *München unterm Hakenkreuz. Die Hauptstadt der Bewegung: Zwischen Pracht und Trümmern.* Munich: Ehrenwirth, 1980.

Prüller, Wilhelm. *Diary of a German Soldier.* Ed. H.C. Robbins Landon and Sebastian Leitner. London: Faber & Faber, 1947.

Reck-Malleczewen, Friedrich Percyval. *Diary of a Man in Despair.* Trans. Paul Rubens. London: Macmillan, 1966, 1970.

Sauer, Paul. *Württemberg in der Zeit des Nationalsozialismus.* Ulm: Süddeutsche Verlagsgesellschaft, 1975.

Schirach, Baldur von. *Ich glaubte an Hitler.* Hamburg: Mosaik, 1967.

Schluckner, Horst, Hans-Joachim Else, and Siegfried Marohn. *Überlebende. Nach Erlebnisberichten von. . . .* Berlin: Kongress-Verlag, 1956.

Schmitz, Hubert. *Die Bewirtschaftung der Nahrungsmittel und Verbrauchsguter, 1939-1950. Dargestellt an dem Beispiel der Stadt Essen.* Essen: Stadtverwaltung, 1956.

Scholl, Inge. *Students against Tyranny: The Resistance of the White Rose, Munich, 1942-43.* Middletown, Conn.: Wesleyan Univ. Press, 1970.

Schramm, Percy Ernst. *Neun Generationen. Dreihundert Jahre deutscher "Kulturgeschichte" im Lichte der Schicksale einer Hamburger Bürgerfamilie (1648-1948).* 2 vols. Göttingen: Vandenhoeck & Ruprecht, 1964.

Schultz, Joachim. *Die letzten 30 Tage: Aus dem Kriegstagebuch des Oberkommandos der Wehrmacht.* Ed. Jürgen Thorwald. Stuttgart: Steingruben, 1951.

Speer, Albert. *Inside the Third Reich: Memoirs.* New York: Macmillan, 1970.

Spiwoks, Erich, and Hans Stöber. *Endkampf zwischen Mosel und Inn. XIII. SS-Armeekorps.* Osnabrück: Munin, 1976.

Staden, Wendelgard von. *Darkness over the Valley.* Trans. Mollie Comerford Peters. New York: Penguin, 1981.

Steinert, Marlis G. *Hitler's War and the Germans: Public Mood and Attitude during the Second World War.* Ed. and trans. Thomas E.J. de Witt. Athens: Ohio Univ. Press, 1977.

Strölin, Karl. *Stuttgart im Endstadium des Krieges.* Stuttgart: Vorwek, 1950.

Studnitz, Hans-Georg von. *While Berlin Burns: The Diary of . . . , 1943-1945.* London: Weidenfeld & Nicolson, 1964.

Timm, Willy. *Freikorps "Sauerland" 1944-1945. Zur Geschichte des*

Zweiten Weltkrieges in Südwestfalen. In *Veröffentlichungen aus dem Stadtarchiv Hagen,* no. 3. Hagen: Stadtarchiv, 1976.

Vietzen, Hermann. *Chronik der Stadt Stuttgart, 1945-1948. Veröffentlichungen des Archivs der Stadt Stuttgart,* Vol. 25. Stuttgart: Klett, 1972.

Wahl, Karl. *" . . . es ist das deutsche Herz." Erlebnisse und Erkenntnisse eines ehemaligen Gauleiters.* Augsburg: Selbstverlag, 1954.

Warlimont, Walter. *Inside Hitler's Headquarters, 1939-1945.* New York: Praeger, 1964.

Wendel, Elsie. *Hausfrau at War: A German Woman's Account of Life in Hitler's Reich.* London: Adams Press, 1957.

Wolff-Mönckeberg, Mathilde. *On the Other Side: To My Children, from Germany, 1940-1945.* Trans. and ed. Ruth Evans. London: Peter Owen, 1979.

Zittel, Bernhard. "Die Volksstimmung im Dritten Reich im Spiegel der Geheimberichte der Regierungspräsidenten von Schwaben." *Zeitschrift des Historischen Vereins für Schwaben* 66 (1972): 1-58.

3. Newspapers Consulted (varied selections and runs):

Deutsche Allgemeine Zeitung
Frankfurter Zeitung
Münchener Neueste Nachrichten
Völkischer Beobachter, Süddeutsche Ausgabe
Westfälische Landeszeitung

4. Secondary Accounts

Abelshauser, Werner. *Wirtschaft in Westdeutschland, 1945-1948; Rekonstruktion und Wirtschaftsbedingungen in der amerikanischen und britischen Zone.* In *Schriftenreihe der Vierteljahreshefte für Zeitgeschichte,* no. 30. Stuttgart: Deutsche Verlagsanstalt, 1945.

Allea, Peter. *One More River: The Rhine Crossing of 1945.* New York: Scribners, 1980.

Andrews, Allen. *The Air Marshals: The Air War in Western Europe.* New York: Morrow, 1970.

Bailey, Ronald H. *The Air War in Europe.* In *Time-Life World War II,* vol. 16. Alexandria, Va.: Time-Life Books, 1979.

Baird, Jay W. *The Mythical World of Nazi War Propaganda.* Minneapolis: Univ. of Minnesota Press, 1974.

Bauer, Yehuda. *A History of the Holocaust.* New York: Franklin Watts, 1982.

Beck, Earl R. "The Allied Bombing of Germany, 1942-1945, and the German Response: Dilemmas of Judgment." *German Studies Review* 5, no. 3 (Oct. 1982): 325-37.

Becker, Peter. "The Role of Synthetic Fuel in World War II Germany:

Implications for Today?" *Air University Review* 32, no. 5 (July-Aug., 1981): 45-53.

Bekker, Cajus (Berenbrok, Hans Dieter). *The Luftwaffe War Diaries*. Garden City, N.Y.: Doubleday, 1968.

Bewley, Charles. *Hermann Goering and the Third Reich: A Biography Based on Family and Official Records*. New York: Devon-Adair, 1962.

Bidinian, Larry J. *The Combined Allied Bombing Offensive against the German Civilian, 1942-1945*. Lawrence, Kans.: Coronado Press, 1976.

Blond, Georges. *L'Agonie de l'allemagne, 1944-45*. Paris: Fayard, 1952.

Blumenstock, Friedrich. *Der Einmarsch der Amerikaner und Franzosen im nördlichen Württemberg im April 1945*. Stuttgart: Kohlhammer, 1957.

Bracher, Karl Dietrich. *The German Dictatorship: The Origins, Structure, and Effects of National Socialism*. New York: Praeger, 1970.

Brenner, Hildegard. *Die Kunstpolitik des Nationalsozialismus*. Reinbek bei Hamburg: Rowohlt, 1963.

Brockdorff, Werner. *Flucht vor Nürnberg: Pläne und Organisation der Fluchtwege der NS-Prominenz im "Römischen Weg."* Munich-Wels: Wesermühl, 1969.

Bundeszentrale fur politische Bildung, Bonn. *Germans against Hitler, July 20, 1944*. Wiesbaden: Wiesbadener Graphische Betriebe, 1969.

Caffey, Thomas M. *Decision over Schweinfurt: The U.S. 8th Air Force Battle for Daylight Bombing*. New York: David McKay, 1977.

Carnes, James Donald. *General zwischen Hitler und Stalin. Das Schicksal des Walther v. Seydlitz*. Düsseldorf: Droste, 1980.

Clark, Alan. *Barbarossa: The Russian-German Conflict, 1941-45*. New York: Morrow, 1965.

Conway, J.S. *The Nazi Persecution of the Churches, 1933-1945*. New York: Basic Books, 1968.

Dawidowicz, Lucy. *The War against the Jews, 1933-1945*. New York: Bantam, 1975.

Davis, Franklin M. *Across the Rhine*. Vol. 22 of *Time-Life World War II*, Morristown, N.J.: Silver Burdett, 1981.

Deakin, F.W. *The Brutal Friendship: Mussolini, Hitler, and the Fall of Italian Fascism*. New York: Harper & Row, 1962.

Deutsch, Harold C. *The Conspiracy against Hitler in the Twilight War*. Minneapolis: Univ. of Minnesota Press, 1968.

Dickinson, John K. *German and Jew [The Life and Death of Sigmund Stein]*. Chicago: Quadrangle, 1967.

Diehl-Thiele, Peter. *Partei und Staat im Dritten Reich. Untersuchungen zum Verhältnis von NSDAP und allgemeiner innerer Staatsverwaltung 1933-1945*. 2nd ed. Munich: C.H. Beck, 1971.

Dietrich, Richard. *Berlin. 9 Kapitel seiner Geschichte*. Berlin: de Gruyter, 1960.

Farquarson, J.E. *The Plough and the Swastika: The NSDAP and Agriculture in Germany, 1928-45*. In *Sage Studies in 20th Century History*, vol. 5.

London and Beverly Hills: Sage Publications, 1976.

Fest, Joachim C. *Das Gesicht des Dritten Reiches. Profile einer totalitären Herrschaft.* München: R. Piper, 1963.

Frankland, Noble. *Bomber Offensive: The Devastation of Europe.* New York: Ballantine, 1970.

Fritsch, Ludwig A. *Amerikas Verantwortung für das Verbrechen am deutschen Volk. Ein Gewissensappell an die amerikanische Führungsschicht.* 5th ed. (*Deutsche Hochschullehrer Zeitung,* 6.) [Reprinted, "Grabert," n.p., n.d., Institut für Zeitgeschichte München.]

Glum, Friedrich. *Der Nationalsozialismus: Werden und Vergehen.* Munich: Beck, 1962.

Gordon, Sara. *Hitler, Germans and the "Jewish Question."* Princeton: Princeton Univ. Press, 1984.

Gross, Leonard. *The Last Jews in Berlin.* New York: Simon and Schuster, 1982.

Grunberger, Richard. *A Social History of the Third Reich.* London: Weidenfeld & Nicholson, 1971.

Hanser, Richard. *A Noble Treason. The Revolt of the Munich Students against Hitler.* New York: G.P. Putnam's Sons, 1979.

Herington, John. *Air War against Germany and Italy, 1939-1943.* Canberra: Australian War Memorial, 1962.

Herzstein, Robert Edwin. *The War that Hitler Won: The Most Infamous Propaganda Campaign in History.* New York: G.P. Putnam's Sons, 1978.

Higham, Robin. *Air Power.* New York: St. Martin's, 1972.

Hilberg, Raoul. *The Destruction of the European Jews.* Chicago: Quadrangle, 1961, 1967.

Hillgruber, Andreas, and Gerhard Hümmelchen. *Chronik des Zweiten Weltkrieges. Kalendarium militärischer und politischer Ereignisse.* Düsseldorf: Athenaeum/Drosche, 1978.

Höhne, Heinz. *The Order of the Death's Head: The Story of Hitler's S.S.* New York: Ballantine, 1971.

Homze, Edward L. *Foreign Labor in Nazi Germany.* Princeton: Princeton Univ. Press, 1967.

Howsell, Haywood S. *The Air Plan That Defeated Hitler.* Washignton, D.C.: U.S. Air Force Headquarters, 1972.

Huber, Karl-Heinz. *Jugend unterm Hakenkreuz.* Berlin: Ullstein, 1982.

Hüttenberger, Peter. *Die Gauleiter, Studie zum Wandel des Machtgefüges in der NSDAP.* Stuttgart: Deutsche Verlagsanstalt, 1969.

Irving, David. *The Destruction of Dresden.* New York: Holt, Rinehart, and Winston, 1963.

_____. *Hitler's War.* London: Hodder and Stoughton, 1977.

_____. *The Rise and Fall of the Luftwaffe: The Life of Field Marshal Erhard Milch.* Boston: Little, Brown & Co., 1973.

Johé, Werner. *Die gleichgeschaltete Justiz.* Forschungsstelle für die Geschichte des Nationalsozialismus in Hamburg, *Veröffentlichungen,* vol. 5. Frankfurt: Europa Verlagsanstalt, 1967.

Kershaw, Ian. *Der Hitler Mythos. Volksmeinung und Propaganda im Dritten Reiche.* In *Schriftenreihe der Vierteljahrshefte für Zeitgeschichte,* no. 41. Stuttgart: Deutsche Verlagsanstalt, 1980.

———. *Popular Opinion and Political Dissent in the Third Reich: Bavaria, 1933-1945.* Oxford: Clarendon Press, 1983.

Koehl, Robert L. *RKFDV: German Resettlement and Population Policy, 1939-1945: A History of the Reich Commission for the Strengthening of Germandom.* Cambridge: Harvard Univ. Press, 1957.

Kurowski, Franz. *Der Luftkrieg über Deutschland.* Düsseldorf: Econ, 1977.

Lang, Jochen von, and Claus Sibyll. *Der Sekretär. Martin Bormann, der Mann der Hitler beherrschte.* Frankfurt a.M.: Fischer, 1980. (English: *Bormann: The Man Who Manipulated Hitler.* Trans. Christa Armstrong and Peter White. London: Weidenfeld & Nicholson, 1979.)

Laqueur, Walter. *The Terrible Secret: An Investigation into the Suppression of Information about Hitler's "Final Solution."* London: Weidenfeld and Nicholson, 1980.

Lochner, Louis P. *Tycoons and Tyrant: German Industry from Hitler to Adenauer.* Chicago: Regnery, 1955.

Lukas, Richard C. *The Strange Allies: The United States and Poland, 1941-1945.* Knoxville: Univ. of Tennessee Press, 1978.

Majdalany, Fred. *The Fall of Fortress Europe.* Garden City, N.Y.: Doubleday, 1968.

Middlebrook, Martin. *The Battle of Hamburg: Allied Bomber Forces against a German City in 1943.* London: Allen Lane, Penguin, 1980.

———. *The Nuremberg Raid, 30-31 March 1944.* London: Allen Lane, 1973.

Milward, Alan S. *Die deutsche Kriegswirtschaft, 1939-1945.* In *Vierteljahrshefte für Zeitgeschichte,* no. 12. Stuttgart: Deutsche Verlagsanstalt, 1966.

Mosley, Leonard. *The Reich Marshal: A Biography of Hermann Goering.* New York: Dell, 1974.

Musgrove, Gordon. *Operation Gomorrah: The Hamburg Firestorm Raids.* London: Jane's, 1981.

Overy, R.J. *The Air War, 1939-1945.* London: Europa, 1980.

Paul, Wolfgang. *Der Heimatkrieg, 1939 bis 1945.* Esslingen am Neckar: Bechtle Verlag, 1980.

Poliakov, Leon, and Josef Wulf. *Das dritte Reich und die Juden: Dokumente und Aufsätze.* Munich: K.G. Saur, 1978.

Price, Alfred. *Battle over the Reich.* New York: Scribner's, 1973.

Prittie, Terence. *Germans against Hitler.* Boston: Atlantic-Little Brown, 1964.

Roon, Ger von. *German Resistance to Hitler: Count von Motlke and the Kreisau Circle.* New York: Van Nostrand, Reinhold, 1971.

Roper, Edith, and Clara Leiser. *Skeleton of Justice.* New York: AMS Press, 1975.

Rothfels, Hans. *The German Opposition to Hitler.* Hinsdale, Ill.: Henry Regnery, 1948.

Rumpf, Hans. *Das war der Bombenkrieg. Deutsche Städte im Feuersturm. Ein Dokumentarbericht.* Oldenburg-Hamburg: Stalling, 1961.

Rupp, Leila J. *Mobilizing Women for War: German and American Propaganda, 1939-1945.* Princeton: Princeton Univ. Press, 1978.

Ryan, Cornelius. *A Bridge Too Far.* New York: Popular Library, 1974.

Schaffer, Donald. "American Military Ethics in World War II: The Bombing of German Civilians." *Journal of American History* 67, no. 2 (Sept. 1980): 318-34.

Schorn, Hubert. *Der Richter im Dritten Reich: Geschichte und Dokumente.* Frankfurt a.M.: V. Klostermann, 1959.

Schröter, Heinz. *Stalingrad.* Trans. Constantine Fitzgibbon. New York: Ballantine, 1958.

Steinert, Marlis G. *23 days: The Final Collapse of Nazi Germany.* Trans. Richard Barry. New York: Walker, 1969.

_____. *Capitulation, 1945: The Story of the Doenitz Regime.* London: Constable, 1969.

Stephenson, Jill. *The Nazi Organisation of Women.* London: Croom Helm; Tatowa, N.J.: Barnes & Noble, 1981.

Thorwald, Jürgen. *Die grosse Flucht. Es begann an der Weichsel, das Ende an der Elbe.* Rev. ed. Stuttgart: Steingrüben, 1968.

Toland, John. *Adolf Hitler.* 2 vols. New York: Doubleday, 1976.

_____. *The Last 100 Days.* New York: Random House, 1966.

Verrier, Anthony. *The Bomber Offensive.* New York: Macmillan, 1969.

Webster, Sir Charles, and Noble Frankland. *The Strategic Air Offensive against Germany, 1939-1945.* 4 vols. London: HMSO, 1961.

Werth, Alexander. *Russia at War, 1941-1945.* New York: E.P. Dutton, 1964.

Wheeler-Bennett, John W. *The Nemesis of Power: The German Army in Politics, 1918-1945.* New York: Viking, 1967.

Wood, Tony, and Bill Gunston. *Hitler's Luftwaffe: A Pictorial History and Technical Encyclopedia of Hitler's Air Power in World War II.* New York: Crescent, n.d.

Wright, Burton K. "Army of Despair: The German Volkssturm, 1944-1945." Ph.D. dissertation, Florida State Univ., 1982.

Zawodny, J.K. *Death in the Forest.* Notre Dame: Univ. of Notre Dame Press, 1962.

Ziemke, Earl F. *The Battle for Berlin: End of the Third Reich.* New York: Ballantine, 1968.

Index